An Illustrated History
of the GAA

An Illustrated History of the GAA

Eoghan Corry

Gill & Macmillan

Dedicated to all the footsoldiers of Gaelic games who toil so that others may enjoy.

For my mother, whose sense of fair play, sense of place, sense of fun and sense of duty were drawn from the same well of wisdom that inspired a fellow countyman of hers to found the GAA.

For Paddy King, who has seen the GAA he loves grow and prosper and who can be found at the heart of the action in Croke Park each Sunday of the season ministering to referees.

In memory of Fr Senan Corry of Cranny, Clare and Willow Park, a great sportsman and an inspiration to many, including the writer.

Gill & Macmillan Ltd
Hume Avenue, Park West, Dublin 12
with associated companies throughout the world
www.gillmacmillan.ie
© Eoghan Corry 2005
0 7171 3951 4
Design and print origination by Designit
Colour reproduction by Typeform Repro, Dublin
Printed and bound by Scotprint, Haddington, Scotland

This book is typeset in Bembo 9.5pt on 12pt.

The paper used in this book comes from the wood pulp of managed forests. For every tree felled, at least one tree is planted, thereby renewing natural resources.

A CIP catalogue record for this book is available from the British Library.

5 4 3 2 1

Contents

The six GAA games: who plays them and why • GAA clubs: demographics, penetration, and their importance in political and cultural life • The personnel who work in the GAA: who they are and where they come from • The structures and agendas which guide the GAA • Croke Park and the provincial stadiums

Nineteenth-century politics, attitudes, and the way they determined how the GAA came about • The GAA's inspiration: O'Donovan, O'Curry, Wilde, Davin and Cusack • Players, athletes and officials in the early days • The first inter-county games • Rivals and rivalry: the IAAA, rugby, soccer, and how they affected the games in Dublin • The 1903 All-Ireland final

The first national heroes in football and hurling: Kerry and Kilkenny • The decline of athletics • Women join the ranks • War, rebellion and reconciliation • The roaring twenties • Telling the story: ballads, newspapers and radio • The 1931 All-Ireland final

The rise of the GAA in Connacht and Ulster • The GAA's alternative Ireland and the rhetoric of nationalism • The emergency, foot and mouth, saving the harvest and the Polo Grounds • The glory days of the Munster hurling championship • Ring and Mackey: hurling's never-ending debate • Seán Purcell and the heroes of football

The rise of Down football and how it transformed the GAA • American and Australian influences • Playing rules and the soccer/rugby ban • The quest for threes and fours • Dublin's urban revolution • Kerry's greatest team • Eddie Keher and the new hurling heroes • The unwanted club championship and its rise • Dark days in Ulster and the troubles

The Australian Rules series and how it changed the GAA • Leinster football and the stadium it helped build • Hurling's Riverdance days • The re-emergence of Ulster and Connacht • TV and the commercial revolution • Higher standards, higher goals • The GAA's future and its inspiration to indigenous sports everywhere

Preface

The great events in modern sport are being supplied by an increasingly shrinking number of sports. Only a few can command attendances of over 82,000 or television viewing figures of over half a million.

Well-established international sports are in danger of falling off the schedules. Somehow, Ireland's Gaelic games have retained their position as the most popular sports on a highly globalised western island.

This is the story of how that happened. But it does not disguise the scale of the crisis across the world, that thousands of games played by children and athletic young men and women are being wiped out in the sporting equivalent of an ecological or linguistic disaster.

This is a modest attempt at the story of how indigenous sports survived in Ireland and the cultural, political and social context in which it happened.

It is a tribute to all our sporting heroes, the inspiration of our sporting joys and sorrows.

Acknowledgments

All photographs are reproduced courtesy of the GAA museum and archive, except the following:

Artane Band p. 42; Cambridge University Library p. 38 (*both*); Celtic Art pp 120–21 (*bottom*); Colman Doyle pp 138 (*bottom*), 140 (*both*), 142, 173, 177, 188 (*bottom*), 182–83, 209 (*top*), 210 (*top*); Commissioners for Public Works p. 10; Davin collection pp 23, 24–25 (*bottom*), 29; Dr Noel Kissane p. 22; Eoghan Corry p. 212; F. J. Biggar p. 62; *Irish Examiner* pp 48, 107, 108, 109, 110, 111, 113, 115, 117, 118, 122 (*both*), 123, 124 (*both*), 125 (*both*), 127 (*both*), 132, 135 (*both*), 136, 137 (*both*), 138 (*top*), 144, 174, 175 (*both*); *Irish Independent* pp 59, 74 (*both*), 80 (*top*), 81, 82, 84, 87 (*bottom*), 93, 106; *Irish Press* p. 53; Jim Connolly collection (*Sportsfile*) pp 132 (*bottom*), 164, 165, 166, 168, 169, 171, 178, 179, 181 (*both*), 183 (*both*), 184 (*top*), 185, 186 (*both*), 187, 203 (*bottom*); *Kerryman* pp 119, 120, 126 (*bottom*); Monaghan County Museum p. 18; National Library of Ireland pp 14, 15, 19, 25 (*top*), 27, 28, 29, 30, 31, 35, 36, 52, 65, 68; National Museum of Denmark p. 11; National Museum of Greece p. 8; National Museum of Ireland p. 12; Scottish National Portrait Gallery Edinburgh p. 16; Séamus J. Ryan collection p. 91; Sportsfile pp 2, 4 (*both*), 5, 170, 190, 191, 192 (*both*), 184–202 inclusive, 203 (*top*), 204–6 inclusive, 207 (*bottom*), 209 (*bottom*), 211 (*top*), 218–42 inclusive; *Tipperary Star* p. 80 (*bottom*).

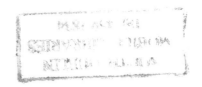

The 2,000 Associations

On four successive Sundays every September, Ireland is confronted with its own soul. Combining ritual, history, culture and sporting event, the four All-Ireland finals in hurling and football for men and women have served to inspire generations of Irish people at home and abroad.

And, uniquely, for what are essentially ball games, have caused them to reflect a little on what they are.

The Gaelic Athletic Association (GAA) has always described itself as 'more than a sporting organisation'. Previous generations, critics and defenders alike, assumed that that meant it is a political organisation as well.

They were right.

But it doesn't stop at that. The GAA did not follow the sporting, cultural or political norms in Ireland: it helped to define them. The GAA has created its own unique sporting culture on the island and among Irish people abroad.

It led rather than followed the country's faltering moves from colonial to post-colonial status to a modern nation.

In the North it helped stabilise and bring focus to a minority community entrapped by a sectarian crisis not of its own making. In England, Scotland, America and Australia it gave solace to economic migrants at a time of high emigration.

In recent years the phrase 'more than a sporting organisation' has been re-examined and extended.

Hurlers, handballers, footballers, musicians and set dancers talked of the GAA's contribution to a wider culture.

Sociologists talked of the GAA's role as a focus for the communities under the pressure of economic hardship and emigration.

Historians talked of its role in raising national consciousness in Irish history.

Economists talked of its contribution to the business life of the small towns which staged its matches.

Architects talked of the symbiosis between the landscape and the clubhouse that the GAA's capital development has represented.

Sports sociologists talked with wonder about this museum-piece amateur sporting organisation which has been guided by professionals to compete successfully in the media marketplace of the twenty-first century.

And it became increasingly clear that 'more than a sporting organisation' is an open-ended term.

The key to understanding the GAA is not found in the large-scale pageantry of the All-Ireland final which dominates the September weekend. That, after all, is the way that all ritualised climactic ball games transpire throughout the developed world.

Instead, the key to what makes the GAA special can be found on St Patrick's Day, when a very different event takes place in Croke Park to celebrate the Irish national festival. The club finals do not fill the 82,000 seats of the national stadium, but they are closer to the heart of the association.

Every spring, each of the 2,000 GAA teams sets out to achieve one ambition, to bring glory and honour to their village, suburb or townland. Croke Park on St Patrick's Day is where the best clubs end up.

Some of these places don't exist on the map. They are communities of rural households brought together by allegiance rather than the fancies of a medieval cartographer.

They sometimes represent units which exist only in the minds of the GAA and its followers. Each is different from the next parish, the next townland, the next county. Administrators have a full-time job trying to understand local allegiances and local rivalries and the complex relationships between them.

During a dispute over electoral procedure at a club in Monaghan in 1982, the absence of membership cards was queried by Seán Kilfeather, a visiting journalist. 'Membership of the GAA is a state of mind', he was told.

The GAA is a patchwork of 2,000 different associations, each one existing in its own state of mind.

● ● ●

Since its foundation in 1884, the GAA has spread unevenly through the country. Founded in Thurles as a counterweight to the sporting establishment growing in Dublin, its initial influence was in Munster and the southern counties of Leinster.

Andy Comerford and Derek Lynch of Kilkenny oppose John Reddan and Colin Lynch of Clare for the throw-in, a tradition in hurling that predates the GAA. Michael Cusack's initial rules suggested that a woman on horseback should throw in the ball at the start of the match. Until 1970 it was common for an invited dignitary, usually a civil or religious leader, to throw in the ball. Among those accorded the honour was the Archbishop of Perth, Redmond Prendiville, who had defied seminary rules to play for Kerry in the 1924 All-Ireland final. In Kerry they still joke about how Tadhgie Lyne tackled Archbishop Thomas Morris at the start of the 1960 All-Ireland football final after he had thrown in the ball.

In hurling the boundaries are even more pronounced. Hurling was compacted in east Munster and south Leinster at the time the GAA was founded and has not spread out from those regions since.

The game is played in just one city, Cork, seriously in ten counties, and has a reasonable number of participants in ten more. Three teams, Cork, Kilkenny and Tipperary have dominated the game throughout its history. Each of these hurling counties has a football area (even Kilkenny) where hurling is a secondary pursuit.

Previous generations ascribed this to a genetic factor: 'Hurlers are born, not made.' The most noted exception must be Seán Óg Ó hAilpín. As the GAA's much-loved broadcaster Micheál Ó Muircheartaigh commented in one of his famous mid-broadcast asides: 'His father's from Fermanagh, his mother's from Fiji, neither a hurling stronghold.'

The hurling boundary can be easily marked on a map. In Clare the border runs from Tubber in the north to Labasheeda on the Shannon through Corofin and Kilmaley. To the north, hurling stops on a straight line from Ballinasloe to Galway city, and then at the Corrib bank. Roscommon's hurling parishes, Ballygar, Four Roads and Tremane, just make the line, and north of that the Antrim Glens and the Ards Peninsula are the only remnants of a ground hurling tradition that once extended to Derry and Donegal.

In Limerick it runs the boundary dividing the hills of west Limerick from the limestone lowlands of east Limerick. Kerry's hurling parishes, Ardfert, Ballyheigue, Causeway and Bluss are just inside the border.

In Cork the hurling border loops from Mallow to the city and the coast at Cloyne, home of Christy Ring, who once said the best way to promote hurling in Cork was by stabbing a knife through every football found east of this line.

To the east it stops on the Grand Canal and at the Blue Ball on the road between Birr and Tullamore, just beyond the Slieve Blooms in Camross in Laois, in Ballylinan in north Kilkenny, halfway through Carlow, and on the foothills of the Wicklow Mountains between Ferns and Carnew.

Many of the better players in non-hurling counties like Dublin, Kildare and Meath are the sons of hurlers who migrated, including the iconic Dubliner Niall Quinn who scored some of the most memorable goals in Irish soccer history.

Art Ó Maolfabhail's *Camán: 2,000 Years of Irish Hurling* pointed out that the ground hurling of the beach and coastal regions (camánacht) prevailed in the north along Antrim, Derry and Donegal with an outcrop in Kerry, and the more expansive wide-bas field hurling (iománaíocht) prevailed in Munster and south Leinster, but the two forms of hurling appear to have co-existed in many areas.

Historians have locked camáns on the issue. In 1993 the Wexford-born geographer Kevin Whelan developed his wetland-dryland thesis, that the boundaries between hurling and football areas also mark those between the big farms from the small, the fertile land from the hungry, the ash from the rushes, 'the transition from fertile, drift-covered limestone lowland to hillier, hungrier, wetter shales, flagstones, grits and granites. If ash is emblematic of hurling areas, the rush is the distinctive symbol of football territory.'

Whelan feels that when the patronage of the gentry ended, hurling went into a tailspin. It collapsed into shapeless anarchy and declined so swiftly that it was lost everywhere except in Cork city, south-east Galway and north of Wexford town. He argues that the kingdom of east Thomond extends through some of the richest hurling lands of the counties of Clare, Galway, Limerick, Tipperary and Offaly. The southern hurling zone coincides with the area where, in the late medieval period, the Norman and Gaelic worlds fused to produce a vigorous culture and coincides with the well-drained level terrain.

A simpler explanation would be that hurling is a more difficult game to learn, and a strong hurling culture is necessary to support the vast number of young people to sustain a successful county or club team. But traditions, as the GAA has learned again and again, can be hothoused and grown.

The Kildare team that went to the 1976 Leinster senior semi-final had a collection of Wexford and Galway *émigrés*, but they also had home-grown players such as Pat Dunny, Tommy Christian and Mick Dwan. Kildare's hurling tradition reaches back to 1949, when two Johnson brothers from Callan came and settled in two townlands, from which grew the Ardclough and Éire Óg clubs. Asked for the secret as to how hurling had grown from nothing in Ardclough, one player credits Mick Johnson's wife from Mullinahone who gathered the youngsters together in her back field for practice.

Football — slower, more ponderous and easier to master — has permeated the nation but made little progress outside of the Irish communities abroad.

The two games share the same playing field, slightly larger than soccer or rugby, and H-shaped goals with one point for a score over the crossbar and three points (a goal) under the crossbar.

The skills of fielding, the solo run where the ball is released to the foot and taken back again, and the devilishly difficult lift with the toe, are honed in long evenings of effort. Hurling advocates look down at the slower game, but football is played on a wider scale.

Kerry, the proud home of one of the ancestors of modern football, the inter-parish game caid, has dominated the sport. Cork has the most clubs, followed by Dublin. Most of the 32 counties have enjoyed a level of success at provincial, under-age or graded championships. Fermanagh and Wicklow are the only counties which have not won a provincial championship. Fermanagh, ironically, have contested two All-Ireland semi-finals, and a Wicklow club won an All-Ireland representing Dublin.

Six sports are organised or supported by the GAA. Separate women's associations for hurling (camogie) and women's football are in the process of being integrated into the association, as happened with women's golf, hockey and basketball into dual-sex associations in recent years.

Handball is played with the bare hand (or gloved) against a wall. A one wall game or games in two court sizes are played to a high level by Irish players and players in six other countries. Irish players have recently won the world singles championship and professional tournaments in America.

Rounders is organised by a separate association, the Rounders Association of Ireland. Americans would see similarities with fast pitch softball. The sport is dominated by four counties, Carlow, Cavan, Derry and Dublin.

Athletics was organised by the GAA until 1922, and the GAA had a hand in developing the athletes that won 20 gold medals at the modern Olympics, as well as the inclusion of the hammer throw and triple jump on athletic programmes.

But it is the unique sports of hurling and Gaelic football that draw the biggest crowds, the biggest television audiences, and the most attention.

Their story, and the story of the communities that play them, is as gripping as the games that inspired it.

The making of hurleys remains a local, although increasingly mechanised, industry, with periodic shortages of the required ash timber leading to supply problems. A competitive match can leave 20 hurleys broken and splintered on the sideline, so a supply of spares is essential. The size of the base (bas) of the hurley has never been regulated, and from the 1970s on it was not unusual for goalkeepers to pick a broader-based hurley for puck-outs than for general play.

Battered, bruised and somewhat the worse for 70 years of celebrating, the Sam Maguire cup was retired to the GAA museum in Croke Park and replaced by baby Sam. Here one-week-old Eoin Browne from Dublin samples a little of the glory in 2002.

Donal Daly and Darragh Ó Sé of Kerry and John Toal and Paul McGrane of Armagh jostle as Longford referee John Bannon throws in the ball. Man-to-man marking has been a tactical staple of Gaelic football since the early twentieth century.

chapter two

The Prairie Fire

Who founded the GAA, and why? In more certain times we know that the Gaelic Athletic Association was founded at a poorly attended meeting in the billiards room of Hayes's Hotel in Thurles on 1 November 1884.

The seven founders were named in Thomas F. O'Sullivan's *History of the GAA* (1916): schoolteacher and hurling revivalist Michael Cusack, champion athlete Maurice Davin, Cusack's past pupil and rugby team mate police District Inspector Thomas St George McCarthy, journalists John McKay from Cork and John Wyse Power from Waterford, Carrick-born solicitor P. J. O'Ryan, and John K. Bracken, a stone-mason who played cricket for Templemore.

The meeting was as much about identity as athletics. Cusack's call for self-determination in sporting matters, 'A Word About Irish Athletics', had been published in William O'Brien's Land League journal, *United Ireland*.

The new movement tapped into more than one popular idea: that articulated by Parnell's political machine, the National League; Michael Davitt's agrarian Land League; and a third, largely apolitical popular movement, a sporting revolution that was transforming rural Ireland.

The clues as to what was happening throughout rural Ireland can be found in advertisements in provincial newspapers. From May through to October, the new newspapers springing up in provincial towns carried advertisements for local athletics sports.

The form varied from place to place, but generally a notice appeared indicating that the annual sports would be held at a local field, with a local aristocrat named as patron, and a committee of middle-class organisers listed. Some of the events were borrowed from the programmes of high-profile athletics sports in the cities. The sports at Trinity College in Dublin, for instance, had been running since 1857, Galway University since 1863, and Cork University since 1871. Cash prizes were offered for individual events. Running, jumping, pitching and tossing were rewarded accordingly. By 1881 there were over a hundred of these annual meetings. The question of affiliation to London or Dublin did not arise.

But with a land war festering in the background, issues such as patronage did. And in 1879 in Balla there was a stand-off.

The Balla sports enjoyed the patronage and the use of grounds from Sir Robert L. Blosse. A resolution from Blosse, which was not adopted, to the Mayo Grand Jury in 1879 so incensed a section of the local community that they staged a rival sports to his on William Nally's farm in Lagaturu. Pat Nally organised these sports.

The club wanted at first to hold their annual sports as usual, but without Blosse's patronage. He refused, and when a nationalist band, the Emmet Band from Dundalk, was engaged to play at the dissident sports, he ran them off his land.

Blosse held his own sports, followed by one of the most spectacular fireworks displays ever seen in Mayo. Then the people, with the support of the Land League which had been formed in Castlebar two months earlier, held theirs.

The patrons for Pat Nally's sports were Charles Stewart Parnell and James Lysaght Finigan, who had just been elected Home Rule MP for Ennis in a by-election.

Although neither patron showed up, 2,000 people supported the meeting and 16 police were dispatched to keep an eye on things. One banner at the meeting read 'God Save Ireland' on one side and 'Pay Not' on the other. Significantly, the programme of 19 events included a 300 yards 'race for labourers'.

In 1881 Nally met Cusack and they talked about the issues of control of athletics in Ireland, the fact that labourers were excluded from those sports run under English AAC rules, and the possibility of a separate new movement which would give Ireland autonomy in sporting matters.

The strength of the personalities behind the new GAA were important in securing its survival. This was the eighth attempt to kick-start an Irish athletics organisation, counting the Dublin Amateur Athletics Club of 1867, Henry Dunlop's Irish Champion Athletics Club of 1872 which was credited as the national association in the 1879 edition of the *Encyclopaedia Brittanica*, Val Dunbar's Irish National Athletics Committee of 1877 which was to have led to the Irish AAA in 1878 but disappeared without trace, Cusack's 'National Athletics Meeting' of 1880, Henry Dunlop's Amateur Athletics Association of Ireland of 1881, and the Dublin Athletics Club of 1882.

Cusack had been involved at committee level with six of them, and had come into contact with all the people who were behind the organisation of sporting culture in Dublin.

They included Henry Dunlop, instigator of the Lansdowne Road project, the Hones and Barringtons of Trinity and its offshoot Civil Service sports, the four Davin brothers of Carrick-on-Suir who were the inspiration of the Munster athletics circuit, and the two journalists who invented modern sports coverage in Ireland, Fred Gallaher and John L. Dunbar, editors of the nationalist sporting journal, *Sport*, and its unionist counterpart, the *Irish Sportsman*. Another forgotten inspiration of the GAA was the Dublin-based Scottish journalist, Morrison Miller, who organised the Caledonian Games that attracted 20,000 spectators to the RDS in May 1884.

Cusack was 37 by this time and brimming with the obsessive energy that was to bring his involvement with the organisation he founded to a premature end. He was also turning his back on Dublin's sporting culture.

He had not always been hostile to urban or colonial influences. In 1881 he had advocated cricket as Ireland's national game. He was also passionately interested in athletics and joined all the Dublin athletics organisations, the Irish Champion Athletics Club, the City and Suburban Harriers, the Irish Cross Country Championship club, and the Dublin Athletics Club, and became heavily involved at committee level in all of them. He first proposed a new body to control Irish athletics in three letters to the *Irish Sportsman* in 1881.

He had come to Dublin in December 1878 and founded a private school to assist young people entering the civil service or universities, using his own notes and publishing question and answer books. It was a huge success and Cusack started a school rugby team and, crucially, a hurley club, the Civil Service Academy Hurley Club.

The set of rules drawn up by Trinity College Hurley Club were not the oldest in the game (Paddy Larkin had put together a hurling code for the Killimor club in 1869), but they were the first to be published. They did not permit handling the ball, allowed the ball to be struck only with the left side of the stick, and the clubs which played it eventually affiliated to the hockey union.

But it excited the interest of Cusack in Ireland's oldest game, enriched with a semi-mythical status in the annals and heroic literature and references in the Brehon laws which had been enthusiastically gathered and reissued over the previous three decades by John O'Donovan, William Wilde and Eugene O'Curry.

Cusack, who played hurley enthusiastically, turned his attention to the Irish language on the foundation of a 'Gaelic Union for the Preservation and Cultivation of the Irish language' in his academy in 1882.

From this sprang the *Gaelic Journal* of November 1882, and directly as a result of the journal, the Dublin Hurling Club in December 1883. One of Cusack's biographers, Marcus de Búrca, believes Cusack only decided on the revival of hurling in 1882 to get at his opponents of the athletics establishment, who were hurley men. His club lasted just four months but had played one high-profile, if poorly regulated, match against the Killimor club in Galway, and from the experience he planned for a new association which would combine the organisation of hurling and athletics. From his language movement and journal he borrowed the 'Gaelic' aperture which was to become the new association's most successful brand.

Cusack allied with Castlederg-born Methodist and Hardwicke school headmaster John Huston Stewart in 1882 and his RIC past pupil Owen Harte, exploiting the public feeling caused by the Phoenix Park murders to get the 'no police' rule removed by the Dublin Athletics Club in 1882.

In 1881 Cusack had proposed that 'English standards of excellence be accepted' by Irish clubs, but he shared the concern of Val Dunbar at the foothold the English AAA was gaining in Ireland.

The athletics section of the Ulster Cricket Club affiliated to the English AAA in 1882 and the Trinity College Sports of 1883, hitherto an independent event, were held under English AAA rules.

Dunbar's normally unionist-inclined *Irish Sportsman* called for 'Home Rule in Irish athletics', fairly unambiguous terminology in the political context of the time, in January 1884. The argument was joined by Cusack and his friends, stressing especially that weight-throwing was not emphasised by English AAA rules.

The Cusack who attacked R. J. O'Duffy of the Society for the Protection of the Irish Language at their congress of April 1882 for being 'too nationalist' unashamedly used the political machinery of nationalism to construct his own sports body two years later.

● ● ●

In 1884 a campaign was launched by Fred Gallaher that English AAA rules should apply to the network of unregulated summer sports throughout the country.

Cusack may have already decided on his alternative. In 1883 he had attended athletics meetings in Munster on what one of the organisers of Cork sports called his 'Gaelic mission'. Despite a mixed reaction there, in 1884 he decided to bypass Dublin altogether and use Munster to launch the new association.

Let the games begin. The earliest representation of a stick and ball game is found in the Athens archaeological museum. One of three, probably forming the base of a pedestal in a gymnasium, it was found in Athens in 1922 and dates from the fifth century B.C. The players at the side may be waiting for leaders to start the game, or to engage in single combat themselves. The figure on the left may be signalling the start of the match. Ireland's heroic and romantic literature suggests that the men of Ireland were hurling around this time. The Arabs, Greeks, Persians and Romans each had their own version of a stick and ball game.

At what appears to have been short notice, he decided that November 1884 would be a suitable date to found the GAA. Samhain is one of the most significant Celtic festivals, and it was the legendary date on which the battle of Cath Gabhra had been fought in A.D. 294, where the elite and athletic force of the Fianna had been defeated. The small attendance in Thurles that day may reflect the impulsive nature of Cusack's decision to start the movement.

The GAA's founder remains an enigma. Biographer Liam Ó Cathnia passionately opposed the theory that Cusack was the model for the rather unsympathetic character of the Citizen in James Joyce's *Ulysses*. The bigoted, alcoholic anti-Semite that Bloom meets in the Circe chapter is how Cusack is presented through literature to modern generations.

According to Ó Cathnia, Cusack was not anti-Semitic or anti-Protestant, and did not favour the IRB or Invincible violence. Marcus de Búrca's biography of Cusack is less convinced, calling Cusack 'colourful and often controversial'.

Somewhat appropriately, even the site of his birthplace in Carron, restored by the GAA in 1984, is disputed.

Three weeks before the meeting in Thurles, Cusack wrote an address to Irish athletes in the Land League journal *United Ireland*. It would have been read by a small and highly politicised readership.

No movement having for its object the social and political advancement of a nation from the tyranny of imported and enforced customs and manners can be regarded as perfect if it has not made adequate provision for the preservation and cultivation of the national pastimes of the people. Voluntary neglect of such pastimes is a sure sign of national decay and dissolution.

A few years ago a so-called revival of athletics was inaugurated in Ireland. The new movement did not originate with those who have ever had any sympathy with Ireland or the Irish people. Accordingly labourers, tradesmen, artists, and even policemen and soldiers were excluded from the few competitions which constituted the lame and halting programme of the promoters.

Two years ago every man who did not make his living either partly or wholly by athletics was allowed to compete. But with this concession came a law which is as intolerable as its existence in Ireland is degrading. The law is that all athletics meetings should be held under the rules of the Amateur Athletics Association of England and that any person competing at any meeting not held under these rules should be ineligible to compete elsewhere. The management of nearly all the meetings held in Ireland since has been entrusted to persons hostile to all the dearest aspirations of the Irish people.

Every effort has been made to make the meetings look as English as possible — foot-races, betting and flagrant cheating being their most prominent features. Swarms of pot-hunting mashers sprang into existence. They formed harrier clubs for the purpose of training through the winter, after the fashion of English professional athletes, that they might be able to win and pawn the prizes offered for competition in the summer.

We tell the Irish people to take the management of their games into their own hands, to encourage and promote in every way every form of athletics which is peculiarly Irish, and to remove with one sweep everything foreign and iniquitous in the present system.

The vast majority of the best athletes in Ireland are nationalists. These gentlemen should take the matter in hands at once, and draft laws for the guidance of the promoters of meetings in Ireland next year. The people pay the expenses of the meetings, and the representatives of the people should have the controlling power. It is only by such an arrangement that pure Irish athletics will be revived, and the incomparable strength and physique of our race will be preserved.

The vast library of correspondence and journalism that Cusack left has overshadowed the association's first president, Maurice Davin, and the role he played in founding the GAA. But while Cusack had lined up political support, Davin was responsible for the success of the body in the sporting world.

A former holder of the world hammer throw record, he was hugely respected across the south. His throws of a short-handled hammer, using one arm, against M. M. Stritch, who used a long-handled hammer and both arms, were the highlight of the Civil Service sports of 1872 (which Davin won) and the first Irish

Hammer Championship staged by the Irish Champion Athletics Club in 1873 (when Stritch won). These were scenes not out of place in Charles J. Kickham's *Knocknagow*, published in book form the same year.

Davin's brother Tom competed in the English championship for the first time in 1874 and Maurice's two weight-throwing victories at the first English AAA championship in 1881 helped to earn it the description as a 'world championship' in the English press.

Davin may have been responsible for bringing football into the GAA. An officer of Carrick-on-Suir Cricket and Football Club, he was aware of the growth of rugby clubs across Munster, significantly in the future GAA heartland of Kerry where Killorglin was among the affiliates. In the month before the GAA was founded, he wrote: 'Irish football is a great game and worth going a long way to see when played on a fairly laid out ground and under proper rules.' He set about drafting those proper rules.

Few organisations can have had three initial meetings as widely divergent as the GAA. The press reports of the foundation meeting divide into two categories: those written by Cusack, McKay or Wyse Power, listing seven founders; and those written on second-hand information which list 12. The billiards room meeting in Lizzie Hayes's hotel in Thurles brought together an eclectic bunch, Cusack, Davin, three IRB men and two men who never took any further part in the association, a solicitor friend of Davin and an RIC officer who played rugby for Ireland.

Six other names were listed as attending the meeting in the *Freeman's Journal*, including a colleague of Davin he had rowed with in Carrick-on-Suir, William Foley, John Butler of Ballyhuddy, and four others from Thurles, the 1878 mile champion T. K. Dwyer, C. Culhane, William Delahunty and M. Cantwell. The image is suggested of Frank Maloney of Nenagh skulking around the environs of the room, perhaps with colleagues from the IRB, perhaps deterred from attending by St George McCarthy's presence. It is likely they came to express their support but did not attend the meeting which, if press reports are to be believed, largely consisted of reading congratulatory telegrams and letters of support.

All that was achieved in Thurles was to secure the valuable patronage of Dr Thomas W. Croke, Charles Stewart Parnell and Michael Davitt, the most powerful ecclesiastical and political figures of nationalist Ireland.

The second meeting in the Victoria Hotel in Cork in January 1885 saw the GAA effectively taken over by the Irish Parliamentary Party. Davin was not in the chair; politician and lord mayor elect Paul Madden presided. John O'Connor, another prospective MP, did most of the talking. The central committee of the GAA was packed with the 25 members of the organising committee of the National League, the officers elected at Thurles, and a vague 'two delegates' from every registered athletics club. Marcus de Búrca speculates this was part of a deal done with Parnell as a price for granting patronage, particularly if Parnell was aware of the Fenian background of three of the seven founder members, or it may just be that Cusack and Davin wanted to utilise the National League network, something suggested in letters to the provincial press two weeks beforehand.

The third meeting on 17 January 1885 saw the GAA, after marking its cards with both the IRB and the Irish Party, draw up rules for the sports it sought to promote. Two of the delegates at the meeting (Frank Maloney and John Fahy) represented Nenagh Cricket Club, and two the North Tipperary Hurling Club. Rules were adopted.

The fifteenth-century grave slab at the ruined church of Clonca near Malin Head in Innishowen is the oldest visual representation of a hurley. The inscription on the stone says it was made by Ferghas Mac Állain to the memory of Manas mac Mhoireasdáin of Iona. The stone depicts a sword, a cross and a narrow-bas camán and ball.

Panel from an altar set depicting a stick and ball game in medieval Denmark. It dates to 1333 and relates to the monastery of Soro which was dissolved in 1586. During the Middle Ages a French stick game called hoquet was played, and the English word hockey may be derived from it.

One of the vice-presidents appointed at this meeting never attended a GAA meeting — John Stewart, the Tyrone Methodist who had campaigned with Cusack against the 'no-labourers rule' at the Dublin AC.

Hammer throw record-holder William 'Jumbo' Barry, who was also appointed vice-president, seems to have taken no part in association affairs and instead given his allegiance to the Irish Amateur Athletics Association founded by Dunlop, Dunbar and Lloyd Christian the following month.

A third vice-president, J. F. Murphy of the Lees club from Cork, was soon to lose his position because his club continued to play football under what appeared to be rugby rules, despite being affiliated to the GAA.

J. E. Kennedy of the Cork Athletics Club was also appointed, indicating the southern bias of the new association.

There was no Dublin representation, and eventually it was the Dublin clubs which called the two meetings to form the Irish Amateur Athletics Association, expressing alarm at the close connections between the GAA and the Irish National League evident at the meeting in Cork. Cork AC, the club of one of the GAA founders, John McKay, was among several which associated with both bodies for much of 1885.

Cusack said the new organisation spread like a 'prairie fire'. It did so because there was a pre-existing athletics circuit where Davin's name was well known, and a political network of National League branches which set up sporting branches.

'Although I am not a member of the National League', Cusack wrote to Davin in April 1884, 'I think I am not without influence with several of its leading members.' In the same letter he declares 'the whole business must be worked from Munster', and 'I have found it to be a hopeless cause to revive our national pastimes without the assistance of the leaders of the people.'

Cusack had a clear idea who his main supporter would be. Four days after the first rules of football and hurling were drawn up, Charles Stewart Parnell made his famous speech declaring that no man has the right to fix the boundary on the march of a nation.

In the eight weeks between the first and second meetings of the GAA, the Irish National League connection seems to have been reinforced. *Irishman's* circular letter to the provincial press within a fortnight of the foundation of the GAA in November 1884, urged that every branch of the Irish National League should organise 'athletics and gymnastics clubs' and to affiliate with the parent body 'to maintain our position as a distinct nation'.

It has been suggested that Cusack made a deal to gain Parnell's patronage of the infant GAA, particularly as Parnell might have recognised IRB fingerprints on the proceedings at Thurles, but it is much more likely that the deal was secured well in advance of the August letter to Davin.

Some of the trappings of the Catholic and Repeal Association meetings were inherited, including the patronage of the clergy, the use of bands which played 'national tunes', banners, green flags and harp motifs. A green flag with the gold harp floated over some early GAA sports meetings. At the revival hurling match in Nenagh 3,000 spectators attended Captain O'Carroll's field in Lisenhall. It was bedecked in green and white flags for the occasion and a banner at the entrance proclaimed 'God Save Ireland'.

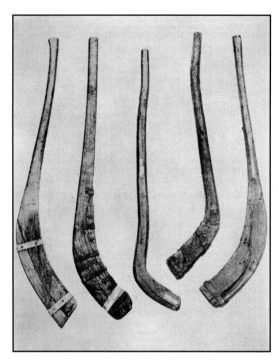

Camáns from the collection of the National Museum, from County Wexford (*c*.1900), County Clare (*c*.1905), Tuam, Co. Galway (*c*.1850), unknown (late nineteenth century) and Wexford (*c*.1900). Horsehair balls, also part of the collection, were displayed for the first time when the museum extension at Collins Barracks was opened in 1997.

The original three patrons were Parnell of the Irish Party, Davitt of the Land League, and most significantly Thomas William Croke, Archbishop of the province where the GAA had been established and enjoyed its greatest support.

Within months two more patrons were added, the Irish Republican Brotherhood founder John O'Leary and the Nationalist MP William O'Brien. The tradition of Catholic churchmen holding honorary presidencies of GAA clubs continues to this day, as does that of seeking the patronage of the Archbishop of Cashel at national level.

Church support gave it an advantage over the IAAA, and on three occasions the archbishop criticised the excesses of the early association.

The archbishop intervened to solve several further GAA crises, most notably after the convention of November 1887.

The association was by no means exclusively a Catholic one, but after the Thurles convention of 1887 few of those early Protestant members were left.

The Gaelic Athletic Association was founded by sportsmen with a passing interest in politics, rather than politicians with a passing interest in sport. This can finally be established despite claims made by Tom Markham in 1934 that an IRB subcommittee planned the GAA at a series of meetings in Dublin in 1883.

Ireland's political police, the Royal Irish Constabulary (RIC), were suspicious but thought the association doomed to a political future, and their bulky files on the association have served as valuable source material since. They have helped to justify the argument that the GAA served mainly as a cover for subversive activity, but in the meantime may have put undue emphasis on the IRB influence on the association. RIC men didn't track the National League members who joined up.

Of the historians who trawled through those files, Bill Mandle and Pádraig Puirséal felt the motivation was largely political. Liam P. Ó Cathnia and Marcus de Búrca did not.

It appears that the existence of a ready-made political structure extending into hundreds of parishes throughout rural Ireland proved too great a temptation for the Clare herdsman's son to resist when he started the association. Once this political skeleton had been uncovered, it proved difficult for the GAA to find a cupboard to contain it.

When Cusack identified this structure, it was about 60 years old and undergoing its third incarnation. It was the handiwork of none other than Daniel O'Connell, admiration of whose penchant for populist politics is one of the few things that has united historians of the nineteenth century. On one Sunday in 1828 the Catholic Association had organised 1,500 simultaneous meetings around the country.

The model of O'Connell's Catholic and Repeal Association is suggested by the list of branches in small and obscure townlands recorded in RIC files compiled immediately before the Parnell split of 1890.

The parish organisation was inaugurated so effortlessly as to mirror the political organisation of the Catholic and Repeal Associations of pre-famine times. To this day, parish priests are often granted honorary presidencies and curates become presidents of clubs associated with chapels of ease. The use of local patron saints or historical figures, the identity with the landscape and spirit of the district, the strong sense of neighbourliness and the lack of clear membership structures all invoke something that dates back to the age of Dan O'Connell and run deeper than sport.

That the GAA was grafted on to the populist political movement of rural Ireland, descended from O'Connell's times, made it very parochial but gave it a resilience which enabled it to survive the crises of the Parnell split and the later Civil War.

The localised structure proved a useful model for other national organisations. It also explains the rapid growth of the GAA. There were 31 soccer clubs in the whole of Ireland in 1885, half of them based in Belfast.

The GAA peaked at 875 clubs immediately before the 1890 Parnell split, a level it was not to approach again for 20 years.

Crucially, Cusack's piggy-back on the organisation of O'Connell's movement meant that the parish club came to be accepted by the GAA, accepting diocesan but ignoring county boundaries, with often incongruous results. It remains the basic unit of the GAA today.

●   ●   ●

Davin drew up rules for four sports, football, hurling, athletics and handball, but little or no effort was made to regulate handball until the birth of a rival organisation, the Irish Amateur Handball Union, in 1912.

Most handball activity in the 1890s and early 1900s seems to have taken place outside GAA control, with large sums of money changing hands in breach of the association's amateur rules.

Cusack's *Celtic Times* reported on another widespread Munster activity. Road bowling was believed to have been introduced by soldiers or perhaps by English and Scottish weavers in the eighteenth century. A 28 ounce ball, 2.5 inches in diameter, resembling a cannon ball, is thrown along a road. The game was relatively widespread in the 1880s and there were moves to get the GAA to include it in its list of sports, but little became of it and it had declined sharply by the time it was eventually organised by J. F. Cadden's All-Ireland Bowl Players Association in the 1920s. A scheme to bring coursing under GAA control in December 1901 fell through.

Rounders, included from the beginning, was also largely ignored, although it was widespread enough to secure its inclusion in the Tailteann programme of 1924.

None of the other local games mentioned by Croke in his acceptance letter was codified. 'Ball-playing, hurling, football-kicking according to Irish rules, casting, leaping in various ways, wrestling, handy-grips, top-pegging, leap-frog, rounders, tip-in-the-hat, and all such favourite exercises and amusements amongst men and boys may now be said to be not only dead and buried', he wrote in 1884, 'but in several localities to be entirely forgotten and unknown.'

Samuel Carter and Anne Maria Hall's *Ireland: Its Scenery, Character* etc. published in 1842, described the game of hurling as they encountered it or, more likely, were told about it. (Mrs Hall had grown up in Wexford.) This famous illustration, with its oversized ball high in the air and a gate that probably served as the goal to the left, accompanied an account of hurling in Kerry given in the third volume published in 1840. The Halls related an apocryphal tale about a great hurling match held in the Phoenix Park, got up by the Lord Lieutenant at the end of the eighteenth century and attended by all the nobility and gentry of the vice regal court. They were told that the winning goal was struck through the window of the vice regal carriage. By the time the book came on the scene, the game appeared to be in near terminal decline.

The long-established 'meggers' (horse-shoe throwing) did not merit a mention. It is not clear if the organisation of boxing and wrestling was considered — in his youth Davin had once travelled to seek a sparring match with Jem Mace who was staying in Clonmel.

On the same day that the rules were being agreed, Killimor defeated Ballinakill by two goals to nil in the first hurling match, presumably under Paddy Larkin's 1869 hurling rules. A month later, three football matches were played under the new GAA rules. At St Canice's Park in Kilkenny town, two clubs, St Patrick's and St Canice's, met. In Naas, Co. Kildare, Naas played Sallins. All three were scoreless draws.

The football rules that were adopted in January 1885 and published in *United Ireland* would be virtually unrecognisable even five years later. A soccer goal was used as the model. There is no mention of off-side, nor do the rules mention how long a player could handle the ball. The rules for hurling, which closely paralleled those for football, stipulated that the ball may not be lifted off the ground with the hand.

They give no idea of whether it was a carrying or a propulsion game, although Cusack claimed in April 1885 that under GAA rules 'the ball must not be carried'.

When Maurice Davin, the author of the rules, was present at another scoreless hurling match on 14 June in Dublin, he suggested that Nenagh should be declared the winners against Athenry because they 'had hit the ball over the crossbar, Galway having gained no point'.

Scores were soon being counted unofficially as 'overs', and a 4 July meeting suggested that 'going over the end line five times should count as a point'. On 10 October the concept of a point was defined further when a rule was made that point posts be erected 21 yards on each side of the goal posts.

A trial period until 1 November met with great enthusiasm and the rules were altered for the third time in a six-month period.

Points were soon to become a feature of Gaelic matches, both football and hurling.

A goal outweighed any number of points until 1892. A goal was then made equal to five points, and finally in 1895 to three points, scored over the soccer-

This engraving of a boy keeping sentry in case the priest should break up a hurling match accompanied a description of just such an incident in Thomas Crofton Croker's *Fairy Legends and Traditions of the South of Ireland* in 1825. His description of summer hurling was the most famous English-language account of the game at the time the GAA was founded. Both hurlers in the background have their right hand underneath.

style posts and between point posts on either side of the goal.

Another improvement came in 1888 when the number of players on each team was reduced from 21 a side to 17 a side.

The second major amendment to the original rules for GAA football abolished wrestling and handigrips, but not without severe opposition from Waterford and Kilkenny.

Cusack too was dissatisfied, suggesting that they might as well ban the hand-pass as well and 'then we have the Association game'. GAA football had evolved into a propulsion game seventeen months after rules were first drawn up. Clubs seemed to move freely between the codes. Wicklow town started out life as an Association club but entered their local county Gaelic football championship in 1887.

That led to the first of many splits in the GAA. Lees club in Cork preferred the carrying game. The rules that were in use in Cork city, particularly by the Lees club, were described as 'rugby undisguised' at a GAA meeting in October 1885.

J. F. Murphy of Cork was removed from the vice-presidency of the association the following February because he had 'framed the so-called National Football Rules in opposition to the GAA'.

Within a fortnight a meeting in the Foresters' Hall in Cork formed the Munster National Football Association (MNFA) and elected Murphy president. The GAA claimed at their special convention in Thurles that May that 'several clubs in the south are playing football under rugby rules' and that 'opponents of the GAA were present at the meeting in the Foresters' Hall'.

The MNFA resolved not to play under rugby rules. Maurice Davin advised the Cork footballers that they could play under the Munster rules and still be recognised by the GAA as athletes. In August, founder member John McKay resigned as Cork secretary, and in September he resigned from the vice-presidency of the association. But in November Lees had applied for admission to the GAA and had been accepted, apparently happy with changes to the rules of the football game which had now been abbreviated with the title 'Gaelic' after the association which controlled it.

Almost certainly at Cusack's behest, another Cork group from Blarney, Riverstown and Little Island, met to reinforce the GAA in the county.

In August, the Wexford county board arranged a county championship with the most remarkable scorelines in Gaelic history. Rosslare beat Lady's Island by two tries to nil, Ballymore by three tries to one, and Crossabeg by three tries to two after extra time to win the first GAA county championship.

Internationally, the GAA was the second athletics body to be established worldwide. It is a measure of the country's capacity for bifurcation that Ireland also supplied the third.

While the football split was quickly solved, the GAA had a rival athletics body to contend with within three months of its foundation. The Irish Amateur Athletics Association was established by Val Dunbar and many of his Champion Athletics Club colleagues, drawing from the colonial constituency that Cusack had discarded.

After a head-to-head between the rival bodies in Tralee in June 1885, the IAAA was largely confined to Dublin and Belfast, while the GAA managed a populist athletics movement in the provincial towns. The long-term consequences were serious, however. For only three years subsequently, 1922 to 1925, was there unity in Irish athletics and the mess that ensued destabilised the entire Irish sports culture for over a century.

When an English official, Harry Abrahams, became involved in the 1930s, it led to Ireland being excluded from international competition, costing at least two Olympic gold medals and probably more, and the

One of the more evocative pre-GAA hurling scenes features a heavily stylised group of hurlers playing before the O'Connell homestead in Derrynane, etched by John Fogarty around 1831. Hurling was described along the western seaboard in poems, folklore and in scenes such as this, but was no longer played there at the time the GAA was founded.

non-recognition of Pat O'Callaghan's world hammer record. The athletics dispute, as much as the sordid political context of the games, led to Ireland's boycott of the Berlin Olympics in 1936. A resolution of the issue in 1967 succeeded only in killing the popular athletics movement in rural Ireland, and even as the final efforts are being made to solve the problem at the present time, the level of participation in athletics is nowhere near that achieved in the very first year of the GAA's existence.

The athletics achievements of those early GAA years are astonishing. They already had two world record holders (and three records) when the association was founded, Maurice Davin in the hammer and Pat Davin's unprecedented double record in the high jump (6 feet 2¾ inches at Carrick in 1880) and long jump (23 feet 2 inches at Monasterevin in 1883).

Despite scenes such as this famous, probably imaginary, depiction of camanachd of around 1840 in the Scottish National Portrait Gallery in Edinburgh, the Scottish revival of the 1820s failed to lift the game that would become known as shinty. Instead it generated international football matches between England and Scotland 50 years before their official revival, one of which was attended by Walter Scott. By the 1980s, research by Art Ó Maolfabhail and others suggested that camanachd was closer to the ground hurling played in Ulster and north Leinster than modern hurling, and that the GAA founders had rendered ground hurling extinct by adapting the wider-bas Munster and south Leinster form of the game. In reality, the references to hurling in classical, romantic and heroic literature, in poems and in oral and legal sources, are dreadfully vague, do not describe the game and have led to some modern scholars suggesting not all of them may refer to hurling at all.

Seven months after the association was founded, J. C. Daly of Emly provided the GAA with its first new world record when he jumped 44 feet 4 inches in what is now known as the triple jump.

World records began to tumble at rural meetings throughout Ireland. Dan Shanahan of Kilfinane passed the triple jump record three times in a few months in 1886, and at other GAA meetings John Purcell and O. D. Looney of Macroom both pushed the record further until Shanahan jumped 50 feet and half an inch in 1888 to set a record that would stand until 1909. When it was beaten, it was by another GAA athlete who had emigrated to the United States, Dan Ahearne, whose brother Tim won an Olympic gold in 1908. Ahearne's world record stood for a further 13 years.

James Mitchell broke the hammer record twice to take it past the 130-foot mark in 1888 when he went to America with the 'invasion' athletes and never returned, getting a job as a sports-writer with the *New York Sun*.

John Flanagan of Kilmallock took the record from Mitchell at the 1895 GAA championships with a throw of 145 feet 10½ inches and went on to break the record 14 times. He lost it for two brief periods to Tom Kiely of Ballyneale in 1899 and Matt McGrath of Nenagh in 1907, but Flanagan kept winning it back. He was 41 when he broke the record for the last time and retained it until his throw of 185 feet (56.08 metres) was beaten in 1911 by Paddy Ryan of Pallasgreen.

Two other GAA world records survived for over a decade. Tommy Conneff of Clane ran 4 minutes 17.8 seconds for the mile in 1888, a record that was not broken until 1904 (Conneff's world record for the three-quarters of a mile was not broken until 1931).

Peter O'Connor set a long jump record of 24 feet 11¾ inches in Ballsbridge in 1901, breaking his own world record by four inches. It stood as a world record for 20 years and as an Irish record until 1990.

Eighteenth-century football as depicted by an English artist. The first English and Anglophile sports historians saw the history of football as a rough and tumble street festival game that was tamed and codified by English public schoolmasters in the era of Kingsley's 'muscular Christianity'. The truth may be more complex, with broader influences helping football evolve from game to organised sport within a wider European and world context.

• • •

That GAA connection with the National League came undone in the most unpredictable of circumstances. Kerry Nationalist MP Edward Harrington acted as patron for the Kerry County Cricket Club sports in June 1885 without the gift of foresight to realise that this was the single most important confrontation between the GAA and the IAAA in the athletics war of that summer.

Cusack was glad to see off the clutches of the National League, having borrowed and in some cases taken over its organisational structure. The League was seriously damaged by the defeat of the Home Rule movement, only to re-emerge in other political guises. But its impact on the GAA structure can be seen to this day.

There was a high price to be paid for Cusack's use of a political model for his sports body. The GAA wins the championship of Irish sports history with the library of books it has produced, and since Mark Tierney first foraged through the RIC files on the GAA in the 1960s, many of them have dwelt on how the association was so successfully taken over by the Irish Republican Brotherhood.

In fact the take-over of the GAA seems to have been virtually the only achievement of the sieve-like secret society before the 1916 Rising. Few of these historians have even acknowledged how the GAA escaped from the clutches of the National League a few months beforehand. It would help them to see how virtually unavoidable that brush with the Brotherhood was, and how easily the Brotherhood gained control.

Three years after he had founded the GAA, Cusack had a gun pulled on him in Thurles the night before the convention of the association he had founded. It was a reflection of how high tensions could run when a sports organisation was dressed in political clothing.

Even if they had no political allegiances to start with, which is likely despite a reference in Davin's obituary that he had been a Fenian in his youth, the biographies of Cusack and Davin indicate that the founders of the GAA would have a tough time trying to keep control of the organisation they had started.

Davin was the only non-Brotherhood man among the first seven presidents of the GAA, and the second non-Brotherhood president was not elected until 1924, although Cusack appears to have been one of several non-Brotherhood secretaries in the same period.

The downturn in the national mood of 1886 and the demoralisation of the nationalist movement after the defeat of the Home Rule Bill was at least partly responsible for this.

Three Irish Republican Brothers attended the foundation meeting, and the Brotherhood took half the seats on the executive in 1886. During the year Murphy, McKay and Cusack left the executive. Many of the purely sporting activists who had become involved in the association in its infancy left and the GAA retained scarcely any of the original Protestant members such as William Fisher of Waterford and John Stewart, a Methodist professor from Tyrone who was appointed a GAA vice-president in 1885.

The biggest casualty of the Brotherhood take-over was Cusack himself, removed from office in August

1886. Because he came into conflict with the powerful Edmund Gray and his newspaper, the *Freeman's Journal*, and also simultaneously with Archbishop Croke, Cusack has had a bad press from those events of 1886.

An 1882 altercation with Edmund Dwyer Gray meant that the *Freeman's Journal*, the most powerful newspaper of the nineteenth century and perhaps the most powerful in Irish newspaper history, had him in its sights. As a result, although Ó Cathnia and de Búrca have both entered pleas on his behalf, the common perception of Cusack's last six months is that he was the architect of his own destruction.

● ● ●

The oldest representation of handball, 'Castle Blayney', painted in 1785 by John Nixon. Eighteenth-century handball courts often had their construction date engraved on the court in the manner that pelota courts in the Basque region still do.

Cusack at this stage had fallen out with his erstwhile colleagues, Dunlop, Christian and the Dunbars. Even J. F. O'Crowley, who was to prove crucial in the early development of the GAA, had had a row with Cusack at the Cork sports of 1883, complaining that Cusack had come south 'on his Gaelic mission'.

Cusack sued Dunbar's *Irish Sportsman* for libel after it published a parody, part of which went:

> *If he ever gets a pass for his much neglected class*
> *What an awful fluke 'twill be*
> *Then at every Gaelic meeting*
> *You have no chance of competing*
> *Except Irish you can speak*
> *And pronounce the Celtic names*
> *Of the Grand Olympic Games*
> *We have pilfered from the Greeks.*

He had also alienated Fred Gallaher, the editor of *Sport*, and the *Freeman's Journal* editor, Edmund Gray.

The two most important allies he still possessed were the *United Ireland* editor, William O'Brien, and Maurice Davin. O'Brien allowed him the space for his crucial 'word about Irish athletics' and Davin pledged support, and by default much of Munster's, to the new association.

Cusack's legendary truculence is best indicated in his one-liners. His reply to an approach by the IAAA secretary John Dunbar about amalgamation ran to ten words: 'I received your letter this morning and I burned it.' He then called the IAAA (during compromise negotiations) a 'ranting, impotent, West British abortion'. But when he took on Gray, Cusack may have miscalculated. The first salvo was a series of resolutions from Nenagh GAA club sponsored by Cusack. They criticised the *Freeman's Journal* for its reluctance to cover GAA affairs, its failure to publish a speech by Croke, and its criticism of Cusack's refereeing.

Gray himself replied to Cusack. The *Freeman's Journal* used a passing reference to Archbishop Croke to recruit the bishop to their side against Cusack, and published a letter from Cusack to Croke which ended with another classic Cusack expression: 'As you faced the Pope, so I will, with God's help, face you and Gray.'

The *Freeman's Journal* published Croke's counter-claim that it was he who had requested the *Freeman* to delay publication of his speech so that he might vet its

An Illustrated History of the GAA – The Prairie Fire

'Handball Playing in Ireland' as depicted by *Illustrated Sporting and Dramatic News*, 16 February 1884. Despite being included in the early rule books, little was done to promote the game until 1922.

text. Croke added: 'If Mr Michael Cusack is allowed to play the dictator in the GAA's counsels, to run a reckless tilt with impunity and without rebuke' then he, Croke, could not continue as patron.

Cusack defended himself at a May meeting when a motion was passed without a vote requiring his letters to be countersigned by another secretary and Maurice Davin. As Davin lived in Carrick-on-Suir, and the GAA had no full-time staff, this effectively brought the administration of the association to a halt. In June, Cusack was rebuked again by the executive for criticising the Dublin Grocers' Assistants club which had appointed its own and not the GAA's official handicapper. In July, the *Freeman's Journal* journalist and Cusack's co-secretary, John Wyse Power, wrote to Davin complaining about Cusack's secretarial incompetence.

The summit meeting in July at which Cusack was dismissed seems to have been something of a show-trial. Cusack was now completely marginalised and hecklers were pre-appointed to interrupt his defence, all gleefully reported in the *Freeman's Journal*.

After his dismissal, with the backing of Morrison Miller (the Scot who had staged the Caledonian Games in 1884), Cusack launched the *Celtic Times*. His misfortune continued. The newspaper lasted only a year, its circulation declining from a claimed 20,000 in mid-summer to 10,000 by December, and at the end of the year the financial and intellectual toll had also closed his academy. The image of Cusack as a self-destructive impulsive still prevails.

A year later Davin followed him, but this time Croke and the *Freeman's Journal* opposed the ejection. At the elections to office at the 1886 annual convention held at Thurles on 15 November, the Brotherhood virtually took over the executive, a fact noted with alarm by the RIC.

Davin was unable to be present at a meeting in Wynn's Hotel in February 1887 when the Brotherhood tightened its control of the organisation and curtailed the powers of the new county committees. (One of the moves at the meeting, a ban on members of the Royal Irish Constabulary, had repercussions that lasted until 2002.)

Davin resigned in protest, later claiming he had two courses open to him, either to call for a special convention with all the political dissensions it would arouse, or to resign and 'see how things went on'.

At another 'packed' executive meeting held in Limerick on 28 May, Davin's resignation was considered and accepted.

Seen through police eyes, the Brotherhood take-over was alarming. The March 1887 divisional commissioners' and county inspectors' monthly report for the south-western division in the State Papers Office, Crime Branch Special describes the growth of the GAA as 'a good opportunity of a general communication of all the leading conspirators in the county'.

By June the police feared that the extremists were eroding 'the good influence of the priests and that the growth in the GAA was hardly to be accounted for by a sudden love of athletics'.

The stormy November 1887 GAA convention at Thurles must be one of the most acrimonious sports council meetings ever to have taken place anywhere. During the summer of 1887 proceedings had vacillated from farce to high comedy.

The unwieldy structure of the Gaelic Athletic Association in 1887 contributed to the chaos. There were by now over 600 clubs in the GAA, many of

Pat Nally was in prison when the GAA was founded, but the success of his athletics meeting under the patronage of Charles Stewart Parnell in Balla in 1879, in opposition to a sports organised by the local landlord, served as an inspiration to the GAA. The old corner stand in Croke Park (1954–2003) was named in his honour.

recent foundation and each with the right to send two delegates to the convention; and Gray's *Freeman's Journal*, admittedly a hostile source, was highlighting cases of sharp practice.

The 1887 GAA convention was an action-packed event, featuring a dispute over the election of the chairman, a walk-out by some priests of the Killaloe diocese, and a counter-meeting outside. The traditional interpretation of events is that the Brotherhood party took control of the meeting inside the courthouse and the constitutional or clerical party formed the counter-meeting.

In fact, the division appears to have been much more complex. The president elected by the courthouse faction may not have been in the IRB at all, despite

RIC suspicions. To further confuse the issue, the counter-meeting in the street was attended by some of those that the RIC's intelligence files claimed were Brotherhood men.

Tales told to the Castle might not all have been tenable and some of the quotes from the RIC files may have been fanciful. The informer who alleged he accompanied P. J. Hoctor to the post office and saw him send a telegram to John Torley, the Scottish representative on the supreme council of the Brotherhood, 'victory all along the line' may also have been providing the RIC with what they wanted to hear.

Brotherhood man Frank B. Dineen is reported to have told police agent O'Reilly in November 1887 that 'the priests who had come to oppose the IRB were about a year too late'. Archbishop Croke's intervention helped restore Davin to the presidency, and constitutional nationalists, which may serve as a euphemism for clerical interests, recaptured control of the association the following January.

Davin walked out of the 1889 convention, prompting a second take-over by the Brotherhood. This time a financial crisis caused by his ill-advised tour of the US had destroyed his credibility. Peter J. Kelly, who had attended an exploratory meeting in Loughrea in 1884 where, according to Marcus de Búrca, the game plan for the GAA was first discussed, was elected president. The Brotherhood retained control of the central council until the Parnell split reduced the association to chaos.

Throughout Munster, Leinster and parts of Connacht and Ulster, unaffiliated counties and clubs organised independently of the executive. Coincidentally interest in soccer was at its highest in rural Ireland as a result of Hibernian's victory in the Scottish cup and the subsequent defeat of the English cup-holders Preston North End for the 'world championship'. Soccer clubs sprang up in GAA districts with clerical support, some with unlikely names such as the Athenry Dr Crokes and the Cloondarone and Cloonmore Campaign F.C. Within two years the soccer ban on Sunday matches had caused most of them to die out.

Out of the chaos the GAA had pulled off its most successful innovation, the All-Ireland championship. It seemed like an organisational impossibility. The 657 GAA clubs (or as many of them as cared to enter)

would play each other in the same competition until a winner had emerged. In the summer of 1887 and the spring of 1888, the GAA did just that.

Not everyone entered. There were seven counties in the hurling championship and 12 in the football. The rail services which had been introduced over the previous 50 years also helped. Special trains were chartered by GAA clubs to travel to grounds situated beside railway lines, Athlone, Dungarvan, Mountrath, and Inchicore in Dublin. The semi-final of the first All-Ireland football championship in 1887 was played at Limerick Junction.

The country was used to big sporting occasions such as horse races but had seen nothing like this before. The GAA's very first football all star was Malachy O'Brien of the Limerick Commercials club, not yet 17, man of the match against Meath, Kilkenny, Tipperary and Cork. When he kicked the winning goal from midfield against Dowdstown of Meath, he was invited to tea by Lord de ffrench, who hosted the game.

Limerick Commercials, a club formed by the drapers of the city, beat Dundalk Young Irelands from Louth

in the final in front of a crowd that paid £300 (the equivalent of €30,000 today) in sixpences and three-penny bits to watch the match. Dundalk's team included an uncle of the future GAA president Alf Murray.

William J. Spain, later to win a hurling medal with Dublin, scored the winning goal after a long dribbling run almost from his own 21-yard line by Thomas McNamara, and a three-man hand-passing movement.

Commercials were fêted back to Limerick and greeted by cheering crowds. They had only won the Limerick championship by default when five of the St Michael's team were barred from a replay by the new rule preventing rugby players from playing Gaelic football.

Within a generation the sons of these champion footballers were to form the backbone of the great Limerick rugby teams. But for now, Limerick was a GAA city.

In hurling, the favourites came from a club from the town where the GAA was founded and the district where hurling rules had first been drawn up in 1869. Before they had won the Tipperary championship the reputation of Thurles, under team captain Jim Stapleton, had leaked out. The *Celtic Times* reported on Thurles's defeat of Twomileborris in the county championship: 'The players swept along with the speed and dash of the Fianna of ancient Ireland. . . . No shoes were worn by either side. . . . Dozens were knocked out. . . . 'Tis easily seen Kickham never described the match in Knocknagow for no imagination, not even that of the genius of Mullinahone, could picture what Tipperary hurling was like.'

Cork withdrew after a dispute and never got their county championships finished. After Galway beat Wexford, Wexford's Jack Lowery, who had all his front teeth knocked out, was given £2 to replace them by the owner of Elm Park, Lord de ffrench, but never did.

The final took place in Birr. Thurles travelled by special train while the Galway team, formed from a combined Meelick and Killimor panel with some players from the Shannon islands in Lusmagh parish, came on 'McIntyre's brake' across the Shannon.

Both teams togged out in nearby Cunningham's Hotel (now the Wayside Inn), Meelick in green jerseys with white stripes and Thurles in green jerseys

From its foundation in 1879 until its effective winding-up in October 1883, James J. Herne's athletics, cricket and football club in Carrick-on-Suir was as much a precursor of the GAA as those organised by Michael Cusack in Dublin and Pat Nally in Mayo. It prepared an enclosed running track and printed rules. Herne, who had witnessed the evolution of games into organised sport in America in the 1860s, first introduced the Davin brothers to developments in sports administration and legislation, prompting Maurice Davin to draw up organised rules for hurling and football and a constitution for the GAA.

with stars 'artistically worked in the centre'. They marched in military fashion in two lines, marshalled by the Meelick IRB man and former American Army officer Captain Lynam to John Farrell's field at Moorpark, now a retail development.

Galway had heard Tipperary would not come and, having had a few drinks, were about to start a meal when the Tipperary team arrived by special train and were fêted through the town.

Tipperary won by a goal, scored according to the *Midland Tribune* by Tommy Healy of Coolcroo when, 'by means of a dextrous left hander, he sent the ball flying from the middle of the field under the rope, thus scoring a goal for Thurles.'

Maurice Davin, the GAA's first president, was also the first of a line of Munster-based athletes to win recognition on both sides of the Irish Sea for his weight-throwing ability. He threw a world record distance for the hammer at the Ireland-England athletics international organised by the Irish Championship Athletics Club at Lansdowne Road in 1876.

But in 1880s Ireland politics was never far away. The Meelick club was devastated by a series of evictions within six months of the final and did not even enter the 1889 Galway championship. Among those evicted were James Lynam, team captain Pat Madden, the Mannions of the strand and Willie Madden, who had played against Castlebridge, while Paddy Larkin was jailed for six months for taking the hay of an evicted widow to market to sell on her behalf.

• • •

It was a great start. Attendances of 5,000 at the hurling final and 9,000 at the football were high by the standards of the time. Ireland's soccer international with England attracted an attendance of 7,200 in 1888. But ambition overcame the infant GAA, whose entire organisational staff and 48 'invaders' went on a promotional tour of the United States. The trip lost money through bad weather but mainly because of appalling organisation and the fact that the GAA allied itself with the AAC in an athletics war with the AAU for control of the sport in America. And 17 of the 'invaders' never came home, including the world hammer throw record-holder.

Interest was in danger of petering out. The 1890 hurling final was not finished because Cork walked off the field. Only three counties entered the 1892 All-Ireland hurling championship, Cork, Kerry and Dublin. The GAA forgot to get the grass cut for the 1893 final!

Sport declared: 'The preliminary arrangements were entrusted to an utterly irresponsible person with the result that not alone were the proceedings of a very disappointing happy-go-lucky nature, but were also a complete financial failure.'

The GAA was less popular in 1892 than it was in 1885, with just 200 clubs affiliated. Its best athletes had gone to America and were winning medals for the US at the first Olympics in Athens. In some counties only two or three clubs bothered to affiliate. Only a dozen counties were playing the games, all of them south of the railway line from Galway to Dublin. There were no championships in Connacht or Ulster.

While Dublin footballers and Tipperary hurlers were bringing new skills to the fields, some of the All-Ireland finals attracted fewer than a thousand spectators.

Between 1890 and 1894 four separate All-Ireland finals were left unfinished because of crowd invasions or rough play.

The *Irish Sportsman* of February 1891 declared: 'The game as it is played at present is fraught with danger and, so far as I can gather from looking on, it is simply a helter-skelter, hit-or-miss business carried on without any attention to rules at all.'

In the gloom it was scarcely noticed that two Kerry clubs had changed the GAA's All-Ireland championship for ever. For the 1891 competition, Kilmoyley club disbanded altogether and re-registered with Ballyduff so that eight of their players could represent Kerry in the All-Ireland. One of their best defenders was 'P. County' (in fact P. Quane, who gave a false name because he was from Kilmoyley). The following year the Cork county champions, Redmonds, selected three players from Blackrock and two from Aghabullogue. The GAA consequently decided to change the rules.

Maurice Davin at Deerpark with his sister Bridget, Pat and Ellen Davin and their daughter Mary Bridget.

Henceforth, the team could be picked from all the clubs in the county, not just the club which had won the county championship. Inter-county GAA rivalry as we know it was born in Kilmoyley.

While the IRB seem to have secured the top offices, the GAA in the towns and villages was more closely allied to Parnell's political movement. The events of 1887 had weakened the GAA and set it up for virtual collapse in December 1890, when the Irish Parliamentary Party split over Parnell's leadership after details emerged of his affair with the wife of another MP.

Throughout the country local GAA units suffered parallel splits. The anti-Parnell central council expelled pro-Parnell county boards. GAA membership plummeted from nearly 900 clubs to less than 200.

A Dublin Parnellite MP, William Field (who had defeated William Martin Murphy in the 1892 election), began canvassing support for a new no-politics policy among clubs.

Sportswriter P. P. Sutton and the 1891–2 secretary Patrick Tobin from Dublin contacted 500 clubs which had lapsed since 1891. They were joined in the exercise by the resourceful Navan man, Dick Blake, better known as a football enthusiast and reformer (he wanted

the team size reduced from 17 to 14 a side) rather than for his political views.

In 1893 the GAA had revoked its ban on British Army and police members, and in 1896 the ban on rugby players was also dropped. Soccer scarcely featured in the debates of the time. The rugby ban was seen as a battle for control of the game akin to that between the rugby union and league movements in the north of England. Dropping the ban on IAAA athletes was also considered, but initial talks stalled on suspensions and records.

The reform movement reached full flow when Blake was appointed secretary at the 1895 convention, and with Tobin and Limerick man Frank Dineen set about reforming the association. The number of clubs increased from 217 in 1895 to 360 in 1897, 768 in 1907, and grew steadily until independence and then experienced two decades of rapid growth, having 1,000 clubs in 1924, 1,686 in 1935, 2,010 in 1945, 2,226 in 1950 and 2,850 in 1960.

Blake's three-year term of office, before he was dismissed in controversial circumstances because of the finances of the association in 1898, is held up by Marcus de Búrca as a valuable period of reform, arresting the decline of the GAA.

He incurred the wrath of the Cork and Limerick boards because of his no-politics position and had the misfortune to referee a controversial All-Ireland final involving Cork. Cork disaffiliated for two years as a result.

Blake's more nationalist successor as secretary, Frank Dineen, continued to steer the GAA towards recovery. More importantly, when Alderman Maurice Butterly's 14 acres in Jones's Road came up for sale in 1908, he bought them for £3,250 (equivalent to €300,000 today) and held them in trust until the GAA could buy them from him for £3,645 8s. 5d in 1913. The site became Croke Park.

●　●　●

Clubs still jealously picked the teams which contested the All-Ireland championship, even if the teams of the 1890s were beginning to resemble modern county teams.

Blackrock had three players on the successful Cork team of 1892. By the time Cork completed three in a row in 1895 they were picking the team and being described as 'the home of hurling'.

The Tubberdora team which won five All-Irelands in six years between 1895 and 1900, 'a team without parallel in GAA history', according to the county's historian Canon Philip Fogarty, used an average of five outside players on their selections, including Paddy Riordan from Drombane who is said to have scored 6-7 in the final of 1895.

It might have been six All-Irelands had Tubberdora not withdrawn from the 1897 Tipp county championships. Mikey Maher prepared his team on Walsh's kiln field where he had his forwards shooting at the band of a wheel.

Neighbouring Limerick had perfected the art of 'hooking' the opponent's hurley to win the All-Ireland of 1897, the year Suir View put out that last one-club selection to represent Tipperary.

A one-club selection won the final for Tipperary in 1895 thanks largely to the star footballer of the decade and scorer of the late winning free, Willie Ryan. Until 1903 it appears county teams were regarded as the domain of the champion club. Dublin sent out contrasting selections in 1897 and 1898 to win the first two legs of a three in a row in football because they were selected by different clubs.

It took exceptional players like Mikey Maher of Tubberdora and Tom Semple of Thurles on the Twomileborris team in 1900 to make the final 17.

Left:
The GAA founder Michael Cusack complete with bas-gan-saggart. Cusack continued his involvement with the GAA at local level after his removal as secretary.

Right:
Three articles in a Land League newspaper served as Cusack's entirely self-generated pre-publicity for the foundation of the GAA in November 1884. More concerned with matters of identity than sport, they reflect contemporary political sentiment that power was shifting away from colonial towards indigenous Irish interests. Cusack's output in the 1880s was truly prodigious, writing articles for 20 different newspapers and journals, as well as running campaigns for the preservation of Irish sport and the Irish language and his private grind school in Dublin.

THE IRISHMAN

OCTOBER 11, 1884.

A WORD ABOUT IRISH ATHLETICS.

No movement having for its object the social and political advancement of a nation from the tyranny of imported and enforced customs and manners can be regarded as perfect if it has not made adequate provision for the preservation and cultivation of the National pastimes of the people. Voluntary neglect of such pastimes is a sure sign of National decay and of approaching dissolution.

smoking and card-playing. A few years later a so-called revival of athletics was inaugurated in Ireland. The new movement did not originate with those who have ever had any sympathy with Ireland or the Irish people. Accordingly labourers, tradesmen, artists, and even policemen and soldiers were excluded from the few competitions which constituted the lame and halting programme of the promoters. Two years ago every man who did not make his living either wholly or partly by athletics was allowed to compete. But with this concession came a law which is as intolerable as its existence in Ireland is degrading. The law is, that all Athletic Meetings shall be held under the rules of the Amateur Athletic Association of England, and that any person competing at any meeting not held under these rules should be ineligible to compete elsewhere. The management of nearly all the meetings held in Ireland since has been entrusted to persons hostile to all the dearest aspirations of the Irish people. Every effort has been made to make the meetings look as English as possible—foot-races, betting, and flagrant cheating being their most prominent features. Swarms of pot-hunting mashers sprang into existence. They formed Harrier Clubs, for the purpose of training through the winter, after the fashion of English professional athletes, that they might be able to win and pawn the prizes offered for competition in the summer. We tell the Irish people to take the management of their games into their own hands, to encourage and promote in every way every form of athletics which is peculiarly Irish, and to remove with one sweep everything foreign and iniquitous in the present system. The vast majority of the best athletes in Ireland are Nationalists. These gentlemen should take the matter in hands at once, and draft laws for the guidance of the promoters of meetings in Ireland next year. The people pay the expenses of the meetings, and the representatives of the people should have the controlling power. It is only by such an arrangement that pure Irish athletics can be revived, and that the incomparable strength and physique of our race will be preserved.

OCTOBER 18, 1884.

Irish Athletics.

TO THE EDITOR OF THE IRISHMAN.

DEAR SIR—I am much pleased to see that you take an interest in Irish Athletics. It is time that a handbook was published with rules, &c., for all Irish games. The English Handbooks of Athletics are very good in their way, but they do not touch on many of the Irish games which, although much practised, are not included in the events on programmes of athletic sports. Weight-throwing and jumping appear to be going out of fashion in England; but such is not the case in Ireland, although those events are too often left out of programmes of what might be called leading meetings. I have some experience of those things, and see numbers of young men almost daily having some practice. It is strange that for one bystander who takes off his coat to run a foot race, forty strip to throw weights or try a jump of some kind. Irish football is a great game, and worth going a very long way to see, when played on a fairly laid-out ground and under proper rules. Many old people say that hurling exceeded it as a trial of men. I would not care to see either game now, as the rules stand at present. I may say there are no rules, and, therefore, those games are often dangerous. I am anxious to see both games revived under regular rules. I cannot agree with you that Harrier Clubs are a disadvantage, as I believe they are a good means of bringing out long distance runners, and we want some more good men at this branch of sport. I am sorry to hear that it became necessary to make some other remarks, which appear in the article on "Irish Athletics" in UNITED IRELAND of the 11th inst. I thought we in Ireland were pretty free from the abuses you mention. I know they are said to be a great blot on the sport in England, but I understand the management there are doing all they can to remedy it. If a movement such as you advise is made for the purpose of reviving and encouraging Irish games and drafting rules, &c., I will gladly lend a hand if I can be of any use.—Yours truly,
MAURICE DAVIN.
Deer Park, Carrick-on-Suir, Oct. 13, 1884.

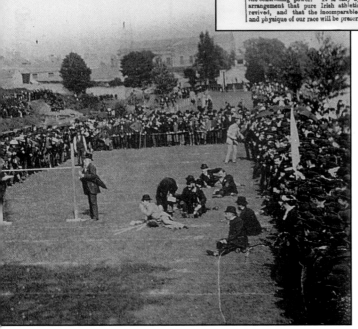

Pat Davin preparing to jump at Clonmel sports in 1882. The only man to have simultaneously held world records for both the high jump (1.84 m in Carrick-on-Suir in 1880) and the long jump (6.98 m in Monasterevin 1883), and younger brother of the first president of the GAA, Carrick-on-Suir solicitor Pat Davin (1857–1949) was the greatest of Ireland's pre-Olympic athletes. When Davin took Marshall Brooks' world high jump record at Carrick in July 1880, the record was only accepted in London because it had been verified by a distinguished panel of judges that included Val Dunbar, editor of the *Irish Sportsman* and J. P. V. Veale of the English AAA. Officially ratified IAAF world records were not instituted until 1921.

The original hurling revivalists came from Trinity College, where a sporting movement had emerged in the 1850s. College rowing and tennis clubs go back even further. As well as establishing the earliest football club and annual athletics meeting on the island, and perhaps in Europe, it fostered an eclectic group of sports which included the hurley club whose hockey-inclined rules were published in the sixth edition of Lawrence's Cricket handbook in 1870. Michael Cusack was an enthusiastic hurler before he founded the GAA. Back: G. Y. Dixon, (unknown), John Ross, George Frasier Fitzgerald, W. Kelly, Travers Smith. Middle: C. W. Welland, T. S. Lindsay, A. F. Flood. Front: George Seawright, R. J. Polden, F. W. Caulfield, G. H. Garret, F. S. Seawright. John Ross was afterwards the last Lord Chancellor of Ireland, George Francis Fitzgerald became a pioneer of air travel and radio broadcasting, while John Henry Bernard, later Archbishop of Dublin and provost of Trinity College, was on the 1880 team. Most famously, Edward Carson, later leader of the Ulster Unionist Party, also played.

Michael Cusack (second from left in front) as a member of the Phoenix rugby team. He advocated rugby, cricket and hurling, the precursor of hockey, as Ireland's 'national' games before founding the GAA. Back: C. S. Bowles, R. W. Ellis, E. Waring, R. H. Lowry, W. M. Russell, F. E. Rainsford, E. J. O'Reilly, E. O. Bailey. Front: V. Guerrini, Michael Cusack, R. Code, G. A. Drought, T. Askin (captain), G. Paton, M. Sweeney.

THE DUBLIN METROPOLITAN HURLING CLUB.

To the energetic exertions of Mr. Cusack, of the Civil Service Academy, Dublin, we are indebted for the revival of hurling in Ireland. A club called the Dublin Metropolitan Hurling Club, consisting mostly of young men preparing for Civil Service appointments, has been started under his management. The club meets on Saturdays for practice, and some scratch matches have been played with an energy and skill which augurs well for the future excellence of this club. If we may judge by the constantly increasing number of spectators attending those matches, the game is likely to become even more popular than its kindred sport polo, or hurling on horseback. The rules of the game as played by this club, and adopted by county clubs started since, are few and simple, consisting of the following :— The ball to be made of cork and thread covered with leather, the ground selected to be quite level, the size to be regulated by the number of players; two poles are placed about five yards apart in the centre of the end boundaries, and through which the ball must be driven to secure goal; if the ball should go beyond the end boundaries, but not through the poles, the goal-keeper is to drive it back opposite to where it passed the boundary. The hardest possible hitting, both right and left, is encouraged, to develop both sides of the body, except in a crush, when the timber is not to be "lifted," as the ball is sure to be stolen from a "swiper." But in the open the ball is to be "coaxed" and "lifted," with the hurley—never with the hand—and when off the ground hit with the full strength of the player. Play begins by a lady on horseback galloping across the field and tossing the ball in the centre amongst the players—a custom which seems to have been followed in all matches of which we have any authentic record. In an historic match played between Kilkenny and Waterford some years ago, the parties being led by Lord Beresford and Sir Thomas May respectively, the leaders themselves galloped across the field in opposite directions after having dropped the ball in the centre.

The first indication of Cusack's 'improvements' on the rules of hurley, as played in Trinity College, came with this report in the *Irish Sportsman* in 1882. His Metropolitan club rules have not survived, but the hope that it would surpass polo indicates the popularity of polo at the time. It was capable of drawing crowds of 15,000 to matches in the Phoenix Park. The Beresford family is still associated with the sport.

In 1883 the *Irish Sportsman*'s 'hurley notes' reported that Michael Cusack had set up a club 'for the purposes of taking steps to re-establish the national game of hurling … so far as is practicable rules shall be framed to make a transition from hurley to hurling as easy as the superiority of the latter game will permit.' *The Irish Times* reported that eight matches were played by Cusack's hurlers at the polo grounds in the Phoenix Park in 1883. In December 1883 the Dublin Hurling Club became the Metropolitan Hurling Club. These illustrations featured in the London-based *Illustrated Sporting and Dramatic News*, 22 March 1884.

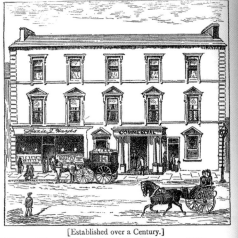

[Established over a Century.]

THE COMMERCIAL AND FAMILY HOTEL,

AND POSTING ESTABLISHMENT,

THURLES.

LIZZIE J. HAYES, Proprietress.

The anniversary of the downfall of the Fianna of heroic literature, Thursday, 1 November 1884, was chosen as the foundation date for the GAA in the billiard room in Hayes's hotel in Thurles. By Michael Cusack's choosing, this key railway town was a venue central to Munster but not to Connacht, north Leinster or Ulster.

Patronage was the nineteenth-century equivalent of celebrity endorsement. At a time when every other sporting initiative sought the patronage of the imperial representative in Ireland, the Lord Lieutenant, Cusack's choice of Archbishop Thomas W. Croke of Cashel, Irish Party leader Charles Stewart Parnell and Land League founder Michael Davitt was a gamble. He calculated that embracing the emerging religious, political and agrarian movements that had been gathering force in the five years before the foundation of the association would give the GAA an advantage in the newly independent Ireland. After the anticipated Home Rule failed to materialise in 1886, IRB founder and nationalist MP John O'Leary also became a patron of the GAA. The choice of Croke was most significant, enabling local clergymen to serve as patrons in individual branches, a practice that continues to this day.

Archbishop Croke's letter to Maurice Davin of 26 March 1886 sought an end to the controversy between the archbishop and Michael Cusack, who felt Croke was over-stepping his mark as patron in intervening in a dispute over the status of a dissident Dublin club. Within a year Davin had fol-lowed Cusack out of the association both had helped to found.

National Pastimes.

Gaelic Athletic Association.

The following are the rules for hurling and football adopted at the meeting held at Thurles :—

HURLING.

1. The ground shall, when convenient, be 200 yards long by 150 yards broad, or as near that size as can be got.

2. There shall be boundary lines all around the ground, at a distance of at least five yards from the fences.

3. The goal shall be two upright posts twenty feet apart with a crossbar ten feet from the ground. A goal is won when the ball is driven between the posts and under the crossbar.

4. The ball is not to be lifted off the ground with the hand, when in play.

5. There shall not be less than fourteen, or more than twenty-one players at the side in regular matches.

6. There shall be an umpire for each side and a referee, who will decide in cases where the umpires disagree. The referee keeps the time and throws up the ball at the commencement of each goal.

7. The time of play shall be one hour and twenty minutes. Sides to be changed at half time.

8. Before commencing play hurlers shall draw up in two lines in the centre of the field opposite to each other and catch hands or hurleys across, then separate. The referee then throws the ball along the ground between the players or up high over their heads.

9. No player is to catch, trip, or push from behind. Penalty, disqualification to the offender and a free puck to the opposite side.

10. No player is to bring his hurley intentionally in contact with the person of another player. Penalty same as rule 9.

11. If the ball is driven over the side lines it shall be thrown in towards the middle of the ground by the referee or one of the umpires; but if it rebounds into the ground it shall be considered in play.

12. If the ball is driven over the end lines and not through the goal, the player who is defending the goal shall have a free puck from the goal. No player of the opposite side to approach nearer than twenty yards until the ball is struck. The other players to stand on the goal line, but if the ball is driven over the goal line by a player whose goal it is, the opposite side shall have a free puck on the ground twenty yards out from the goal posts. Players whose goal it is to stand on the goal line until the ball is struck.

N.B.—Hitting both right and left is allowable.

UNITED IRELAND

[SATURDAY, FEBBUARY 7, 1885

FOOTBALL.

1. There shall be not less than fifteen or more than twenty-one players aside.

2. There shall be two umpires and a referee. Where the umpires disagree the referee's decision shall be final.

3. The ground shall be at least 120 yards long by 80 in breadth, and properly marked by boundary lines. Boundary lines must be at least 5 yards from fences.

4. The goal posts shall stand at each end in centre of goal line. They shall be 15 feet apart, with a cross-bar 8 feet from the ground.

5. The captains of each team shall toss for choice of sides before commencing play, and the players shall stand in two ranks opposite each other until the ball is thrown up, each man holding the hand of one of the other side.

6. Pushing or tripping from behind, holding from behind, or butting with the head, shall be deemed foul, and the player so offending shall be ordered to stand aside, and may not afterwards take part in the match, nor can his side substitute another man.

7. The time of actual play shall be one hour. Sides to be changed only at half time.

8. The match shall be decided by the greater number of goals. If no goal be kicked the match shall be deemed a draw. A goal is when the ball is kicked through the goal posts under the cross-bar.

9. When the ball is kicked over the side line it shall be thrown back by a player of the opposite side to him who kicked it over. If kicked over the goal-line by a player whose goal-line it is, it shall be thrown back in any direction by a player of the other side. If kicked over the goal-line by a player of the other side, the goalkeeper whose line it crosses shall have a free kick. No player of the other side to approach nearer than 25 yards of him till the ball is kicked.

10. The umpires and referee shall have during the match full power to disqualify any player, or order him to stand aside and discontinue play, for any act which they may consider unfair, as set out in Rule 6.

———

Tulla (Co. Clare).—The second meeting held under the auspices of the Gaelic Athletic Association for the révival of Irish sports and pastimes, came off on last Sunday evening. The principal winners were—220 yards, T. O'Grady; half-mile, J. O'Dwyer; mile, P. Giltinane; subscribers' race, G. l'epper; sack race, B. Meehan; pole jump, B. Meehan. Amongst those who won juvenile races were M. Ryan and M. Mealy. The day was most beautiful, and it was gratifying to witness the interest which the people are taking in our National pastimes. The next meeting will take place on Sunday evening, 15th inst., when it is expected we will have a copy of the rules from Mr. Cusack, of the Central Association, Dublin.

Clara.—This club now numbers 144 members. Their afternoon meetings have been most successful. Mr. White is working strenuously on the exact lines laid down by the G.A.A.

Opposite:

The first rules of football and hurling were drawn up by Maurice Davin and published in January 1885. A preponderance of scoreless draws meant they were revised within months and the distinctive three points equals one goal scoring system had evolved by 1895.

Report of the GAA convention in Thurles in 1889 in the short-lived official journal of the GAA, the *Gael*.

The letter from Thomas Croke accepting patronage of the GAA, which later served as a preface in the GAA rule book and became known as 'the charter of the GAA'. It was published in the Christmas 1884 edition of *Nation*.

The winning All-Ireland teams of 1887 were not photographed, or indeed awarded their medals, until 1910. By that time some of the excitement generated by that initial championship had been dissipated, and some of the players had emigrated. The championship went into almost instant decline in 1888. Attendances plummeted and only three counties entered the hurling championship of 1890. Tipperary. Back: D. Maher, J. Sullivan, Ned Murphy, Jer Ryan, M. Maher, E. Leamy, Tom Burke, C. Callaghan, D. Davoren, Matty Maher. Middle: P. Ryan, D. Maher, Jim Stapleton (captain), Tom Maher, G. Leamy, J. Ryan, Jer Dwyer. Front: Mick Carroll, Martin 'Mack' McNamara, T. Butler. Missing: Pat Leahy, Andy Maher, Ned Bowe, John Mockler, Tom Stapleton, Tom Carroll, Dan Ryan, John Leamy, Tommy Healy, Tim Dwyer and Ned Lambe.

Limerick Commercials were not photographed until 15 years after their All-Ireland success. The group includes the then teenage star of the 1887 championship, Malachi O'Brien, in the front, and the first dual All-Ireland medallist William J. Spain. Back: Timothy Fitzgibbon, Ned Nicholas, Edward Casey, T. McMahon, Phil Keating. Middle: D. Liddy, P. S. Reeves, James Mulqueen, Michael Slattery,

GAA central council members after the reconstruction convention in 1888 had replaced the fractious Thurles convention. Thurles was more than a split between the IRB and clerical supporters. The county structure was unable to cope with the rapid growth of the association and only recovered after the organisation of provincial councils in 1901. Back: J. J. O'Reilly (Dublin), Dr Charles J. O'Connor (Kildare), Rev. J. Concannon, John Cullinane (Tipperary), George F. Byrne (Meath). Middle: Rev. C. Buckley (Cork), Alderman Mangan (Louth), William Prendergast (Clonmel, hon. sec.), James O'Connor (Wexford), Rev. E. Sheehy (Limerick), J. J. Cullen (Dún Laoghaire, records sec.). Front: R. J. Frewen (Tipperary, treasurer), Maurice Davin (president, Tipperary), T. O'Riordain (Cork, hon. sec.).

Patrick Kelly, Timothy Kennedy, John Hyland, Robert Normoyle, Denis Corbett (captain), William Gunning, W. Cleary, R. Breen, Pat Treacy (non-playing captain). Front: Thomas McNamara, Patrick J. Corbett, Malachi O'Brien, Tom Keating, Jeremiah Kennedy. Missing: John Hyland, William J. Spain.

'After Thurles we may look upon the GAA as a purely Fenian society', Crime Special Branch concluded in 1888. The colonial administration took great interest in the GAA, leaving behind extensive records for historians. Recent re-examination of the files suggests that many of the suspects made unlikely Fenians and local constables may have overstated the extent of IRB infiltration of the infant association. Within the central administration the battle for control led to several heated meetings until the mid-1890s.

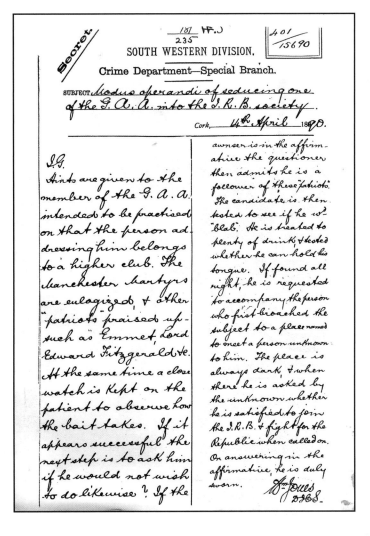

Opposite:

Pat Davin was among the GAA champion athletes which gave exhibitions when a group of GAA 'invaders' toured 11 east coast American cities in 1888, including New York, Boston and Philadelphia in September–October 1888. The tour originated as the return leg of an international contest between the US and Ireland in July 1888 and had the effect of almost bankrupting the infant GAA and its president. The athletes selected were Pat Davin (Carrick, world long and high jump record-holder), Jim Mitchell (Emly, world hammer throw record-holder), Dan Shanahan (Kilfinane, world triple jump record-holder), Pat T. Keoghan (Dungarvan, standing jump champion), T. M. O'Connor (Ballyclough, high jumper), William Phibbs (Glenville, 880 yards champion), Mike and Jack Connery (Staker Wallace, Limerick, high jump and pole vault), Pat Looney (Macroom, triple jump), Tim O'Mahoney (Rosscarberry, 440 yards champion), William McCarthy (Macroom, miler), J. C. Daly (Borrisokane, former hammer record-holder), William Real (Pallaskreen, hammer thrower), P. O'Donnell (Carrick, hammer thrower), J. McCarthy (Staker Wallace, sprinter), T. Barry (Dungarvan), D. Power (Shanballymore, hurdler) and J. Mooney (Ballyhea, sprinter).

The hurlers selected to travel were H. Burgess (Dún Laoghaire, Dublin), J. Cordial (Kinnitty, Offaly), F. Coughlan (Kickhams, Dublin), Michael Curran (Castlecomer, Kilkenny), J. Dunne (Rahan, Offaly), J. Fitzgibbon (Ogonelloe, Clare), John Fox (Mooncoin, Kilkenny), T. Furlong (Davitts, Dublin), James Grace (Tullaroan, Kilkenny), J. Hayes (Faughs, Dublin), M. Hickey (Carrickbeg, Waterford), J. McEvoy (Knockroo, Laois), P. Minogue (Tulla, Clare), P. J. Molohan (Monasterevin, Kildare), P. Muleady (Birr, Offaly), J. Nolan (Dunkerrin, Offaly), John O'Brien (Moycarkey, Tipperary), Tom O'Grady (Moycarkey, Tipperary), William Prendergast (Clonmel, Tipperary), J. Rourke (Kilbane, Clare), J. Royce (Albert Hill, Wexford), P. Ryan (Rathdowney, Laois), Thady Ryan (Clonoulty, Tipperary), Jim Stapleton (Thurles, Tipperary), P. P. Sutton (Metropolitans, Dublin). Of the 54 who travelled, 17 stayed on in America including world hammer record-holder, Jim Mitchell. Pictures show the 'invasion' team in Thurles and on board ship.

Cartoon from the *Dublin Weekly News*, 11 June 1887, on the occasion of the GAA presentation to Gladstone. Gladstone's presentation was the subject of much fun and lampoonery in newspapers of the time.

Although the 1695 Sunday Observance Act remained in force at the time the GAA was founded, the Act proved unenforceable when often militant Sabbatarians tried to prevent GAA matches taking place. GAA matches were interrupted by mobs, and teams and spectators were showered with missiles. Sabbatarianism held up the development of the GAA in the north-east by several decades.

Be it further Enacted, by the Authority aforesaid, That no person or persons whatsoever, shall Play, Use, or Exercise any Hurling, Commoning, Foot-Ball Playing, Cudgels, Wrestling, or any other Games, Pastimes or Sports, on the Lord's-Day, or any part thereof. And if any person or persons shall Offend therein, and be thereof Convicted in such manner, as hereinafter Directed; Every such person and persons, shall Forfeit the Summ of Twelve Pence sterl. for every such Offence, to be immediately paid to such Justice of the Peace, Officer or Officers, before whom such Conviction shall be.

First Olympic decathlon gold medallist Tom Kiely from Ballyneale, Co. Tipperary, was the most important figure from the golden age of GAA athletes. According to folklore he rejected offers from both the American and British teams to represent them and paid his own way to the St Louis Olympics so that the medal would be credited to Ireland. He later became a prominent official within the GAA and its successor, the NACA. He had held the world hammer record for 46 days in 1899 until it was superseded by Limerick man John Flanagan, three times Olympic gold medallist. From the first recorded world record throw by Maurice Davin at Lansdowne Road on Whit Monday 1876 until Imrem Nemeth's record of 1948, all the world's longest recorded hammer throws were by Irish athletes.

The GAA spread slowly in Ulster, perhaps because of the prevalence of Sabbatarianism. When Thomas O'Reilly and John Alex Clancy's Ballyconnell's First Ulsters, by reputation the oldest club in the province, played their first match on 13 March 1886, they were approached by the local constabulary and warned they were breaking the Sunday Observance Act of 1695. The constables took names but failed to get a justice of the peace to sign the summonses. This team photograph of Ballyconnell dates from 1888. Clancy is in the braces, fourth from the left in the middle. Co-founder O'Reilly is on the extreme right in the front.

Peter O'Connor jumping at Crystal Palace. O'Connor's long jump of 7.61 m at the RDS in 1901 stood as a world record for 20 years and was not beaten as an Irish record until 2 June 1990. After he had won a silver medal in the long jump at the 1906 intercalated Olympics in Athens, O'Connor climbed a flagpole with a green flag to indicate his nationality in protest at an attempt to raise the British Union Jack. Ironically, the GAA Central Council had declined an invitation to send an Irish team to the first modern Olympics in Athens in 1896 on the grounds that Ireland could expect to win gold medals in only two events, the shot and the high jump.

Pat and Mick Leahy of the famous athletics family.

One of the great athletics champions of the early GAA, Cork-born Pat Leahy (1877–1926), clearing the bar at Crystal Palace in 1898. GAA athletes dominated the field events at the 1896–8 AAA championships, described as the athletics championships of the world by English-speaking newspapers, despite the revival of the Olympics which had just got under way. Pat Leahy won silver in the high jump and bronze in the long jump at the 1900 Olympics. Elder brother Con also won three Olympic medals.

The anti-Parnellite MP Pierce O'Mahoney was still alive when the GAA team in Navan was named in his honour. His team had a brief ascendancy and a long legacy. It proved one of the most innovative in early GAA years. Although only the first of its three encounters with Willie Ryan's Arravale Rovers for the 1895 championship counted as a championship match, the three matches did much to boost the sport of Gaelic football just six years after Thomas Nulty, Bishop of Meath, had tried to proscribe it in the county. County chairman Dick Blake's steward-ship of the club started a trajectory that led to his becoming secretary of the GAA and temporarily ridding it of its more overtly political trappings, although the enthusiastic support of the Irish Party members for his stewardship suggests the process may have been more complicated than some his-torians have suggested. Blake improved the rules of football to make it safer. One of his legacies is the seven-yard square. Though long replaced by the parallelogram, the phrase 'in the square' is still used nationwide. This is the team that won the county championship for Navan. Back: J. Reilly, C. McCann, John Elliott, P. Fitzpatrick, K. Connor. Middle: Dick Blake (county chairman), Mick Rogers, Joe Sharkey, Hugh Pentleton, Mick Murray (captain), Jack Shaw, Paddy Daly, M. McCullen, Jim Russell, J. P. Timmons. Front: John Hegarty, Peter Clarke, J. O'Brien, P. Fox.

Retiring in the manner of a champion boxer, Mike Maher's Tubberdora team disbanded and merged with Horse and Jockey in 1899, having been undefeated in championship hurling and winning three All-Ireland titles in four years. They scored 71-108 in 14 county and inter-county championship matches. While training in Walsh's kiln field, the forwards practised by shooting at the spokes of a cartwheel. They withdrew from the 1898 championship after a player was injured in training. Back: Watty Dunne, Will Devane, Ed Brennan, Mikey Maher (captain), D. Ryan, John Ryan, Tim Condon. Middle: Thomas Leahy (chairman), Phil Byrne, John Connolly, Jack Maher, Denis Walsh, Jim O'Keeffe, Dick O'Keeffe, Michael Conlon (secretary). Front: Tommy Ryan, Jack 'Field' Maher, Ed Maher, Johnny Walsh.

Tipperary defeated Meath by a point in the 1895 All-Ireland football final with 17 Arravale Rovers players, the first to be played in what is now Croke Park. This was the match that established Willie Ryan's reputation as the outstanding foot-baller of his generation, scoring the winning free. The referee wrote to the *Freeman's Journal* after the match saying he should not have allowed one of their goals because it was scored from inside the 21-yard line. As late as 1952 one of the surviving spectators still nominated it as the greatest match of all time. Mick Ryan went on to play rugby 17 times for Ireland, participating with his brother Jack in the tumultuous 1899 triple crown-winning match against Wales. Back: John Luddy, Willie O'Shea, W. Dwyer (treasurer), Phil Dwyer, Paddy Glasheen, Mick Ryan, J. Wyse (assistant secretary). Middle: Jerry O'Brien, Paddy Daly, John Carew, Bob Swords, Jim Riordan, M. Butler. Front: J. Ryan (chairman), Willie Ryan, M. 'Terry' McInerney, Bob Quane, Willie P. Ryan (captain), M. Connery, W. P. Quane, J. J. Burke (secretary).

Denis Grimes's 1897
Limerick hurling team was
the first to perfect the art of
hooking. The GAA patron
T. W. Croke was a spectator
at the final in which they
beat Kilkenny. Back: Pat
Mulcahy, John Hynes, Mick
Downes, James 'Seán Oge'
Hanly, Mick Finn, Jim Flood,
Paddy O'Brien, Jim Cottrell.
Front: Paddy Flynn, John
Reidy, T. Casey, Pat Buskin.
Maurice Flynn, Tony Brazil,
Denis Grimes (captain),
John Finn, F. Dunworth.
Missing: Dan Riordan,
John Condon, Pat Butler.

The band of the Artane Industrial School has been associated with the GAA since 1885 and played for the 1895 All-Ireland finals, but it was only in the 1950s that it became the automatic choice for All-Ireland finals. After the closure of the school in 1969 it evolved with the GAA's help to become the premier young person's marching band in Dublin. It started recruiting girls in 2002.

The only surviving issue of the *Gaelic News* shows photographs of the two leading football teams of the era, Dublin and Tipperary, playing in the Croke cup football final of 1896. Dublin's Young Ireland team was built around employees at the Guinness brewery and were among the first to have organised training. Luke O'Kelly is seated to the left of the man with the ball in the front. Tipperary were 1895 All-Ireland champions. Third from the left in the front is Willie Ryan.

chapter three

Homes for Heroes

Most of the organisational problems associated with the early years of the GAA were solved with apparent ease when provincial councils were established in 1901. The new councils took over the burden of running the competitions and crucially gave each of the four provincial championships an identity they were to proudly retain. For the next century the provincial councils were the engine room of the GAA, generating the funds and support that the network of clubs required. After 1905 the association was profitable. By 1909 all 32 counties were organised for the first time.

This improved the structure of the games, and the new century also found new heroes on the playing field to boost the profile of the games.

Key among them were the footballers of Kerry in 1905 and the hurlers of Kilkenny in 1906.

The Killarney and Tralee clubs, great rivals for the Kerry championship, came together under the inspirational leadership of Jim 'Thady' O'Gorman. A sprightly 17-year old from Killarney called Dick Fitzgerald joined O'Gorman in the attack.

At the end of an exhaustive 1903 championship that was completed two years behind schedule, they came up against a new Kildare team in the All-Ireland final led by Joe Rafferty, a football-obsessed cowherd who carried a football with him when he walked around the Mount Armstrong demesne.

Three times the sides met before Kerry resolved the issue and won the All-Ireland for the first of many times. Crowds of 12,000, 18,000 and 12,000 dwarfed anything seen before in the games, smashing a previous record attendance of 10,000 at the 1894 All-Ireland final, and approaching the 20,000 attendance records for the 1898 Ireland-Scotland rugby match in Belfast and the Ireland-England soccer match in Belfast in 1903.

A few ghostly images from photographs are the only clues we have of the intensity of these famous games. But folklore preserved the rich legacy they left the game. The toe-to-hand was first demonstrated at these matches. The phrase 'Up Kerry' was invented for the game, according to *Kerryman* writer Pat Foley, borrowed from John Baily's 1898 council election slogan in Ballymacelligott, 'Up Baily!' Kildare's Mick Kennedy was reputed to have developed the long, low hand-pass along the ground.

Kildare dyed their boots white to match their glamorous new colours of white shirts and togs; Kerry wore red. The grateful GAA allocated an extra £25 expenses to each team and presented defeated Kildare with gold medals to mark their achievement.

Dick Fitzgerald, who was to become the greatest player of his generation, reminisced afterwards: 'In my long career I never remember [having] seen more determined games. Both counties gave football a fillip that marked, as it were, the starting point of the game as we know it today.'

Fitzgerald's reputation dominated the opening decades of the new century, from the 1903 and 1905 finals with Kildare to the epic finals with Wexford in 1913 and 1914 that marked the end of Kerry's first harvest.

His 1914 book, *How to Play Gaelic Football*, was the first instruction manual. His advice was simple and direct, and he showed that man-marking was now an important feature of play.

Crucially, there was more room on the playing field as teams were reduced to 15 a side in 1913. The first 15-a-side match between Kerry and Louth stunned the spectators and became one of the many to enter into folklore as the 'greatest ever'. Fitzgerald himself wrote: 'Never in the history of outdoor games in Ireland have people gone home so well pleased with what they saw.'

Play also required greater accuracy as point posts were abolished in 1907 and the goal posts took an 'H' shape that is still familiar today.

Fitzgerald believed team sizes could be further reduced to 13 a side. 'Gaelic football of the present day is more scientific than any existing football game', he wrote. 'In other forms of football, such is the constitution of rules governing them, there is very often too much of the element of luck. In the native game, however, there is no such preponderance of luck, and this is to be accounted for by the fact that the rules provide the two kinds of score.'

When Kilkenny won the All-Ireland final for the first time in 1904, it was not yet clear that it was set to become the third great hurling county. Football was more popular in Kilkenny when the GAA was first played there. Indeed, there were more cricket clubs than hurling clubs in the county in 1900.

The team was built around Dick Doyle and his brothers and Jim 'Drug' Walsh from Mooncoin. In 1904 what was described as a 'miracle save' by goalkeeper hero Pat 'Fox' Maher of Tullaroan sealed a two-point victory for Kilkenny and he was carried off the field on the shoulders of their supporters amid a 10,000 attendance at Carrick-on-Suir.

In 1905 Kilkenny came back to win again. Jimmy Kelly scored a record-equalling five goals and two points in a replayed All-Ireland against Cork which brought victory for Kilkenny and 19-year-old captain Dan Stapleton.

Another new rule had created the necessity for a replay in the first place. Cork had already beaten Kilkenny, but their goalkeeper Daniel McCarthy was a British Army reservist.

Under an 1895 rule revived in 1905 and, amazingly, retained until 2002, members of the British Army were now banned from playing Gaelic games.

Kilkenny made up for lost time and won seven All-Irelands in the next ten years, capturing the 1911 title without playing Limerick in the final. It was cancelled because of a waterlogged field to the dismay of both teams and 12,000 supporters who had come by special train to Cork. A scheduled replay in May was cancelled because of a religious retreat in Limerick. Limerick then turned down a second replay in a dispute over the venue for the match, and Kilkenny were awarded the title.

Irish women were among the very first to join men on the sportsfields of Europe. Women's bowls, croquet, tennis and hockey were organised in Dublin by the turn of the twentieth century. In 1903 women turned their attention to hurling as well.

It began as a decidedly urban movement, away from the hurling heartlands of Munster and south Leinster as the academics and professionals of the National University and the Gaelic language movement were the first to take up camáns.

The group was led by Máire Ní Chinnéide, subsequently the editor of the memoirs of Peig Sayers. She was among members of the Keatings branch of the Gaelic League who started practising women's hurling in Drumcondra Park in the summer of 1903.

Tadhg Ó Donnchadha named the new sport Camóguidheacht, from the alternative word for a hurl, camóg.

Other organisers included Seán Ó Ceallaigh, who wrote under the pen-name Sceilg and afterwards became Minister for Education in the second Dáil, and Séamus Ó Braonáin, later Director General of the first Raidió Éireann who drew up a code of rules for a 12-a-side game on a pitch that was 60 to 100 yards long and 40 to 60 yards wide.

A well-publicised demonstration match between Craobh Céitinn (Keatings) and a second club, Cúchulainns, took place at a feis in Navan on 17 July 1904. 'It was the time of the hobble skirts, when the girls went down like nine pins when they tried to run', Agnes O'Farrelly later told Pádraig Puirséal.

The first camogie competition, the Ashbourne cup for universities, was organised by Una O'Flaherty, UCD professor of Gaelic poetry, in 1915. The kilt-wearing Edwin Ashbourne, Gaelic League president and son of the sponsor of the 1904 Ashbourne Land Act, donated the trophy.

By then camogie was played in 11 counties as well as London and Glasgow. Dublin beat Louth in the first inter-county match at Jones's Road in July 1912. The real revolution in camogie, in the hurling heartlands, would take many more decades.

● ● ●

'As far as I know, and I have been a patron for years, the Association is purely an athletic body and that alone', Archbishop Croke had told a delegation in 1895. But the GAA wasn't so certain. The move by Dick Blake and others to make the association less political had helped it regain momentum. The naming of clubs after inspirational historical and political Irish figures suggested this athletics body was conscious of deeper patriotic roots.

'Besides reviving our national sports, the GAA has also revived national memories, the names of its clubs perpetuating the memory of many great and good Irishmen', Douglas Hyde had said in 1892.

Clubs went further during the Boer War, choosing the names of Boer heroes: de Wets (Rahoma and Athenry), Krugers (Tuam and Dublin Francis St) and 'The Irish Brigade Transvaal' (Tralee).

Other clubs were named for the 1848 Young Ireland movement or for Young Ireland leaders such as John Mitchel (Castledawson, Galway and Tralee). They were also named after contemporary figures, Parnell, Joseph Biggar, Michael Davitt (Dublin and Drogheda), William O'Brien (Clane), John Mandeville (Sallins) and local politicians such as L. P. Hayden (Roscommon) or T. P. O'Connor (Galway and Athlone), and for writers such as Davis and Kickham (Dublin). As a result of a spell in Galway

The double in football and hurling had been won by Cork in 1890 and Tipperary in 1895 when Tipperary achieved it again in 1900, beating the unlikely opposition of Kilkenny in the All-Ireland semi-final. By now two of their finest 1890s footballers, Mick and Jack Ryan from the Rockwell club, had gone on to become international rugby players. Five members of the Kilkenny team, the famous 'moving quarrymen', Jim Cooney, Pat Wall, Dan Harney, Bill O'Toole and Jack Shea, all played subsequently for Tipperary when they beat London in the first of the five All-Ireland finals to pitch Ireland's champions against Britain. London unexpectedly won the All-Ireland hurling championship in 1901. The hurling-football double was to be achieved once more, by Cork in 1990. Strangest of all, Jimmy Cooney was a name that attached itself to three separate GAA controversies.
Front: James Lonergan, John 'Farry' O'Brien, James Tobin. Centre: P. Ryan, Jack Dwan, R. Ryan, Jack Tobin (captain), Laurence Tobin, Peter Sweeney, Pat Moloney. Back: T. Hogan (chairman), H. Brennan, P. Dwan, P. Murray, John Long, Mick Aylward, John Kavanagh, David Myers, Willie Tobin, P. Russell, P. Keane.

Dublin's football teams were regarded as the most accomplished in the game at the turn of the last century. When they beat Tipperary in the 1902 final, newspapers reported that a delay in the second half to enable Tipperary to find a sub for an injured player 'did not help the state of the ground, already considerably diminished in width by the spectators'. It was Willie Ryan's last match for Tipperary.

Prison, English liberal Wilfred Scawen Blunt had the Mountrice club in Kildare named in his honour.

Within five months of the execution of the leaders of the 1916 Rebellion, clubs had been registered in Dublin in the names of The O'Rahilly, Seán McDermott and Peadar Macken. Éamonn Ceannt's followed in 1917. A club in Down in 1918, the Little Doreens, was mischievously named for the popular nickname of the Defence of the Realm Act.

In 1925 the GAA congress passed a rule preventing clubs being named for political purposes or after figures who were still alive. The trend has survived to the present day in Northern Ireland.

Republican figures killed in the 1966–94 troubles featured in club and competition names, as in the Sheridan, Bateson and Lee memorial cup for the Derry intermediate championship and the Kevin Lynch club in Dungiven.

The GAA never officially decided that Gaelic matches should be played largely on Sundays, but Cusack firmly believed the ban on Sunday athletics discriminated against the lower classes who worked six days a week.

The columns of his *Celtic Times* are filled with references to the importance of allowing Sunday competition.

Research by Donal MacAnallen shows how Sunday play brought the association into serious conflict with Sabbatarianism in the north-east corner of the island.

Ironically, it was a Tyrone Presbyterian and an early GAA vice-president, William Houston Stewart, who was one of the strongest advocates of Sunday sports. It led to a condemnation of the association's perceived disregard of the sabbath, not only from Presbyterian

and Church of Ireland clergymen, but occasionally from Catholic clergymen as well, usually but not exclusively in Ulster. Those who condemned Sunday games included the Catholic primate Cardinal Michael Logue. MacAnallen points out that there was a significant number of Protestant members of the GAA in Ulster before the Thurles convention of 1887. 'It is worth pondering how Protestants would have shaped the development of the GAA in Ulster had they remained in the association', he says.

Matches too were more likely to be played on weekdays. Sunday games were illegal throughout Ireland under a 1695 Observance Act, but when the Act proved unenforceable some Ulster Protestants began taking the law into their own hands. As MacAnallen says, 'the GAA were the victims of militancy rather than the perpetrator', and police proved the protectors of GAA players at incidents such as Banbridge in 1904, Markethill in 1906, Newtownhamilton and Newbliss in 1910, and Glenavy in 1912.

Sabbatarianism on the part of the board of the Great Northern Railway company also created problems for the GAA. The company refused to allow GAA clubs to charter special trains on Sundays, cancelled trains they discovered were for GAA use and changed their timetables to disrupt the GAA calendar.

This led to the 1903 Ulster final being fixed for Easter Monday and had the effect of denying Fermanagh their first chance of appearing in an All-Ireland semi-final when they were nominated in 1907 but could not get transport to the game. It took 97 years for Fermanagh to play the semi-final the railway authorities had denied them.

The problem receded somewhat after Ulster GAA chairman Paddy Whelan travelled to the railway commission hearings in London in March 1908.

More serious were continued attacks on GAA players and spectators, as happened in Cookstown in 1904 and at a match between Lisburn Keatings and O'Neill Crowleys in 1905, an incident mentioned in the English parliament.

The Lisburn riot effectively killed off GAA in the town for 60 years and MacAnallen suggests that Sabbatarian opposition delayed the popularisation of GAA in Ulster for several decades.

There was an irony, he says, in GAA players being protected from hostile Sabbatarian crowds by the RIC, a police force banned from participation in the association. 'Hurling stones on a Sunday seemed a lesser sin than hurling sliotars' in the eyes of the religious zealots.

The only public GAA grounds in the north-east, Falls Park in Belfast, was closed on a Sunday and therefore of little use to clubs in the city.

Some of the earliest Gaelic football action photographs featured in the *Irish Weekly Examiner* and are from the second replay of the 1903 All-Ireland football final between Kildare and Kerry, showing the old style point posts and soccer goals without nets. Kerry's goalkeeper is Patrick Dillon. Waterford-born Rody Kirwan, Con Healy and Bill Myers are also in action, as is Frank 'Joyce' Conlan of Kildare. The crowd stayed well behind the railings at Cork Athletic Grounds, unlike the chaotic scenes at the first match in Tipperary which ended without a clear winner. Gate receipts were a record £270.

Gaelic football had already surpassed athletics and hurling as the more popular of Gaelic sports before Kerry and Kildare played three times in the 1903 All-Ireland final, but the two replays in Cork and the massive publicity surrounding the games gave football the place at the heart of Irish sporting culture it still retains. It also put the association on a sound financial footing after 21 years of penury.

J. J. O'Reilly's photograph of the 1903 Kildare team. The crest, bizarrely, says KFC. Back: William J. Rankin (chairman), Jack Murray, Larry 'Hussey' Cribben, Jack Gorman, Mick Murray, Jim Wright, Dick Radley (secretary). Middle: Michael Fox (later county chairman), Frank 'Joyce' Conlan, Jem Scott, Mick Donnelly, Jack Fitzgerald, Mick Fitzgerald, J. P. Lacey (official). Front: John Dunne, Ned Kennedy, Mick Kennedy, Joe Rafferty (captain), William Bracken, William 'Steel' Losty, William Merriman.

Although the association passed another 'no politics' motion in 1911, events were soon to overtake them once more. Galway county board proposed in November 1913 that the GAA set up rifle clubs 'for the purpose of training an army' and gave official sanction to the Irish Volunteers when they were established that same month. William Mandle indicates that some GAA clubs set up Volunteer branches, and dual membership was common.

The newly renamed Croke Park grounds were refused for drilling by the Irish Volunteers in January 1914, but that same month GAA president James Nowlan called upon members to 'join the Volunteers and learn to shoot straight'. Delegates sang 'A Nation Once Again' at the 1914 congress. The 1915 GAA congress was cut short to allow members attend a Volunteer parade in Dublin city, having pledged the support of delegates to the British and French in their war against Germany.

A challenge match in Drogheda that same weekend ended with the Louth players calling for three cheers for Kerry. Dick Fitzgerald called for 'three cheers for Eoin McNeill instead'.

On Easter Monday, 1916, the former chairman of the Dublin colleges GAA council was the leader of the group of armed men who seized the GPO and declared the Irish Republic.

The GAA quickly distanced itself from the Rising, but GAA president James Nowlan and well-known

referee Willie Walsh were among those arrested after the event.

Six of the 16 leaders executed after the Rising were GAA members. Of the 40 Dr Croke's club members in Dublin, 32 were in action in Easter week. All the members of the St James's Street Christian Brothers past pupils club, Ollamh Fódhla, were either on the run or in jail after the Rising. Kerry withdrew from the 1917 championship because of the number of footballers who had been interned.

Within five months clubs had been registered in Dublin in the names of The O'Rahilly, Seán McDermott and Peadar Macken. An Éamonn Ceannts club was registered in 1917. When the Clare football team entered the field for the 1917 All-Ireland final, they followed a de Valera flag.

As the British moved to suppress each of the patriotic movements, the GAA was among the bodies it targeted.

Most public meetings were banned in 13 counties on 4 July 1918, with the rules framed to include the GAA, but not rugby, soccer, cricket or lawn tennis. The colonial police force, the RIC, demanded permits for the holding of football matches under their new coercive powers, the Defence of the Realm Act. When the GAA refused to apply for them, confrontation was inevitable. During July 1918 soldiers baton charged matches in Offaly and Down, took down goal posts in Kildare and occupied playing fields in Cork.

The biggest show-down took place before an Ulster championship match between Cavan and Armagh at Cootehill, where a large body of troops occupied the playing field where 3,000 had gathered. Local parish priest Fr O'Connell addressed the crowd, asked them to disperse quietly and no incidents occurred. A match was fixed for the same field on the following day. This time the police were present but bayonets were not drawn and the game took place.

On 4 August the GAA arranged over 2,000 matches on the same afternoon in every county, claiming afterwards they had mobilised 54,000 players. All the matches started at the same time. Parishes and townlands which had not fielded a team for a generation lined out. There was no RIC interference and the permit issue was allowed to die out.

But the harassment did not end there. On the eve of the 1919 All-Ireland final, the *Freeman's Journal* complained that the authorities 'place every obstacle in the movement of devotees to Irish native games'.

A new crisis arose with the firing of the first shots of what would become the Irish War of Independence in Soloheadbeg in January 1919. Tipperary were unable to train for the 1920 All-Ireland final because of martial law restrictions.

Nationalist politicians had always identified closely with the GAA. John Dillon came to throw in the ball at the 1914 All-Ireland final.

The Sinn Féin Party, which had won 73 out of 105 parliamentary

seats in the 1918 election indicating they enjoyed the support of over 80 per cent of the electorate on the island and who had convened the first Dáil Éireann in Dublin, looked to the GAA as a vehicle for public support. Former Kerry full-back Austin Stack and referee Harry Boland were among their new crop of MPs.

Sinn Féin political leaders started coming to GAA matches to show their support. The photograph of Michael Collins, Éamon de Valera and Arthur Griffith together at the 1919 hurling final is the only one of the trio in existence.

Leinster and Connacht were the only two provinces to complete their championships in 1920. By November of that year, the question of whether the inactive Tipperary team or Dublin were the best footballers in the country was to be resolved by a football challenge scheduled for Croke Park.

Bloody Sunday, 21 November 1920, has come to be acknowledged as the turning point in the Irish War of

Cavan's three matches against Armagh for the Ulster championship of 1903, played in 1905, were as important in establishing football as a spectator sport in Ulster as the Kerry-Kildare games were on a national level later the same year. The final was fixed for Easter Monday because the Great Northern Railway Company refused to run excursion trains on Sundays. The victorious Cavan team is pictured.
Back: (unknown), Patrick O'Reilly (secretary), Hugh Maguire, John Maguire, John Fitzpatrick, John McCabe, P. J. Brady, (unknown). Centre: John F. O'Hanlon (chairman), John Brady, Philip McEnroe, Hugh Fitzpatrick, Patrick McGovern, Owen Maguire, William Carolan. Front: (unknown), Bernard Lynch, James Durry, Matthew Smith, Terry Maguire, John O'Reilly, John Smith, Patrick Gilronan, Gilligan.

Tom Semple was emerging as the greatest hurler of his generation when he captained Tipperary to win the 1906 All-Ireland championship, and Paddy Riordan as the greatest marksman of his era. Back: Denis O'Keeffe (chairman), Tom Allen, Jack Cahill, Jack Gleeson, Tom Kerwick, Paddy 'Best' Maher, James M. Kennedy (secretary). Centre: Paddy Burke, Jimmy Burke, Paddy Riordan, Jer Hayes, Martin O'Brien, Phil Molony (treasurer). Front: Jack Mockler, Joe O'Keeffe, Jim 'Hawk' O'Brien, Tom Semple (captain), Tom Kenna, Michael Gleeson, Paddy Brolan.

Dublin Brigade IRA officers had urged the GAA to postpone the match. Jim Nowlan, Dan McCarthy and Luke O'Toole decided not to cancel as it would identify the organisation with the shootings. As there was a news black-out, this meant that the overnight assassinations were not public knowledge.

They also calculated that players and civilians, used to wide-scale British harassment during the previous four years, would be able to cope.

James Gleeson in his book, *Bloody Sunday*, quotes one of the British paramilitaries involved in the operation saying they tossed a coin over whether they would go on a killing spree in Croke Park or loot O'Connell Street instead. Croke Park lost.

Despite the unease in the city that morning, some 10,000 spectators went to Croke Park for the match.

The Tipperary and Dublin teams were regarded as two of the best in the country and indeed met in the 1920 All-Ireland final when it was played two years later.

The ball was thrown in by referee Mick Sammon from Kildare at 2.45 p.m. Shortly afterwards an aeroplane flew over the ground and a red flare was shot from the cockpit. At 3.25 p.m. 15 lorries of military and paramilitaries arrived at Croke Park, preceded and followed by two armoured cars.

According to spectators at the game, a British officer climbed on top of a wall and fired a revolver shot to signal the start of the period of sustained gunfire from the paramilitaries. The crowd thought at first that the raiders were firing blanks, but then the British aimed machine gunfire at some of the crowd.

The crowd stampeded towards the Railway wall, furthest from the gunfire. Two of the players failed to make it off the pitch, Michael Hogan and Jim Egan. Hogan was hit and a young Wexford man who attempted to whisper an act of contrition in his ear was also shot dead. A priest who was a spectator, Fr Crotty, administered the last rites to the player despite the continuing gunfire. Tommy Ryan escaped from the ground but was found in a house in

Independence. Thirty people died in a 13 hour period that day. Eleven British intelligence agents, sent to infiltrate GHQ under the guise of commercial travellers, were killed by Michael Collins's squad in their suburban homes on the morning. An ex-British Army officer who was not a secret service agent and two British Auxiliary paramilitaries were also killed during that operation.

Fourteen civilians, including footballer Michael Hogan, were killed in a British raid on a Gaelic football match in Croke Park on Sunday afternoon.

Finally, Brigadier Dick McKee and Vice Brigadier Peadar Clancy were summarily executed by the British in Dublin Castle that night.

The first incident of the weekend occurred on the day before the match. A fight ensued between some British paramilitaries on the train carrying the Tipperary team to Dublin, resulting in two of the British being thrown off the train.

The team expected repercussions from this incident and did not stay as arranged in Barry's Hotel in Gardiner Place. Instead, they split up into small groups staying in different hotels and the two IRA volunteers on the team, Michael Hogan and Tommy Ryan, stayed with fellow IRA volunteer and former Tipperary player Phil Shanahan in Dublin.

C. S. Andrews' biography captures the mood of the city in the morning and recalls being warned by a fellow officer 'not to go to Croke Park'.

Clonliffe Road by soldiers who were restrained from shooting him on the spot by an officer. His clothes were taken from him and he was marched naked back to the ground. A man who gave him a coat was hit with the butt of a rifle.

The casualties included Jane Boyle, who had gone to the match with her fiancé and was due to be married five days later. Fourteen-year-old John Scott from Drumcondra was so mutilated that medical personnel assumed he had been bayoneted to death. Two other victims were aged 10 and 11 respectively.

As an ambulance man went around the ground with a bucket picking up pieces of bone and in one case a length of thigh, the Tipperary players were rounded up and threatened, before they were set free by an officer who told them he feared he could not restrain his own men's thirst for blood.

● ● ●

Within hours three different versions of the events were being prepared by the British. The first public response was from Basil Clarke, a former *Daily Mail* journalist recruited to head up the propaganda department in Dublin, to counter hostile coverage by London-based newspapers and journalists such as Hugh Martin of the *Daily News*.

Clarke issued a statement saying that the paramilitaries intended to go to the ground and, speaking from a megaphone in the centre of the field, invite the assassins to come forward. In the process of doing so they had come under fire from 'pickets' in the outskirts of the ground and they returned fire, resulting in the large civilian death-toll.

Photographs of the two Irishmen executed in Dublin Castle that evening were also prepared by Clarke, clumsily purporting to show the already dead bodies 'attempting to escape'.

Mark Sugden's Dublin Castle diary indicates the pressure on the colonial administration to come up with such a story. He writes about Clarke's attempt to fabricate a story to justify the atrocity and was satisfied that 'they got good play in London' in the following day's papers.

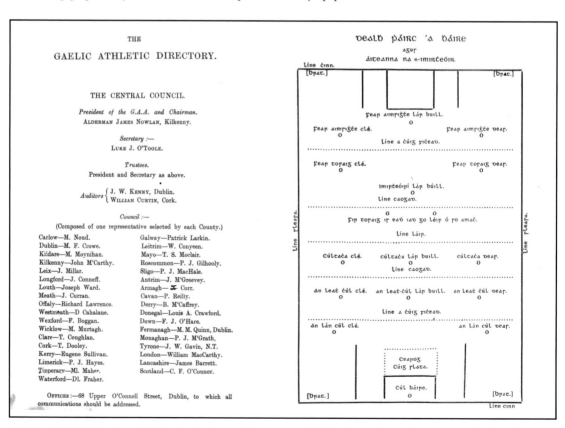

The *Gaelic Athletic Directory* of 1908 with the layout of the teams in Irish. The first edition of the annual carried the obituary of Michael Cusack.

Despite's Clarke's efforts, the atrocity was widely condemned in London as well as Dublin, though the British ambassador in Washington complained about the failure of the American newspapers to accept the British version of events.

Hamar Greenwood, Chief Secretary for Ireland, reiterated a slightly different version of events in the House of Commons the following day. He repeated the claim that 'Sinn Féin pickets at the entrance to the field' had initiated the violence, and said that while he regretted the deaths of innocent persons, 'the responsibility lies with those who are a constant menace to all law-abiding persons in Ireland.'

The earliest action photograph from an All-Ireland final was taken at the Tipperary-Dublin replay in Athy in 1908 and appeared in the *Irish Press* golden jubilee supplement of 1934. It features legendary Tipperary goalkeeper Jim 'Hawk' O'Brien defending the Tipperary goal from a rare Dublin attack. Dominant team of the decade, Kilkenny had opted out of that year's championship.

Despite this attempt at public unity, behind the scenes British military commander General Nevil Macredy was distancing his troops from the RIC and their paramilitary auxiliary forces, saying the paramilitaries had 'arrived ten minutes early' before troops were in position and had returned fire indiscriminately when a spectator in the grandstand had 'fired three revolver shots'. This allowed spectators to escape without being searched, Macredy wrote.

A secret British military inquiry into the events, suppressed until decades later, further contradicted these versions.

In keeping with the official version, a Royal Irish Constabulary policeman said that when the British first got out to the lorries at Royal Canal bridge on Jones's Road, a group of civilians at the start of the passage to the ground turned and ran. According to one of the raiders, one of them fired revolver shots at the paramilitaries.

The evidence from the two local Dublin Metropolitan policemen stationed on Jones's Road contradicted this. They denied seeing any civilians who would have threatened the British forces, but said the raiders from the first car ran down the passage to the ground firing shots. They also said a British

military officer cried out 'Stop that firing. What's that firing about?'

One of his colleagues said that a raiding party of 12 men in RIC uniforms jumped from the lorry and started firing what he thought was blank ammunition in the air, and immediately 'firing started all round the ground'.

One of the British paramilitaries who had been firing at spectators admitted he was operating in plain clothes, with a Glengarry cap in his pocket for identification by his own side. He describes chasing through the crowd 'using his discretion' in firing at civilians with a .450 revolver. He targeted those who were fleeing or 'trying to conceal themselves in the crowd'.

The funerals of the Irish victims were muted, newspaper reports severely censored, but folklore records widespread intimidation and harassment of mourners by the British.

The British agents were buried with pomp and ceremony in London, to the dismay of officers such as Brigadier General Frank Crozier, who was shocked at the honour shown to men who had died 'in the service of the crown while engaged in a murder stunt'.

Nor did Bloody Sunday bring an end to the atrocities. Cork city was burned three weeks later. The attack by the British on a St Stephen's Day dance in Bruff, Co. Limerick, a few weeks later, leaving five dead and a hundred wounded, was equally indiscriminate and brutal. But it was the events in Croke Park that were to resonate most loudly through Irish popular culture.

There was one propaganda victory for the British which featured in Hamar Greenwood's defence of the atrocity before the House of Commons the following day. According to the British, 30 revolvers were found in the grounds.

When Belfast MP Joseph Devlin asked Greenwood in the Commons if any incriminating documents had been found in the grounds, Conservative MPs howled 'revolvers' back at him.

GAA people were genuinely bewildered by the revolvers story and many of them believed Greenwood, Macredy or Clarke had made it up. They hadn't. But it took 70 years to find out where they had come from.

Joe Stynes, an IRA volunteer, Dublin footballer and granduncle of a famous GAA and Australian Rules footballer, was acting as a steward at the game. When the British arrived he cleared the Railway wall, leaving behind several guns he was holding for the IRA.

He also gave his overcoat to an IRA volunteer, 19-year-old Brendan Ryan, to help shield him from the British. Ryan escaped but was shot dead at Mountjoy Prison by the British five months later.

The trophy awarded to the All-Ireland champions of 1904. The Croke cups (1890s) and Railway cups (1910s) were eventually won out, until perpetual trophies in hurling commemorating Liam McCarthy (1922) and in football commemorating Sam Maguire (1928) were instituted.

The debate about Bloody Sunday continues to this day. Tony Geraghty's *The Irish War* (1998) shows how important the event remains in English polemic, particularly in comparison with more recent troubles in Northern Ireland: 'As on another Bloody Sunday in 1972', he writes, 'a republican gun opened fire and triggered off a massacre by the security forces.'

Australian GAA historian William Mandle rejects British claims that the match was arranged as a cover for Collins's operation, but cannot rule out that it served as a cover to help assemble the 120 men he deems necessary for the operation, an argument pursued by Francis Costelloe and others.

But this argument does not stand up well, as the executions of what became known as the 'Cairo gang' were carried out by Collins's trusted Dublin-based squad, not by country volunteers brought to Dublin for the operation. It also disregards the fact that weekly Croke Park fixtures in the weeks leading up to Bloody Sunday were regarded as important for the continuity of the games and again after activity resumed in July 1921.

Mandle also points out that the injured Gael for whom the match was to raise funds was not named, raising the question of another British claim that the match was to raise funds for arms. But matches for prisoners' dependants were commonplace in the run-up to Bloody Sunday and subsequently, as in the supremely bad-taste notice for a match in 1922: 'Desperate shooting at Croke Park (for goals and points). Republicans, Free Staters and separatists (Sinn Féiners all) adjourn to the old venue for a few hours relaxation.'

'At this remove it is hard to imagine the terror of the day', Tim Carey wrote in his *Croke Park: A History*, in which he presents a comprehensive re-creation of the events from eyewitness accounts.

The most famous of the casualties, Tipperary footballer Michael Hogan, had the premier stand at Croke Park named in his honour in 1925.

That same year the IRFU unveiled a memorial to its own war dead in Lansdowne Road. Popular sport was quick to identify its constituencies in post-colonial Ireland.

● ● ●

For good reasons as well as bad, Croke Park was now Ireland's most famous sportsground. It was now also GAA property. Because the GAA could not afford to purchase the Jones's Road grounds, their secretary Frank Dineen did it for them in 1908 and held it in his own name until the GAA got an unexpected windfall of £1,930 from the Kerry v Louth Croke memorial final in 1913 and were able to purchase Croke Park for £3,645 8*s.* 5*d.*

In November 1913 Jones's Road became the GAA headquarters and was renamed after the late Archbishop of Cashel who was the first patron of the association.

Sideline seats were provided for the first time at the 1910 hurling final when 700 chairs were commandeered for the 4,780 attendance. By 1912 a new pavilion had been constructed, offering seats for two shillings.

In 1915 the wall behind the Railway end was raised and another wall erected at the Canal end of the ground. After the 1916 Rebellion rubble from the shelling of Dublin city centre was brought to construct an artificial bank behind the Railway end goal. Initially named Hill 60 after a Gallipoli battlefield, it soon became known as Hill 16 after the date of the Easter Rebellion.

● ● ●

Seven months after Bloody Sunday a truce was signed between the British and what had become the new Irish National Army.

When Tipperary started out in the 1920 championship, Dan Breen was on the run. By the time the

All-Ireland final was played between Tipperary and Dublin eighteen months later, Breen was a hero of the revolution and invited to start the match by throwing in the ball before a crowd of 17,000.

As the new Irish Free State was negotiated, one of the first items on the agenda at the first GAA meeting was the revival of what the founders called the Olympics of Ancient Ireland, the Tailteann games.

On 8 June 1922, J. J. Walsh claimed in the Dáil that the revived Aonach Tailteann would go ahead and promised a festival 'more than twice as large as the Greek Olympic'.

The new government was less enthusiastic when the cost became apparent. Walsh granted £2,000 in 1921, another £2,000 early in 1922, and a further £10,000 (equivalent to €600,000 in 2005) towards the refurbishment of Croke Park. Grants of £10,000 guaranteed from other organisations fell through. The grant-in-aid would not be matched proportionately again by any Irish government until the 1970s.

The Tailteann project was planned for 6–13 August 1922, but it was postponed until 1924. At 4 a.m. on

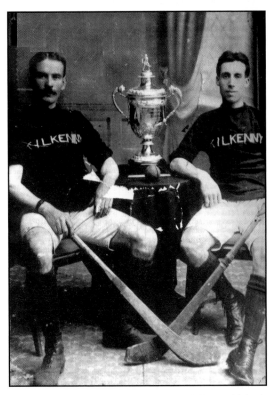

Jack Rochford, star of the 1905 replayed final that established Kilkenny's reputation as the finest hurling team of its generation, with Mick Doyle and the All-Ireland cup for 1907.

A generation of hurling followers believed Kilkenny's victory over Cork in 1907 was the greatest hurling final of all time, a mythologising process begun by the priest who posed with them, J. B. Dollard. Kilkenny went a point ahead and beat off two late Cork attacks to win. Kilkenny were later to the podium than their main hurling rivals, Cork and Tipperary, but Jim 'Drug' Walsh's men won seven All-Irelands in 11 years and established a winning tradition that was to endure. Back: Jack Keoghan, Jack Rochford, Tom Kenny, Dan Stapleton, Danny O'Connor (manager), Paddy 'Icy' Lanigan, John T. Power, Dick Brennan (did not play in final), Sim Walton. Middle: Eddie Doyle, Dick Doherty, Mick Doyle, Rev. J. B. Dollard, Jim 'Drug' Walsh, Jim Kelly, Dick Doyle, Dan Kennedy. Front: Matt Gargan, Jack Anthony. Missing: Dan Grace.

28 June 1922, a series of events were to unfold that changed Irish life for ever. General Michael Collins commenced the bombardment of the Four Courts. Irishman was fighting Irishman over the terms of settlement of the war that had ended twelve months before.

● ● ●

The GAA was the major sporting and cultural organisation in the towns and parishes where the Civil War was most bitterly fought, in west Clare, Kerry, south Tipperary, and north and west Cork.

The association tried to carry on as normal and doggedly refused to abandon its calendar.

An attempt was made to reorganise south Tipperary in August. In September the Cork county board reported difficulties completing its fixtures. The Munster council, working through their fixture pile-up, wriggled out of an impasse with some ingenuity. They decided that the 1920 finalists should contest the delayed 1921 provincial finals.

With fighting especially severe in the Kerry mountains and around Carrick-on-Suir, a November Munster council meeting decided to postpone all championships until 1923.

A Roscommon v Sligo match fixed for Tubbercurry fell through as both districts were controlled by anti-treaty forces during the early stages of the Civil War. Anti-treaty delegates walked out of a meeting of the Kilkenny county board.

In April 1923 Tipperary finally conceded a long-fought, on-again off-again All-Ireland semi-final against Mayo on the issue of the republican prisoners, officially because they found it 'impossible to field a team'.

Among the four republican prisoners shot in the first reprisal shooting on 8 December was the former Cork footballer and hurler Richard Barrett, in response to the killing of TD Seán Hales. The Cork county board proposed votes of condolence to both Barrett and Hales, and sent a proposal for a special peace congress to the central council.

Ulster had a new set of problems as it straddled two regimes in conflict. Most championship matches were held south of the border.

Armagh managed to field a team for the semi-final against Monaghan at Ballybay despite the fact that they had no county board at the time and half their team were on the run on both sides of the newly established border.

The games in Belfast came to a halt as guns were turned on the Catholic population: 257 Catholics were killed and 23,000 burned out of their homes in the turbulent two years between the summers of 1920 and 1922. In Lisburn almost the entire Catholic community was driven from the town, which meant there was no GAA club there for four decades.

Monaghan's preparations for the All-Ireland semi-final included six weeks spent in jail after they were kidnapped by a new paramilitary group established by the Stormont regime, the B Specials, in Dromore, Co. Tyrone, while on their way to play in the Ulster final against Derry on 14 January 1922.

Eoin O'Duffy later recalled that half the Monaghan team were IRA volunteers. These included Dan Hogan, Officer in Command of the 5th Northern Division, and brother of Bloody Sunday footballer-victim Michael Hogan of Grangemockler.

Sergeant Michael Kirk, who was also a veteran of the Anglo-Irish War, was now in the new Free State Army. Pro and anti-treaty factions north and south of the border united in their efforts to get the players released.

The situation grew extremely serious on 8 February when 42 loyalists were kidnapped in retaliation by the IRA and held as hostages for the safe release of the footballers.

A meeting of the north Derry board in Claudy on 13 February was forced to disperse under a hail of bullets from another group of the Stormont regime's new paramilitaries, the A Specials.

• • •

The GAA congress in April 1923 managed to skirt around the treaty issue, although Garda Commissioner and later Blueshirt founder, General Eoin O'Duffy,

provocatively demanded that presidential candidates should declare their attitude to the treaty (both were against).

Clare ended up with two GAA boards after county secretary Pat Hennessy and fellow GAA activist Con MacMahon were executed by the Free State forces in January 1923, just as the Civil War was coming to an end.

A subsequent board meeting offered sympathy to the relatives of 'all the Gaels of Clare who had fallen'.

When county treasurer Seán MacNamara, who was with Éamon de Valera at the time of his arrest at a

Railways were the great beneficiaries of early GAA events, enabling them to run special trains on the underused network. It was a mutually beneficial arrangement as GAA clubs grew along rail lines and key junction towns became venues for major matches. Limerick Junction staged one of the 1887 championship matches. Railway companies were also the first sponsors of GAA competitions spending £50 on two shields as trophies for inter-provincial competitions in 1905. The tournaments, which were to raise compensation funds for injured players, eventually evolved into the Railway cups. Relations with the railway networks were not always cordial. Kerry pulled out of the 1910 All-Ireland football final in a row over rail facilities for its team and supporters. Another row over custody of the railway shield caused Kilkenny to opt out of the competition in 1908 in the middle of one of their most dominant periods.

public meeting in Ennis in August 1924, walked out of the county convention after an adjournment motion was not passed, he established a rival 'Group of Old Gaels' board. It secured the allegiance of 25 clubs as against 26 in the official GAA before unity was re-established in the summer of 1924.

War-scarred Clare was the unlikely venue for a different kind of revolution. Tom Garry from Clonreddin started a women's GAA league in Cooraclare parish in 1926. The idea petered out, but interestingly, Cooraclare was one of the first clubs to reorganise when women's football restarted 50 years later.

Tipperary beat Cork in the 1922 Munster semi-final, having had to travel partly by car, partly by rail and walk part of the way to the game through blocked roads and blown-up bridges.

Kilkenny won the 1922 hurling championship with one of the most dramatic finishes, coming from three points down to win by two points. Corkman Paddy Mehigan, the leading sportswriter of the time,

One of the stars of the 1903 team that won Kerry's first All-Ireland, Dick Fitzgerald was an iconic figure in the early years of the twentieth century, wrote the first instructional book on Gaelic football and has the stadium in Killarney named in his honour.

described the match: 'Alternate scoring, clean, hard hitting, clashing splintering ash, electric movements from goal to goal, frequent blade-to-blade duels for possession, quickly changing fortunes, the best played in the hurling code in modern times.' That the finals were played at all was trumpeted in the *Freeman's Journal* as testimony to the GAA's unifying force over the bitterness of the Civil War. Record receipts of £2,403 were taken, but when the *Freeman's Journal* said there must have been 40,000 there, it was sued by the GAA.

The war effectively ended with the death of Liam Lynch in the Knockmealdown Mountains in April 1923. The president of the provisional government Éamon de Valera surrendered three weeks later. Thousands of sportsmen, now prisoners, were being held without any sense of what was to become of them.

GAA life was not going to return to normal. Sinn Féin in Waterford intervened to prevent football and hurling matches taking place during the course of a hunger strike by prisoners in October 1923. Goal posts were torn down at Turner's Cross and Riverstown in Cork in November.

Although the hunger strike was called off on 23 November, two days later both Cork and Kilkenny county boards were asked to stop all matches until the prisoners were released.

Kerry was in turmoil, with its county chairman and two members of the county team in prison. All five Munster counties refused to play matches until the prisoners were released. After hasty suspensions were dished out to football finalists Kerry, hurling finalists Limerick and junior hurling finalists Cork for refusing to fulfil All-Ireland fixtures, it appeared that the GAA structure might collapse altogether.

A special congress on 12 August 1924 revoked the suspensions after a robust debate. Among those present was one of the greatest players of his generation, John Joe Sheehy, recently released from prison.

He had been constantly on the run from August 1922 to May 1924. He emerged from his Cnocán dug-out to play in a match in aid of republican prisoners in Tralee (700 from the town were in internment camps). No attempt was made to arrest him.

While hiding out 'on the run', Sheehy had heard the landmine blast in Ballyseedy when nine prisoners were killed in one of the most horrific episodes of the Civil War, and rescued a survivor, Stephen Fuller, from the scene.

Only two players had turned up for Kerry's first training session of the year and three players had to be recruited from the sideline to make up the 15 to play Cork in the provincial semi-final. Thirty Kerry footballer internees were released in January 1924, Sheehy among them.

Perhaps the most remarkable selection match in GAA history was then arranged. Pro-treaty players played anti-treaty players for the honour of representing the county in the All-Ireland.

The *Kerryman* report of the game indicates that it was played on a flooded pitch and 'somewhat marred by a large number of fouls, the referee being kept pretty busy'.

The county convention agreed on a second match. The internees defeated the county team by 12 points, 'fought out in a fine sporting spirit which reflected the utmost credit on both combinations'.

As a result there were 11 changes in the team for the All-Ireland championship. Alongside Sheehy on that Kerry team was Con Brosnan, a Free State Army officer later to stand for Cumann na nGaedheal in the 1932 general election.

● ● ●

Handball, which had not thrived under GAA patronage, was given its own association in 1924.

At its third ever meeting on 17 January 1885, the GAA standardised court sizes at 65 feet and the weight of the ball between 1¾ and 2 oz, but virtually ignored handball thereafter.

The sport followed an independent semi-professional model in towns where the few ball courts existed. Courts attached to famous public houses, such as the Boot Inn in Ballymun, staged championship contests in rubbers of 17 matches, usually over two legs at two venues, at which sums of up to £1,000 changed hands. Like boxing champions, the title-holder remained champion until he was successfully challenged and beaten. At the end of the nineteenth and the beginning of the twentieth century, Irish Americans Phil Casey, Mick Egan and James Kelly won highly publicised world title matches against Irish champions. An Irish amateur handball union was established in 1912.

It was not until 1924, when the Irish Amateur Handball Association was founded, that the GAA moved to organise handball on a larger scale.

● ● ●

Athletics also separated from the other GAA sports in 1922, and passed to the National Athletics and Cycling Association (NACA) under the presidency of J. J. Keane. When the IAAA disbanded, the country enjoyed three years of athletics unity.

The NACA selected the team of eight Irish athletes which competed at the Paris Olympics in 1924, including Gaelic footballers Seán Lavan from Mayo and Larry Stanley from Kildare. Considering Irish athletes had won 23 gold medals in individual events in the previous seven Olympics, the games were dis-

Kerry against Wexford in the 1913 All-Ireland football final.

appointing. Stanley was one of two athletes to finish tenth. The rest failed to make it through the heats. Sergeant Patrick Dwyer was best of an eight-strong boxing team in fourth place. Another boxer, William Murphy, reached the quarter-finals, as did the FAI's first soccer team — Irish soccer's greatest achievement until the Northern Ireland team of 1958 and the Republic of Ireland team of 1990 reached World Cup quarter-finals. Jack Butler Yeats won an artistic silver medal.

Athletics unity was short lived. In 1925 an argument over the running of greyhound races at Belfast in Celtic Park caused some of the Belfast clubs to secede from the NACA. When officials of England's AAA intervened, it caused another three-way split in the sport that would take 80 years to sort out.

The oldest surviving programme for an All-Ireland final dates to 1914, pride of the collection of the Limerick GAA historian Séamus Ó Ceallaigh. The programme warned the public against purchasing tickets 'from any person not wearing official badges, green, white and gold', and noted that 'arrangement will also be made with the chief commissioner for police for a car hazard at shilling and sixpence gates'. Advertisers included the Cash tailoring company, 4 Capel Street (John Nelligan proprietor): 'We make Irish Volunteer uniforms for all ranks.'

As soon as the Paris Olympics ended, athletes converged on Dublin for the 16-day Tailteann games. A decision of 5 August meant that the games in Dublin would not, after all, be open to all comers from the Celtic countries.

Despite this, entries came from Australia, Britain, New Zealand and South Africa, and over 100 American and Canadian athletes stopped over on their way home from the Olympics, including the greatest athlete of the era, high jump and decathlon champion Harold Osborne.

There were 6,500 entrants. The opening ceremony brought together, in the words of organiser J. J. Walsh, 'the flower of the Celt lining up under their respective standards', with champion Irish wolfhounds, girls dressed as Celtic queens, artillery salutes and a fly-past of aeroplanes. The main parade consisted of a march-past

by 3,000 athletes, a salute by Captain Tom Byrne of the Irish Boer War Regiment and the 1916 Rising, and a parade of record-breaking athletes such as Tom Kiely, Pat Davin and Peter O'Connor. A choir of 500 sang the Tailteann ode of welcome. The elderly Fenian John Devoy was received as guest of honour.

Attendances peaked at 20,000 for Harold Osborne's high jump battle with Kildare Gaelic footballer Larry Stanley. The Americans fielded a team of recent emigrants which beat the Irish in Gaelic football. Scotland sent a shinty team.

Croke Park staged athletics, cycling, hurling, football and camogie. The swimming events were held in the pool in the Dublin zoological gardens. Australian Olympic gold medallist Andrew 'Boy' Charlton won most of the freestyle swimming events whilst Australia dominated cycling. Light-heavyweight boxing gold medallist Harry Mitchell of England won a Tailteann prize and Sergeant Patrick Dwyer, fourth in the Olympics, contested the welterweight final with Purdy of New Zealand.

Archery was staged in the Iveagh Gardens near St Stephen's Green, billiards in the CYMS club in O'Connell Street, chess in Trinity College's Regent's Hall, claybird shooting at Leopardstown Racecourse, cycling and motor racing in the Phoenix Park, gymnastics in the Mansion House, handball at the Boot Inn in Ballymun and in Clondalkin, rowing on the Trinity regatta course at Islandbridge (two boats a heat), tennis at Fitzwilliam, and tug-of-war at the RDS, Ballsbridge.

Medals were awarded for arts and crafts, dancing, dramatic art, literature, music and national costume, and there was an industrial section. A cultural programme was organised by William Butler Yeats, Oliver St John Gogarty and Count John McCormack.

Press coverage was euphoric. Telegrams of congratulation were sent from Belfast, although Stormont Premier James Craig did not attend due to illness. More significantly, all anti-treaty prisoners were finally released days before the games were about to begin.

Although Munster had suffered most in the Civil War, their teams dominated the All-Ireland championship in the years immediately after the war.

Kerry and Kildare played what was acknowledged as the best All-Ireland final of the era in 1926 before a record attendance of 37,500. Kerry drew level with a late goal and won the replay. It was the finest hour for Kildare's high-jumping midfielder Larry Stanley.

Jack Murphy of Kerry played an excellent game at centre half-back, but apparently put on his clothes without bothering to take off his playing gear afterwards. The following Wednesday a selector, Eugene Ring, noticed that Murphy was in pain. A doctor was summoned and he was sent to hospital in Tralee where he died of pneumonia the following day, leaving his colleagues to win an emotional All-Ireland in his honour.

Kildare returned to win the 1927 and 1928 All-Irelands with the same 15 players, the only time this was achieved, and in 1929 lost to Kerry in front of a new record crowd of 43,839, the first time over 40,000 people had watched any sporting fixture in Ireland.

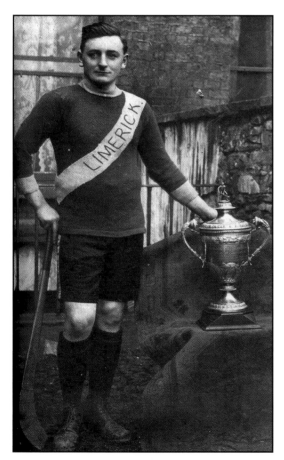

Willie Hough was full-back and captain of the 1918 Limerick team which defeated Wexford in one of the most decisive All-Ireland finals ever. Limerick scored nine goals in the 1918 final and nine in the 1921 final.

Folklore claims that the phrase 'The hay saved and Cork bate' was invented in Tipperary by 1920s hurler Johnny Leahy of Boherlahan, as the old hurling rivalry caught fire once more.

The 1925 Munster semi-final in which Tipperary beat Cork was described as the finest since 1912. Tipperary led 4-2 to 1-0 at half-time. Cork came back to within two points and with the crowd swarming on to the field for the final five minutes, Martin Kennedy struck a goal and a point for victory.

The 1926 Munster final between the same teams went to three matches. The first meeting of the three was a fiasco — abandoned after 16 minutes because the crowd overran the pitch. Cork's cramped Athletic Grounds were too small for the 26,000 who came to see the game.

In the replay Cork went seven points ahead but Tipperary drew level. Martin Kennedy's goal gave Tipperary the lead with five minutes to go before Balty Ahearne equalised again with a goal for Cork.

Third time round Cork won with goals from Eudie Coughlan, and Mick and Paddy Ahearne, but had to withstand a late Tipperary rally before the end.

By now there was a cup for the winners of both All-Ireland championships. The Liam McCarthy cup was first presented to Limerick captain Bob McConkey in 1921 after a final in which he had scored four goals.

Galway hurler Mick Gill developed a new tactic for the 1923 championship. The heavy ball was lobbed high into the square in the hope that the Australian-born Leonard McGrath would get at the end of it.

McGrath got three of Galway's seven goals against Limerick in a high-scoring final and Connacht won their first All-Ireland championship in either code. It was to be 57 years before they would win another All-Ireland in hurling.

Football's Sam Maguire cup was named in honour of a Corkman, a member of the Church of Ireland who had been an intelligence officer in the War of Independence and one of those who helped set up the civil service for the new state.

The Cup, first presented in 1928, was accepted by Bill Squires Gannon of Kildare.

The growing number of supporters wanted more competition. A four-county league set up by Louth, Monaghan, Cavan and Meath in 1924 had proved highly successful.

A hurler poses at Glens feis. Roger Casement umpired one of the hurling matches at this event. A mini revival of hurling took place under the auspices of the Gaelic League after 1904, particularly in Dublin and Ulster. Gaelic League hurling petered out but left a new sport in its wake, camogie.

Corkman Seán McCarthy suggested in 1925 that a national league should be established to provide inter-county competition through the winter months.

Not everyone agreed it was a good idea. Some saw the new competition as a threat to the club, the grass-roots structure of the GAA, and clubs have had a stormy relationship with the league over the playing calendar ever since.

The competitions were low key when they started in 1926. Laois footballers beat Dublin before 1,000 spectators in New Ross in the first final. Cork won the top division of the hurling league with ten points from five matches.

In 1927 an inter-provincial competition was also added to the calendar. The four provinces would play semi-finals in February and a final on St Patrick's Day. The competition proved popular with the players. Spectators were slow to respond to the semi-finals, but crowds of up to 10,000 turned out for the early finals.

The NACA brought ten athletes to the 1928 Olympics. This time they were rewarded with success when Pat O'Callaghan won an Olympic gold medal in the hammer throw.

O'Callaghan was the star attraction at the 1928 Tailteann games later that year, alongside South Africa's 110 metres hurdler Sydney Atkinson and Olympic bronze medallists Charles McGinnis (US, pole vault) and Alfred Bates (US, long jump). The 800 metres champion was Canada's Philip Edwards who had finished fourth at the Amsterdam Olympics.

Motor cycling events in the Phoenix Park attracted an attendance of 20,000. Rowing was moved to Cork and motor boat racing to Athlone, with considerable success.

Rain spoiled the opening ceremony and attendances at the athletics events do not appear to have surpassed 6,000 for O'Callaghan's competition.

In 1932 the third Tailteann games were held in the immediate aftermath of the Eucharistic Congress. They aroused little interest and the Irish Olympic athletes opted not to compete. The athletics events were run off on two rainy evenings and the Tailteann dream fizzled out.

Just four athletes made the expensive trip to Los Angeles for the 1932 Olympics. This became Ireland's most successful Olympics.

Pat O'Callaghan retained his gold medal in the hammer, and former Cambridge University runner Bob Tisdall won the 400 m hurdles, although his 31.7 seconds world record was not allowed under the rules at the time because he had hit the final hurdle. Belfast marathon runner Sam Ferris, who competed for Britain, won a silver medal. Kerry footballer Éamonn Fitzgerald finished fourth in the triple jump and boxer William 'Boy' Murphy also finished fourth.

Within a year of Irish athletics' finest hour, Ireland was debarred from international competition. English official Harold Abrahams had proposed that Ireland be expelled from international competition as early as 1930, and when the 1932 IAAF congress refused to do so, he told hammer thrower Pat O'Callaghan, 'You have the dagoes but we will get you in committee.'

He was true to his word. The NACA was told the following February that they had been expelled at an unspecified meeting at which they were not represented.

The expulsion was probably illegal under the IAAF constitution, but it prevented the best Irish athletes from representing Ireland again. Thomas Moles, a Unionist MP for Belfast, lobbied the IAAF that Northern Ireland athletes be included as part of English AAA teams in future.

It also meant that Pat O'Callaghan's new world record hammer throw of 60.57 m at the 1937 Cork County championships in Fermoy was never ratified by the IAAF.

At Abrahams' urging, three Dublin clubs formed a rival athletics body in 1937 which was subsequently recognised by England's AAA. Eventually nine clubs and 300 members affiliated to the AAUÉ (the É stood for Éire at Abrahams' insistence) and were given responsibility for international team selection over the next three decades, instead of the NACA which had 380 clubs and a membership of 4,500.

The price of the exclusion was high. By the time the athletics split was sorted out Ireland's athletics movement, which had peaked at 10,000, had declined to 500 registered athletes.

It has been assumed by sports historians that Abrahams' campaign to split Irish athletics was based on his personal political beliefs. Recent research shows that he may have been lobbied by the British Foreign Office, worried at the decline in the imperial

order brought about by the 1930 statute of Westminster and the loss of English sporting hegemony due to the rise of federations such as FIFA and the IAAF.

Shinty was lobbied to cut off contacts with hurling at this time because the GAA did not recognise the border. There were simultaneous campaigns to split other sporting bodies. In 1932 RUC boxers and their champion Jim Magill were lobbied not to box for Ireland. Rugby, swimming, cricket, rowing and hockey were also subjected to London-based agitation.

The campaign culminated in 1948 when London hosted the Olympics and the organisers attempted to stop Irish competitors using the name 'Ireland'. Irish swimmers, cyclists and athletes were prevented from competing in the games, but other sports, notably basketball, boxing, fencing, rowing, show jumping and yachting held firm and preserved their unity.

Interestingly, Whitehall does not seem to have targeted the rival soccer bodies, who had split over the venue

Women's hurling, called camogie from its inception, was linked with the Irish language revival associated with the Gaelic League. Female members of the Craobh Céitinn (Keatings) branch held demonstrations in 1904. A highly politicised sport, the first Dublin county committee was formed specifically to participate in a march to O'Donovan Rossa's grave. It was not until 1932 that an All-Ireland championship was organised.

of a cup replay in 1922 and who both picked separate all-Ireland teams until 1948. Soccer was the only major sport to be bifurcated by the Irish border.

It took the election of a British peer, Michael Morris, as Ireland's Olympic representative in 1952 to bring to an end the debate over Olympic sporting jurisdiction. Lord Killanin was eventually to become president of the International Olympic Committee and would preside over a deeper Olympic crisis in 1980.

• • •

The increased interest in Gaelic games meant there was more to talk about, more to write about and more to sing about. Hundreds of ballads were written about the deeds of the sportsmen of the 1920s, great and small, and were sung at the fairs and social gatherings of Ireland.

Long before newspapers bothered to report on hurling matches, the balladeers had been there. Folklorist Thomas Croker collected *The Carrigaline Hurlers* in the 1820s: '*Without exaggeration, our goalers take their station/ For the highest approbation they have won their victory/ 'Twas in no combination, or field association/ But in rural relaxation on the plains of Ownabwee.*'

But the hey-day of the GAA ballad appears to have

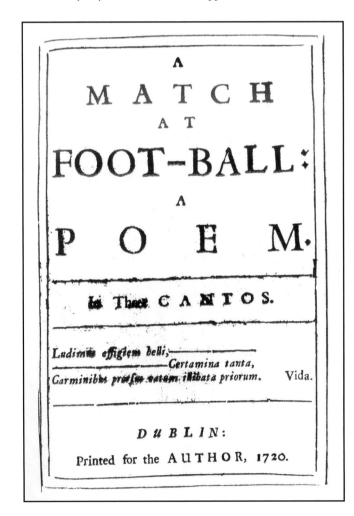

been the 1920s and 1930s. When Phil O'Neill wrote: '*I sing you a song as we steam along/ The well-filled special train/ We're merry and bright and glad tonight,/ Our colours on top again*', he hinted at a new forum for these ballads on the long train journeys to the south and west after matches in Croke Park or Thurles.

An enormous number of ballads and poems appeared in provincial newspapers and publications such as Phil O'Neill's *History of the GAA*, published in Kilkenny in 1931, and Paddy Mehigan's *Carbery's Annual*, published annually between 1939 and 1963.

A verse from O'Neill's 'The Game of the Gaels' (1914): '*Sport with a dash in it/ Clatter and clash in it/ Something with ash in it/ Surely a game*' became a standard end piece for GAA articles, histories and pamphlets.

Readers also warmed to Crawford Neil's 'The Song of a Hurl' (1916): '*Give a rose to a maid or silken braid/ Give a singer his song's full measure/ But give me a lad whose heart is glad/ With the width of a field for his pleasure.*' Crawford was killed in crossfire during the 1916 Rebellion.

Anonymous ballads which typify the style include one commemorating Kildare's 1919 success: '*Three nonpareils Kildare can claim/ Honourable, clean and manly/ Their names can grace the hall of fame/ Dempsey, Conneff and Stanley*', and one commemorating Kerry's 1926 success over Kildare: '*A free to Kerry, Con Brosnan took it/ With steady foot and unerring aim/ He scored the point and again we led them/ 'Twas the final point of the hard-fought game/ Hats off to Brosnan, our mid-field wonder/ He's par excellence in feet and hands/ Oh, where's the Gael can pull down the number/ Of Kerry's idol from Newtownsandes.*'

Sigerson Clifford returned to the 1926 final with Kerry and Kildare: '*These are the men you spoke of in the game your fathers loved;/ These are the men who blazed the trail and made it fair./ In my dreaming now I see them as I saw them long ago,/ Green and gold and white limbs leaping, when our Kerry played Kildare.*'

These ballads are rarely sung nowadays. But tragic laments for Clare goalkeeper Tommy Daly, Cavan's P. J. Duke and John Joe O'Reilly are still in the folk repertoire.

Iconic leader of the 1916 Rebellion, Pádraig Pearse was one of the prime organisers of colleges football and hurling in Dublin, and chairman of the Dublin colleges council in 1910 when his Scoil Éanna hurling team took to the field. Team captain Maurice Fraher, son of the famous hurler Dan Fraher from Waterford, was among Pearse's first pupils. Pearse's successor as headmaster, Kildare-born Frank Burke (second from right in front), became one of the greatest dual players of his generation. Back: M. Caomhanach, D. Ó Conchúbair, S. Mac Garbhaigh, U. Ó Dochartaigh, E. Builfin, P. Ó Conaire, S. Ó Faodagáin, H. Mac Suibhne, Middle: S. Mac Díarmada, A. Ó Goirdin, M. Ó Fearachair (ceannaire), P. Ó Conghaile, P. Dubhshlaine. Front: F. Ó Dochartaigh, D. Ó Cróinín, P. De Búrca, E. MacDáibheach.

● ● ●

The best-known GAA ballad of all, sung and recorded extensively, was about someone who played his greatest matches in his imagination.

The mock-heroic tribute to Timothy 'Thady' Quill was based on an itinerant labourer known for his strength, employed by the author, Johnny Tom Gleeson from Ballinagree, a townland north of Macroom: '*At the great hurling match between Cork and Tipperary/ 'Twas played in the park by the Banks of the Lee/ Our own darling boys were afraid of being beaten/ So they sent for bould Thady to Ballinagree./ He hurled the ball left and right in their face/ And showed those Tipperary boys learning and skill./ If they came in his way sure he surely would brain them/ And the papers were full of the praise of Thady Quill.*'

It became popular after it was included in a Walton's Instrumental Galleries publication.

● ● ●

5

·AN·MACAOṁ·

·EDITED·BY·P·H·PEARSE·AND·WRITTEN· ·BY·THE·MASTERS·AND·PUPILS·OF· ·St·ENDA'S·SCHOOL·

A Note on Athletics.

The first year of a new school is rather a time of organisation and of preparation in the department of athletics than of achievement. The boys must get to know their own and one another's powers, weaknesses, possibilities; in many cases the games have to be taught *ab initio* to raw youngsters. These difficulties were exaggerated in our case by the fact that we had determined to play only Irish games, and the boys who came to us from other schools knew, for the most part, only Rugby or Association and cricket. We had, moreover, all sorts and sizes in a school muster comparatively small, all told. To counterbalance these disadvantages, we had, however, the tremendous advantage of the presence in our midst of two of the very finest hurlers and footballers in the junior teams of Ireland—Maurice Fraher (son of Dan Fraher, of Dungarvan), and Eamonn Bulfin. Admirable material, too, was to be found in such boys as Eugene MacCarthy (son of William MacCarthy, founder of the G.A.A. in London); Frank Connolly, P. Conroy, P. Tuohy. Michael O'Connor, Donal O'Connor, and amongst juniors, Eoin MacGavock, John Power, and Herbert Buckley. We worked quietly and modestly at hurling and football throughout the year—perhaps too quietly and modestly, for had we sought and arranged a match with some other school, quite early in our career, it would, undoubtedly, whatever the result, have encouraged us to make more determined and sustained efforts. As it was, we waited until we were challenged by the St. Kevins, against whom, on Saturday, June 5th, we brought off an overwhelming victory. The match was, indeed, almost one-sided, our team being far superior in speed, endurance, vigour, and, above all, tactics. Fraher captained splendidly, and the result worked out exactly as he had calculated. We quote the *Dublin City and County Observer's* report of the match :—

"Play started briskly, and on the throw-in Senor Bulfin's son could be seen towering head and shoulders over the attacking forwards. He had as a partner in the full-back line Maurice Fraher, a worthy son of that sterling Gael, Dan Fraher, of Dungarvan. Both of these backs played a fine game for the St. Enda's, equal to that of any of backs in Dublin Junior circles. Eoin MacGavock, the St. Enda full forward, opened the scoring with a goal. A weak puck-out by the Kevin full nearly resulted in another score, the ball going over. Kevins visited St. Enda's citadel from the puck-out, but nothing followed, the ball going out, and young Bulfin took the goalpuck and sent into Kevin territory with a splendid stroke. MacGavock was on the ball like a hawk, and scored another goal for St. Enda's from 15 yards out, with an unsaveable shot. Another weak puck-out enabled Eugene McCarthy to add a point for St. Enda's. Midfield play ruled for a time until Fraher, getting the ball on the loose, raised it and scored a high point. Hayes next opened the Kevin scoring with a minor. MacGavock followed this up for St. Enda's with another. Kevins improved their defence after this score, and Hayes added a second point. Withers followed this up with a fine point from 25 yards out, and immediately after Hayes just failed with a good shot. Fraher for St. Enda's soon after this put in two points in quick succession. Hayes again added to Kevins' score, and from uninteresting play Withers scored a grand goal for Kevins. Collins, the midget *cul-baire* of the Kevins, had hard luck in being beaten for a point. It was a hard shot. From its force one would imagine it would require a man to stop it. Withers was again prominent for Kevins, scoring a point, and, soon after, Collins was called on to save in the goalmouth for Kevins. The Kevins effected another change in their defence, the new full-back, Kevin Browner, being unbeatable; but the fulls on the St. Enda team were too strong for the Kevin forwards. Half-time found St. Enda's leading by 2—8 to 1—5. The second half was altogether one-sided, St. Enda's increasing their score to 11—9, while Kevins only added 2 points. Fraher, MacGavock and Bulfin were the best of a very good team. Some of the St. Enda players showed by their play that they come from hurling districts. Kevin Browner, Withers, Hayes, and young Collins were best for Kevins."

Next year we mean to earn a name for ourselves in hurling and football, and hope to bring off—with what fortune remains to be seen—matches with all the leading junior teams in the country.

Our athletic sports (this year a small and wholly private affair) take place on June 17th, too late, unfortunately, to allow of the announcement of the results in AN MACAOMH.

p. mac p.

The rise in the popularity of GAA games also had a literary and artistic impact. Seán Keating's rugged country hurler, currently in the Municipal Gallery, is the major GAA representation among the visual arts of the early twentieth century.

Charles Kickham's *Knocknagow* or *The Homes of Tipperary* (1873) had been inspired by the rural sports revival and helped inspire the GAA revival in turn. The GAA's first president Maurice Davin is said to have served as a model for the village hammer thrower, Matt the Thresher, in the book.

The GAA's many literary journals in the 1890s, 1930s and 1950s boast a rich cast of contributors. The first official newspaper of the Gaelic Athletic Association, the *Gael*, was as devoted to the promotion of literature as it was to Gaelic games. Fenian leader John O'Leary was appointed literary editor. Among the then unknown poets whose work he published was William Butler Yeats, who won the Nobel Prize for Literature in 1923, Douglas Hyde, later first president of Ireland, Thomas William Rolleston, author of eight books, and John's sister Ellen O'Leary, another major poet of the time. Both James Joyce and W. B. Yeats carried GAA references in some of their major works.

There were several attempts to fictionalise the onfield drama of Gaelic games. Patrick Kavanagh, alleged to have lost a valuable match for Inniskeen because he vacated his position in goal to purchase an ice cream, uses Gaelic football as a backdrop to his novel *The Green Fool* and composed a poem based on a camogie final.

Cavan's 1958 goalkeeper Tom MacIntyre used Kavanagh's imagery on stage in *The Great Hunger* and returned to a GAA theme in another play, *The Gallant John Joe*, about an elderly Cavan man haunted by memories of his youth.

GAA life in west Clare is forcefully depicted in William Cotter Murray's *Michael Joe* (1965). Fermanagh journalist Cormac McConnell wrote the only novel based entirely around Gaelic football.

● ● ●

There was a new medium for relaying news of the games to the country, and the GAA led the way here when they staged the first radio broadcast of a sporting event in Europe and the second in the world.

G. A. A.

HELP THE PRISONERS

BY ATTENDING THE

Great Hurling Contest
TIPPERARY v. DUBLIN

AT

CROKE PARK

ON

Sunday next, April 27

IN AID OF

The Republican Prisoners' Dependents' Fund

SPLENDID HURLING ASSURED
SEVERAL BANDS WILL ATTEND

Match at 3.30

An attendance of 10,000 saw Dublin beat Tipperary in aid of prisoners' dependants in 1919, 18 months before the same teams played on Bloody Sunday.

GAA supporter J. J. Walsh became Minister for Posts and Telegraphs when the Irish Free State was established and quickly set about planning a new broadcasting service.

2RN was started on 1 January 1926, and the first broadcast of a field sport in Europe took place on 29 August 1926 when the All-Ireland hurling semi-final between Kilkenny and Galway was broadcast by Cork sportswriter Paddy Mehigan.

It is estimated that up to 25,000 receivers may have tuned in to the 1926 All-Ireland finals a few weeks later.

The second replay of the Munster hurling final became the first provincial match to be broadcast when it was played in Thurles the following October.

GAA historian Pádraig Puirséal quotes a remembered piece of Mehigan's commentary from the 1927 final: 'Cork go sweeping into the Dublin goal. A cloud of dust rises. It must be a goal! Oh! Daly! Daly! Daly! Wonderful!'

The GAA authorities were still suspicious of this innovation and the effect it might have on gate receipts. Radio technicians were refused entry to the 1929 All-Ireland hurling final.

BBC's Belfast station, 2BE, commenced broadcasting on 15 September 1924. When sports results were included in the Sunday news programmes for the first time in 1934, the Northern Ireland Prime Minister Lord Craigavon intervened and GAA results were dropped from the broadcast by director George Marshall on the grounds that they were 'hurting the feelings of the large majority of people in Northern Ireland'. They did not return until the 1960s.

The GAA too was suspicious that the new service would challenge its cultural ascendancy. They objected to the broadcast of results of other sports alongside Gaelic results as early as 1932, but these objections were overruled.

Legends about Mehigan were being told decades after he had stopped commentating. He was said to have persuaded a fiddler to play into the microphone when he went to answer a call of nature. It was also said that his broadcasting career ended when he forgot to come back for the second half of an exciting match.

His successor Éamonn de Barra had his microphone seized briefly by republican gunmen during the 1933 All-Ireland final.

Most spectacularly, commentator Monsignor Michael Hamilton broadcast to the nation that Cavan had won

A football team in Stafford Prison after the 1916 Rising. Entire GAA clubs found themselves behind bars after the Rising. The Kerry team as a consequence withdrew from the 1917 Munster championship.

the 1937 All-Ireland final when the match was in fact a draw.

Another commentator, Dave Hanly, broadcast the 1938 hurling final. By the football final of 1938, Raidió Éireann had found a new commentator, Micheál Ó Hehir.

Spectators were hungry for news of the exploits of their new heroes and were soon to get a new medium to read about it.

Sport played its part in the rise of newspaper circulation in the first third of the twentieth century, in the case of the *Irish Independent,* already the best-selling daily in the country in 1906, from 30,000 to 132,000.

The birth of the *Irish Press* in 1931 is acknowledged to have boosted Gaelic games coverage. But the dominant morning newspaper, the *Irish Independent*, had already increased its coverage during the 1920s in response to the rapidly growing crowds. Even *The Irish Times*, perceived as a pro-British newspaper, which had dismissed the 1920 All-Ireland football final (attendance 25,000) in a report of 230 words, used the heavily stylised reports of the *Irish Weekly Examiner* GAA correspondent Paddy Mehigan on major matches after 1925.

Before it was launched to coincide with the 1931 All-Ireland hurling final, the backers of the new *Irish Press* wrote individually to each county board seeking their co-operation.

When the *Irish Press* was launched on the day before the 1931 hurling final, the Cumbrian-born sports editor Joe Sherwood mistakenly referred to the 'kick off' time. They chose the game well for their launch!

Or rather, three games. Three football matches between Kerry and Kildare had placed Gaelic football at the heart of sporting culture in the All-Ireland final of 1903. Now it was hurling's turn to stage three legendary matches.

In the first two games a familiar pattern had emerged: Cork led in both cases by four points at half-time, Kilkenny took the lead in both cases in the second half, and Cork's two late equalisers were scored by Pat 'Hawker' O'Grady in the first match and Paddy Delea in the second.

It was the swinging fortunes of the second game that fizzled their way into Gaelic folklore. The civil servant and part time sportswriter P. D. Mehigan nominated this match as the best in hurling history.

Cork won the encounter in the end because Kilkenny lost inspirational figure Lory Meagher for the third game and left the way clear for a seven-point win. People started describing hurling as the fastest field game in the world, and possibly the most exciting.

There was a new All-Ireland championship to report, as six counties entered the first camogie championship in 1932. Dublin, captained by association president Máire MacGiolla and helped by two Bray players, beat Galway 3-2 to 0-2 in the final at Galway Sportsfield in the summer of 1933.

It started a pattern. The sport's biggest dilemma was that inter-county competition was too predictable to generate a wide interest, particularly as the provincial model was inherited from its GAA brother. Attendances were pitifully low, even for finals. The 1943 All-Ireland final between Dublin and Cork set a then attendance record of 9,136 which lasted until the 1990s.

In the meantime the camogie association had to negotiate a series of splits and disputes over the presence of male officials, the 'foreign games' rule and occasional bouts of ill-judgment such as the ban on married women playing camogie in the 1960s.

Dublin dominated the first 40 years of the championship, winning 18 out of 19 titles between 1948 and 1966 including a ten in a row and an eight in a row. Kathleen Mills won 15 All-Ireland medals between 1941 and 1962; Sophia Brack won eight All-Ireland medals in succession and competed in nine successive finals; Una O'Connor won ten All-Ireland medals.

They were unbeaten in the Leinster championship between 26 July 1936 and 2 June 1968, when they were surprised by a Kilkenny team spearheaded by Breda Kinsella.

The arrival of the Wexford team of 1968, with the iconic Margaret O'Leary chaired from the field by jubilant supporters, was the start of camogie's emergence from its urban and university roots to national prominence.

The *Freeman's Journal* report of Bloody Sunday. Attempts to manage the coverage of the Bloody Sunday massacre were unsuccessful. Even the heavily censored Dublin newspapers criticised the event and English liberal opinion was appalled, despite the best efforts of Dublin Castle's propagandist, former *Daily Mail* war correspondent, Basil Clarke.

THE FREEMAN'S JOURNAL. MONDAY. NOVEMBER 22. 1920.

FOURTEEN KILLED | AMRITZAR REPEATED IN DUBLIN

Amazing Deadly Round-Up of Military and Auxiliary Officers in Dublin

Armed Forces of the Crown Kill Player and Spectators in Croke Park

STARTLING STREET BATTLE

Civilians Make Sortie From House and Fight With Crown Forces

AGONISING SCENES ON FOOTBALL FIELD

Eleven or Twelve Persons, including a Woman, Killed, and from Eighty to One Hundred Wounded

Dublin was a city of amazing tragedy yesterday.

In a series of morning visits by armed men to hotels and boarding-houses, at least ten officers, two civilians, and two auxiliary policemen were killed, and several officers were wounded.

In Lower Mount street, where a civilian was shot in bed in mysterious circumstances, a regular battle took place between armed civilians emerging from the house where the shooting took place and auxiliary police, and two of the latter, it is said, were mortally wounded.

The attacks by the armed raiders were practically simultaneous, and most of those whom they shot were, according to the Dublin Castle report, military officers associated with the Government's policy in Ireland.

The record we give of the day's events may not be complete, for until a late hour reports were coming in of other shootings in the city—two dead bodies were found in Merrion street—but owing to the operation of the Curfew regulations it was extremely difficult to secure full details or confirmation.

Scenes of bloodshed on a football field, unparalleled in the history of this country, were enacted at Croke Park yesterday by armed forces of the Crown.

Almost 15,000 spectators had gathered to witness a football match between Tipperary and Dublin, when suddenly, the game being in progress, shots rang out, fired by the armed forces, and Michael Hogan, a prominent member of the Tipperary team, fell dead, shot through the mouth. Many of the onlookers were also seen to fall, dead or wounded. A woman is among the killed. The casualty list, the extent of which

has not been definitely ascertained, is a long one. It is estimated that eleven or twelve persons are dead, and from 80 to 100 wounded, in varying degrees of seriousness.

The armed forces, according to many of the onlookers, gave no warning to the spectators to disperse, beyond a preliminary volley of shots in the air. Then the bullets came as thick as hail, dealing out death in their swift passage; a wild scene of panic ensued, and women and children were knocked down and walked on.

A priest, who was a spectator of the tragic occurrence, says: "I found

poor Hogan lying on his back in a pool of blood. His feet were on the playing pitch, and his body on the gravel walk."

The Dublin Castle official report, which gives the number of dead at about 10 and the number of wounded and injured about 54, states "it was believed that a number of gunmen came up to-day under the guise of wishing to attend the Gaelic football match between Dublin and Tipperary, but that their real motive was to take part in the series of murderous outrages which took place in Dublin this morning."

14 KILLED : 5 WOUNDED

The official list of casualties resultant on the shootings of officers yesterday morning is as follows:—

KILLED.
Major DOWLING.
Captain D. L. MACLEAN.
Captain T. H. SMITH.
Captain BENNETT.
Lieut. AIMES.
Lieut. NEWBURY.
Lieut. BAGGALLY.
Lieut. FITZGERALD.
Captain McCORMACK.
Captain PRICE.
Mr MacMAHON.

Mr. L. A. WILD.
Cadets CARLIN and MORRIS.

WOUNDED.
Mr. J. CALDOW.
Captain KINLEYSIDE.
Colonel WOODCOCK.
Colonel MONTGOMERY.
Lieut. MURRAY.

Most of these officers, says an official statement, were connected with courtsmartial, and the attackers were in search of documents found in the typhoid plot. Captain Fitzgerald was some months ago shot at and left for dead in Co. Clare, but by shamming death he got away with a broken arm.

PRIEST DESCRIBES THE SCENES OF BLOODSHED

Terrible scenes took place during the Tipperary and Dublin match at Jones' road yesterday.

being searched individually and allowed to pass through the gate.

Owing to the delay caused by the

a considerable amount of blood oozing from his left side, seemingly. Another priest came over, and he afterwards went for the

The only photograph of Arthur Griffith, Éamon de Valera and Michael Collins together was taken before the 1919 All-Ireland hurling final match at Croke Park, with Dublin Lord Mayor Laurence O'Neill. After the 1918 election civil leaders were asked to throw in the ball at major matches, including de Valera and Dan Breen, who threw in the ball at the start of the 1920 All-Ireland final when it was eventually played.

Michael Collins, GAA secretary Luke O'Toole and All-Ireland medallist, GAA referee and Sinn Féin politician Harry Boland.

Michael Hogan was the only player to die on Bloody
Sunday. The main stand in Croke Park (the original in
1924, then the replacements in 1999 and 2002) has
been named in his honour.

A ticket for the match on Bloody Sunday. Because of events the night before, active volunteers were warned to stay away from the ground. Due to a news blackout, the populace of Dublin had no forewarning that Croke Park would be a target. Official British accounts of the incident were contradicted by their own Dublin Metropolitan Police force.

cumann na ccleas lúit nʒaedealac
(GAELIC ATHLETIC ASSOCIATION)

GREAT CHALLENGE MATCH

(FOOTBALL)

Tipperary v. Dublin

AT CROKE PARK

ON SUNDAY, NOVEMBER 21, 1920

MATCH AT 2.45 P.M.

ADMISSION .: .: .: .: 1/-

44127

Tipperary were awaiting their All-Ireland semi-final against Mayo when they travelled to play Leinster champions Dublin in November 1920, the day that would eventually become known as Bloody Sunday. Back: Ed Cuddihy, John Toohey, Ed Dalton, T. Ennis, P. Kelly, Seán Ryan, T. Carey. Middle: Jim Ryan, A. Carey (secretary), W. Barrett, Jack Kickham, Michael Hogan, Jim MacNamara, Lanigan, Jerry Shelly, Frank Butler, Willie Ryan, Tommy Ryan, Mick Nolan, Tommy Connors, Jim Egan, T. Ryan (south Tipperary board secretary). Front: Jim Doran, Tommy Powell, Ned O'Shea (captain), John Brett, Gus McCarthy.

Dan Breen throws the ball in to start the 1920 All-Ireland football final, delayed for two years by the war in which Breen was one of the Irish army commanders.

Tadhg Barry's 1925 pamphlet, 'Hurling and How to Play it', was sponsored by Whelan's sports providers at a stage when they were anxious to establish their national and GAA credentials.

PEARSE
AND THE
HURLER

"I am certain that when it comes to a question of Ireland winning battles, her main reliance must be on her hurlers. To your camans, O boys of Banba !" (Pearse).

Away back in 1890 we began hurling and Gaelic football with P. H. Pearse, when both of us were attending the Christian Brothers' School at Westland Row, and ever since we have kept in intimate touch with Gaelic games.

We are the only Sports house in Ireland that specialize in G.A.A. Supplies and have done so for over a quarter of a century. Therefore, we know exactly what you want and can supply at once at lowest prices, consistent with good quality, as no other firm in the business can. We have sent our goods to Gaels all over the world—to China, to South America, to U.S.A., to Egypt, to New Zealand, to Australia, to England, and every county in Ireland. Union Jacks were never flown from our premise for we are Irish to the core. When we were in Stafford and Wormwood Scrubbs Jails, and also in Frongoch, the same Gaelic tradition was maintained in our shattered premises. Black-and-Tan raids seriously injured our athletic business. But we are still Gaels and we look to fellow Gaels to remember us when they require anything. Give us a chance to quote for your requirements. Our free athletic lists will help you save money for yourself and Ireland.

WHELAN & SON,
17 Upper Ormond Quay, Dublin.

HURLING
AND HOW TO PLAY IT.

BY
An Ciotóg
(Ald. Tadg Barry, Cork.)

[ALL RIGHTS RESERVED.]

The names of those who died on Bloody Sunday as commemorated in a GAA commemoration programme, including footballer Michael Hogan. The spectator casualties included a woman who had gone to the match with her fiancé, victims aged 10 and 11, and a 14-year-old boy so mutilated that medical personnel assumed he had been bayoneted to death.

✝

The Victims

The following are the names and addresses of the thirteen people who were killed in Croke Park on Bloody Sunday or died of wounds within the following week:

BOYLE, Jane, 12, Lennox Street, Dublin.

BURKE, James, Greenland Terrace, Windy Arbour, Dundrum, Co. Dublin.

CARROLL, Daniel, Ballincara House, Templederry, Co. Tipperary.

FEENEY, Michael, Smith's Cottages, Gardiner's Place, Dublin.

HOGAN, Michael, Grangemockler, Co. Tipperary.

MATHEWS, James, 42 North Cumberland Street, Dublin.

O'DOWD, J., Buckingham Street, Dublin.

O'LEARY, Jeremiah, 69 Blessington Street, Dublin.

ROBINSON, William, 15 Little Britain Street, Dublin.

RYAN, Thomas, Viking Road, Dublin.

SCOTT, John W., 15 Fitzroy Avenue, Drumcondra, Dublin.

TEEHAN, James, Green Street, Dublin.

TRAYNOR, J., Clondalkin, Co. Dublin.

Ar dheis Dé go raibh a n-anamacha

John Synnott of Dublin against Wexford in the 1921 Leinster football final. To the left is Joe Synnott, Paddy McDonnell and with the cap, Leo Synnott.

The first field sports broadcast in radio history outside the US took place in 1926 when the precursor of Raidió Éireann, 2RN, broadcast live commentary of the All-Ireland semi-final between Kilkenny and Galway. John Roberts, seen here in action against Ignatius Harney and the best goalkeeper of the era, John 'Junior' Mahony, scored five goals in Kilkenny's 6-2 to 5-1 victory.

Dublin lost to Bloody Sunday opponents Tipperary in the 1920 All-Ireland final two years late, then won two successive All-Ireland finals in a five-month period as the GAA cleared a backlog of championship fixtures. The team included some of the biggest stars of the era, the Synnott brothers, the McDonnell brothers and dual All-Ireland medallist Frank Burke.
Back: Birra Wood, Jack Carroll, Paddy McDonnell, Jack Reilly, Charles Dempsey, Mick 'Lanty' Fitzsimons, Leo Synnott. Middle: Frank Burke, Bill Donovan, Paddy Kirwan, Billy Rooney, Johnny McDonnell, Tom Pearse, Mick O'Brien, John Synnott, Jackser Kavanagh, Séamus Moore. Front: Joe Norris, Anthony Gibbons, Charlie McDonald, Paddy Carey (captain), Josie Synnott, Billy Robbins, Willie 'Sting' Reilly.

The first minister for Posts and Telegraphs in the new Irish government, J. J. Walsh was an athletics and hurling enthusiast and was instrumental in getting the new national radio service to broadcast the first commentary of a field sports event outside the US, the All-Ireland hurling semi-final of 1926.

A well-known figure as a red-coated judge at coursing meetings, the reports on matches by P. D. Mehigan (1884–1965) in the *Irish Weekly Examiner* and *The Irish Times*, and his Christmas publication *Carbery's Annual*, were enjoyed by a generation of followers. He left the civil service in 1934 to become a full-time sportswriter. One of his favourite subjects was a thrush that set up home outside his house in Dartmouth Square in Dublin. One of his nephews remarked: 'That thrush put all the boys through college.'

HISTORY OF
HURLING
1946 EDITION
"CARBERY"

All Championships from 1887 to 1945.   Full Records.
Pen Pictures. Descriptive Articles. G.A.A. Foundations.

" Slap, cut, parry and a Goal ! "

Hurling Technique.   Instructions to beginners.
Full accounts of recent Finals

PRICE
2/6

P. D. Mehigan was the first full-time Gaelic games correspondent, writing for the *Irish Weekly Examiner* and under the name 'Pato' for *The Irish Times* and serving as the games' first radio commentator for a period after 1926. He played for London against Cork in the 1902 All-Ireland final and for Cork in the 1905 All-Ireland final replay. His *Carbery's Annual* appeared regularly between 1939 and 1963, while he compiled histories of hurling, football and athletics in the 1940s.

For the BEST Report
and Pictures of the Match
Read "Green Flag" to-morrow
in

The Irish Press

Ireland's Greatest Newspaper

It was no coincidence that the *Irish Press* launched on All-Ireland hurling final day, 1931. The newspaper had identified Gaelic games as a means of building up the circulation base it needed. Their correspondent Seán Coughlan wrote under the pen-name, Green Flag. He was ably followed by Pádraig Puirséal, Mick Dunne and Peadar O'Brien. Columnist Patrick Kavanagh also left several inspired accounts of GAA and camogie matches, while lyrical *Evening Press* sportswriter Con Houlihan acquired a cult status among sports followers from the 1970s on.

Clare came back from 16 points down in the sensational 1932 All-Ireland hurling semi-final against Galway at Limerick. Tull Considine, seen on the extreme right, scored seven goals.

Denny Lanigan of Limerick and leading GAA official William Clifford. Lanigan was to referee the 1927 All-Ireland hurling final while still a player.

'Tipp levels up.' Spectators react to a goal from Martin Coughlan during the replayed 1926 Munster hurling final, bringing Tipperary back level after they had trailed by seven points. The match went to a second replay which Cork won. This famous *Tipperary Star* photograph featured in Phil O'Neill's 1930 *History of the GAA*.

Archbishop of Cashel and GAA patron John Harty throws the ball in to start the 1926 Munster hurling final between Cork and Tipperary, which took three attempts to settle. The first match was abandoned when the grounds proved too small for the attendance; the second was drawn, and Cork won the third by five points. The match was broadcast on radio, the first time from outside Dublin by the innovative new government-run radio station, 2RN.

Martin Kennedy of Tipperary clears the ball against Cork in the 1926 Munster hurling final.

Paul Doyle scores Kildare's first point in the 1926 All-Ireland football final, deflected over the crossbar by Johnny Riordan. Kerry earned a replay with a dramatic last-minute goal. Jack Murphy died in hospital before the replay, which Kerry won by three points.

The only team to win two All-Irelands with the same 15 players, Kildare were also the first to take the Sam Maguire cup when Bill Gannon accepted the trophy in 1928.
Back: Jack Hayes, F. O'Toole, Peter Pringle, Matt Goff, Frank Malone, Paddy Loughlin, Jack Connell, Tom Keogh, Paul Doyle. Middle: Jack Higgins, Gus Fitzpatrick, Mick Buckley, Joe Loughlin, Bill 'Squires' Gannon, Paddy Martin, Martin Walshe, Pat 'Darkie' Ryan. Front: Joe Curtis, Bill Mangan, Joe Reilly, Bill Wheeler.

A section of the crowd at the 1926 All-Ireland final which broke GAA attendance records and was the second best attended sports event in Ireland until that time, behind the 1925 soccer international in Belfast between the Irish FA's 32-county selection and Scotland. Since 1929 Gaelic football has consistently been Ireland's most popular spectator sport.

Bishop Matthew Cullen throws the ball in at the start of Kildare v Cavan in 1928, the first final for which the Sam Maguire cup was awarded.

[Handwritten minutes of Central Council meeting, October 4]

oct 4

The Quarterly meeting of Central Council was held at 68 Upper O'Connell St Dublin the President Aldn Nowlan Presiding. The following members of the Council were in attendance. Messrs D Fraher, Mr J Crowe, J J Hogan, Thos Kenny, J Collins, Jim Malone, Stephen Jordan proxy for J Ryan Mayo, J Murphy, J Millar, J Lawlor, M Blake, J Corrigan, J Flynn, P M Graham, P J Gilhooly proxy for Mr O'Brennan Roscommin & L J Toole Secy. The minutes of the previous meetings were read & signed. A deputation attended from the Tipp County board regarding the Council decision in apportioning the Sum of 550 or £60. towards for the Croke Memorial at Thurles afb. he-hearing the representa... the Council decided owing to the objection raised by Tipp board the Council decided in holding over the Amount until the All Ireland Convention.

Mr Crowe proposes That the Council make an offer of £3,500 for Jones Road grounds Mr Lawlor Sec. the notion. Mr Kenny moved an Amendment that the question of purchase be

adjourned to the Annual Convention. Mr Malone Seconded and on being put to the meeting Mr Crowe's motion was carried by 8 votes to 7. Mr Kenny gave notice of his intention of appealing against the Council's decision to Annual Congress. Mr Corrigan proposed that the best thanks of the Council be tendered to the Sub Committee having the investigation & carrying through of the negotiations on behalf the Council namely Messrs Hogan Crowe & Toole Mr Millar Sec. the motion which was carried unanimously. Correspondence having been attended to the meeting terminated. The following motion was also adopted. That a deputation consisting of Messrs Crowe, Hogan & Toole be appointed to wait on the manager Munster & Leinster Bank to make application for a loan of £2000 to enable the Council to purchase Jones Road sports ground. Correspondence having been attended to the meeting terminated—

S. Ua Nuallaíg √
4-1-14

Minutes of the initial purchase of Croke Park. In 1905 the grounds were deemed unsuitable to stage the replay of the Kerry v Kildare All-Ireland football final.

Wexford against Dublin in the 1932 Leinster football championship.

Spectators at Croke Park in 1932, with the Hogan stand and the Long stand now in place.

Croke Park as it was in 1924, after an injection of state funds to bring the stadium up to standard to stage the Tailteann Games.

Fans brave the rain at Croke Park. In the days before all-ticket matches, crowds queued for admittance from early morning and faced a long wait before play began.

ᴀonᴀċ ᴛᴀɪʟᴛéᴀnn

FROM 2—18 AUGUST

GRAND
OPENING CEREMONY
AT CROKE PARK

Saturday, 2nd August, commencing at 3 p.m.

PROGRAMME

OFFICIAL RECEPTION AND MARCH PAST OF
COMPETITORS AND OPENING OF GAMES.

International Shinty-Hurling Contest: SCOTLAND v. IRELAND

Gymnastic Display: ARTANE INDUSTRIAL SCHOOL.

SUNDAY, 3rd AUGUST.
3 p.m.—Ireland v. America. International Hurling. Croke Park.
4 p.m.—Ireland v. England. International Camogie. Bray.
4.30 p.m.—Ulster v. Munster. National Football. Croke Park.
7 p.m.—Ireland v. England. International Football. Croke Park.

MONDAY, 4th AUGUST.
3 p.m.—Connaught v. Leinster. National Football. Croke Park.
4.15 p.m.—Ireland v. England. International Hurling. Croke Park.

TUESDAY, 5th AUGUST.
7 p.m.—England v. America. International Hurling. Croke Park.

WEDNESDAY, 6th AUGUST.
7 p.m.—England v. Wales. International Hurling. Croke Park.

THURSDAY, 7th AUGUST.
7 p.m.—England v. Scotland. International Hurling. Croke Park.

FRIDAY, 8th AUGUST.
3 p.m.—Scotland v. America. International Hurling. Croke Park.
7 p.m.—Ireland v. Wales. International Hurling. Croke Park.

SATURDAY, 9th AUGUST.
2.30 p.m.—Ireland v. Scotland. International Hurling. Croke Park.
4 0 p.m.—Wales v. America. International Hurling. Croke Park

SUNDAY, 10th AUGUST.
2.30 p.m.—Connaught v. Leinster. Hurling. Croke Park.
3.45 p.m.—National Football Final. Croke Park.

WEDNESDAY, 13th AUGUST.
2.30 p.m.—International Athletics and Cycling. Croke Park.

THURSDAY, 14th AUGUST.
2.30 p.m.—International Athletics and Cycling. Croke Park.

FRIDAY, 15th AUGUST.
2.30 p.m.—International Athletics and Cycling. Croke Park.

SATURDAY, 16th AUGUST.
2.30 p.m.—International Athletics and Cycling Finals. Croke Park.

SUNDAY, 17th AUGUST.
2 p.m.—National Hurling Final. Croke Park.

HANDBALL EVENTS AT BALLYMUN AND CLONDALKIN.

For full details and particulars of all items see Official Daily
Programme and Syllabus on Sale during Games.

Visitors Accomodation Bureau, 105 Middle Abbey Street,

ADMISSION 1/- & 2/-   Grand Stand (Reserved) 5/-

Season Ticket, £1 1s. 0d., each admitting to the General
Enclosures AT ALL OUTDOOR EVENTS; can be had from
the following: Messrs. Clerys, Crottys, Elverys, Helys, Leslies,
or at the Central Office, 5a College Street, Dublin.

Chicago-based barrister Paddy Cahill was the promoter behind Tipperary's tour of America in May–July 1926, the first by a GAA team since the ill-fated 1888 'invasion'. The Polo Grounds, used for the first time for Gaelic games, started and ended the tour, which included New York, Boston, Chicago, San Francisco and Buffalo. Martin Kennedy scored 27 of Tipperary's 75 goals. A later tour in 1931 brought another innovation: the first hurling match under floodlights.

The programme for the 1928
Tailteann Games.

The pageantry for the Tailteann opening ceremony in 1924 included pipe bands, Celtic warriors and Irish wolfhounds. The festival gave the new state a sense of purpose just as the last of the Civil War prisoners were being released.

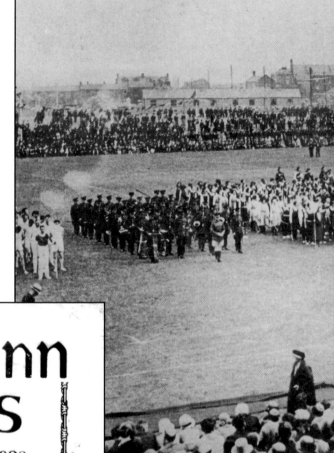

The second of the three great post-independence sporting festivals, the Tailteann Games of 1928 were very different from their predecessor in 1924 or the last festival in 1932.

TAILTEANN GAMES
August 11th—26th, 1928

Daily Programme - 3d.

Thursday, August 16th

Gaelic Press, Ltd., Printers, Dublin.

The opening ceremony for the 1928 Tailteann Games was a less lavish affair than that in 1924. After 1932 there were no further attempts to stage the festival.

The San Patricio hurling team in Buenos Aires. Like the Irish community itself, hurling in Argentina became entwined with Spanish tradition and the players in later years had distinctively Spanish names. Although hurling was played in Argentina in the 1880s, the foundation of the Buenos Aires Hurling Club in 1900 was the first serious attempt to organise the game there. The district of Hurlingham in Buenos Aires still survives, but the hurling club now play hockey as a result of a scarcity of camáns in the 1930s.

South Africa sent a hurling team to play in the 1932 Tailteann Games. Their standard can be gauged by the fact that they drew with Britain: G. Carron, T. Kinna, W. McNicholas, T. Kelly, D. Carron, W. Muldoon, W. Dolan, P. Mulhall, Fr Muldoon, J. McDonnell, M. Muldoon, J. Fitzpatrick, B. Muldoon (secretary), M. O'Hare, J. F. Maher, Fr McGrath, J. Garland, J. McMullen, K. Muldoon (captain), P. McFaul (manager), J. O'Shaughnessy, J. Murphy, L. O'Sullivan (chairman), L. Walsh, F. McFaul, D. Jeoffreys, Liam Burns, H. Burns, W. Jeoffreys.

Action from Cork v Kilkenny in 1931. Many supporters regarded the first replay as the greatest hurling match of all.

Ireland's footballers score a goal against America in the 1932 Tailteann Games. International football matches at a time of high emigration were a highlight of sporting festivals.

Captain of the Cork team that defeated Kilkenny at the third attempt in 1931, Eudie Coughlan had made his first appearance in the 1920 final. Though Cork had dominated the first half in the first two matches, the swinging fortunes of the first replay earned the match a special place in GAA folklore. An eight-point winning margin on the third day flattered Cork.

The pre-match ceremonial when religious dignitaries were asked to start the match involved team captains kissing the ring of the bishop. Here Eudie Coughlan kisses the ring of Archbishop William Hayden of Hobart before the first replay of the 1931 final. Lory Meagher of Kilkenny is at Eudie's right.

Kilkenny goalkeeper Jim Dermody during the 1931 final.

Kerry footballers on board a transatlantic liner on their way to tour the United States in 1931. Kerry drew an attendance of 60,000, then a record for a GAA match, to the 82,000 capacity Yankee Stadium, and came home with enough money to purchase Austin Stack Park in Tralee. A previous tour in 1927 was less successful. An American-based promoter made off with all the money, leaving the Kerry team to be rescued by the local Kerry Association.

The winning of a 'triple crown' All-Ireland in senior, minor and junior was hailed as a magnificent achievement in Tipperary in 1930. The junior grade declined in status over the following decades, leading to its abolition for a ten-year period in the 1970s.

chapter four

The Four Provinces

Founded, according to Michael Cusack's formula, in Munster, the GAA had thrived south of a line from Dublin to Galway and struggled somewhat north of that. There were outposts of activity in the early GAA in Roscommon, Cavan, Monaghan, Antrim, Down, Louth and Derry. But it was 50 years before the All-Ireland semi-finals which matched Munster and Leinster's champions against the other provinces took on real meaning.

Galway had won a farcical All-Ireland in 1925 after a series of objections. Antrim had sprung a surprise on Kilkenny in 1911 and Kerry in 1912 to reach two finals in which they lost heavily. Cavan had lost out to a controversial hand-passed goal in 1928. Mayo actually led Kerry by three points at half-time in the 1932 All-Ireland final. But it was Cavan who eventually ended Kerry's dream of five in a row, two minutes from the end of the 1933 All-Ireland semi-final.

Cavan captain Jim Smith and Patsy Devlin sent the ball into the Kerry goalmouth and Vincent McGovern booted to the net. Tim Landers was just wide on an equalising mission for Kerry and the crowd of 17,000 celebrated the first of many great Cavan moments.

They then beat Galway with goals by Louis Blessing and M. J. 'Son' Magee in front of a record attendance of 45,188. Ulster had its first champions.

A year later it was Connacht's turn. Galway, hurling champions in 1922, had won the 1925 All-Ireland in the boardroom after a bizarre series of objections that saw three of the four All-Ireland semi-finalists chucked out of the competition.

Now they emerged to win an All-Ireland in their own right, beating Cavan in the craziest semi-final in football history. When the match got under way the Tuam pitch was hopelessly crowded, with spectators 15 yards over the sideline and the despairing linesmen giving throw-ins wherever the ball hit a spectator.

The pitch had to be cleared five times in a fragmented, scattered match that one Cavan official described as follows: 'I saw five glimpses of the ball in the second half.'

Six central council members convened at half-time to decide whether the match should continue. Galway were 1-5 to 0-5 ahead at that stage, about to face the wind, and agreed. Cavan's captain apparently said no, although this was disputed vociferously by Cavan at a council meeting afterwards. Instead they said they wanted the match to go ahead as a friendly.

The match went ahead. Son Magee missed a late free and at 6.10 p.m., two hours and four minutes after the throw-in, Galway emerged as the winners.

They went on to win the final with two first half goals from 23-year-old Kerry-born UCG student Michael Ferriter. Martin Kelly got the third at the start of the second half against a Dublin attack led by Clare-born champion sprinter George Comerford.

Cavan re-emerged in 1935, beating Kildare with two goals from Packie Boylan and a third from Tom Reilly on a day that 50,380 spectators crammed into Croke Park.

It had taken a last-minute goal direct from a 50 for Cavan to reach the final, their opponents, Tipperary, having won their last Munster football title when Kerry county convention decided the county should withdraw from all championships in protest at the treatment of republican prisoners at the Curragh.

Beaten finalists Kildare simmered for months afterwards over the dropping of regular goalkeeper Pa 'Cuddy' Chanders, 'a pick and shovel man', in favour of James Maguire, 'a shirt and tie man'.

It would be 53 years before Kildare were back in an All-Ireland final.

Then it was Mayo's turn. Dominant in the National League through the 1930s, they won their first All-Ireland in 1936 when they hammered a stage-struck Laois by 18 points and went 22 matches without defeat.

Laois midfielder Bill Delaney limped through the game with two broken bones in his foot, while Mayo's Paddy Flannelly cleaned up at midfield. 'He raced through and shot to the square, to the net, and high between the posts — he seemed to inspire his side who played runaway football. . . . Flannelly fielded and raced to either wing, paving the way for Munnelly's and Moclair's overwhelming scores', P. J. Devlin reported in the *Irish Independent*.

Laois had four Delaney brothers from Stradbally in action, Jack, Chris, Mick and Bill. Their uncle Tom played at full-back. Goalkeeper Tom was no relation to the others. The four brothers were to win 17 Railway Cup medals.

In 1937 Cavan might have won again. Their goalscorer Packie Boylan had what would have been the winning point disallowed for throwing, three minutes from the end. Few of the spectators noticed a free out was taken instead of a kick-out. It was announced over the loudspeakers that Cavan had won. Radio commentator Fr Michael Hamilton told the nation that Cavan had won and many supporters were greeted by bonfires when they arrived home.

It was the following day before they realised a replay was needed. Cavan missed Jim Smith and Tom O'Reilly for the replay and lost to Kerry by six points.

Kerry were now the replay specialists. In the All-Ireland semi-final they had drawn with a late goal against Laois and won the replay with another late goal.

But the goal of 1937 was for their opponents, a fabulous left-footed drive into the corner of the net from 'Boy Wonder' Tommy Murphy. Just 16 years of age, he was still a student at Knockbeg College.

Not to be outdone, hurling provided another great match, this time also a semi-final. In 1932 Clare came clambering back from 16 points down after half-time to win by five points against Galway. Tull Considine scored six Clare goals, all in the second half.

They lost to Kilkenny in the All-Ireland. Tull Considine got two Clare goals and then rounded full-back Peter O'Reilly, only to be foiled of what would almost certainly have been a third Clare goal.

Instead, it was Kilkenny who triumphed with goals by Matty Power, Martin White a minute later, and Lory Meagher direct from a line ball, a score legalised the previous year.

On the other bank of the Shannon, a young man from Castleconnell was making a name for himself. One of the great stars of the Munster hurling final of 1917 had been John 'Tyler' Mackey. Now his two sons were fronting a great Castleconnell team that was to win 15 club hurling championships including seven in a row, twice.

When Cork beat Limerick in 1932, the newspaper mentioned 'a fine forward' who scored two flash goals at the start of the match. In 1933 Mick Mackey was back to score two goals, but was sent off after an altercation with some Waterford players. The match did not finish because of a pitch invasion.

In 1934 Mackey scored the winning point against Cork, a goal in the Munster final and a crucial goal to give Limerick the lead against Dublin in the All-Ireland final when they won their first title. Dave Clohessy scored four goals in that game.

Limerick went 31 matches without defeat from 1933 to 1935 when, according to P. J. Devlin in the *Irish Independent,* Mackey 'gave one of the most brilliant and spectacular individual displays ever seen' as Limerick hammered Tipperary in the Munster final.

In 1936, now captain of Limerick, Mackey scored five goals and three points in the Munster final, rallied

Limerick against Galway with two goals in the All-Ireland semi-final when the match appeared lost, and zig-zagged through the Kilkenny defence for what old-timers would claim was the best goal in hurling history.

The leading sportswriter of the time, Paddy Mehigan, afterwards recalled 1936 as Limerick's best ever performance and one of the best in the history of the game.

Mackey was back to accept the cup once more as captain in 1940 when his switch to centre-field early in the second half was the turning point in the match as Limerick beat Kilkenny by six points.

Paddy McMahon had scored three goals for Limerick in the Munster final, but their match went to an epic replay.

Bad feeling erupted when Cork's Martin Brennan was struck by an opponent and had to be carried off. A crowd invasion caused a Cork goal to be disallowed, and there was a prolonged exchange of blows in a fracas around the Limerick goal.

Though Cork led, Limerick scored three goals in a ten-minute spell from Paddy McMahon and Richie Stokes. Cork's Jack Lynch got a goal back and Tom O'Sullivan scored again for Limerick after a defensive slip.

'There will never be games, believe me, to equal those two games at Thurles in 1940', Mick Mackey told Raymond Smith in 1974.

The winning goal from Cavan's Vincent McGovern two minutes from the end of the All-Ireland semi-final of 1933 prevented Kerry from winning five in a row.

Mackey never made it back to the podium at Croke Park, but continued to thrill supporters in the Munster championship. His would-be winning goal for Limerick against Cork in the drawn Munster hurling final of 1944 was controversially disallowed with five minutes to go.

He scored another characteristic solo-run goal in the 1945 Munster final, but Limerick lost a four-point lead and Tipperary went on to win the All-Ireland.

Mackey made his last appearance for Limerick when he came on as a sub late in the 1947 Munster semi-final against Tipperary.

Sadly, there is no newsreel footage of him in action, so we will never get a glimpse of a man many rate as the greatest hurler of all time.

Mackey starred for Limerick in the 1935 Munster semi-final against Cork, but there was onfield drama of another kind. Cork's Tommy Kelly was injured and given the last rites on the field of play while players and spectators knelt around him. He was discharged from hospital the following day.

Games were tough, characterised by hard hitting and an occasional crowd invasion, as in that 1936 semi-final between Limerick and Galway when the Gardaí took several minutes to clear the field, the 1933 Munster final between Limerick and Waterford which was unfinished, and the invasion in the 1940 Munster final between Limerick and Cork that caused a Cork goal to be disallowed.

It was not all blood and thunder. In the 1940 Munster semi-final the newspapers reported that just when Limerick's Mick Mackey and Waterford's Christy Moylan appeared to be about to come to blows, Mackey offered half an orange to his opponent during a break in play.

The Munster provincial competition was now the engine-room of the hurling championship, where five of the best hurling counties met each year and old scores were carried from one year to the next.

A special train, an engine and one carriage, was chartered to bring Clare's Jimmy Houlihan and Limerick's Christy O'Brien to Thurles from Dublin, where they had played a club match for Army Metro earlier that day, for a first round match in 1933.

Clare, Tipperary and Limerick all emerged from the province in turn and then Waterford won in 1938 with a Locky Byrne goal to give them the lead and a final, dramatic ten-minute siege of the Waterford posts before they had a first-ever Munster hurling title confirmed.

Runaway All-Ireland champions of 1937, Tipperary had been thrown out of the competition because Jimmy Cooney of Carrick-on-Suir, the star midfielder against Clare, was found to be ineligible because he had attended a rugby international.

Dublin eventually beat Waterford in the All-Ireland final. It was their sixth and last All-Ireland, and the only one in which a Dublin-born player won a medal, Jim Byrne of Eoghan Ruadh. He started the move that led to the crucial Dublin goal scored by Bill Loughnane just before half-time.

• • •

Croke Park was growing, and a towering new stand had been erected in honour of Michael Cusack. The open field which staged its first GAA championship meeting back on 10 September 1892 had become a hotch-potch of pavilions and stands.

In 1924 a new stand was opened for the Tailteann games and in 1926 it was named in honour of Michael Hogan of Tipperary, the most famous casualty of Bloody Sunday. The other stand became known as the Long stand.

The Cusack stand, with 6,000 seats on the upper deck, was opened for the All-Ireland semi-final between Kerry and Laois in August 1938, and concrete terracing was constructed on Hill 16. It was 1949 before the terracing at the Canal end was completed. In 1952 the corner stand was constructed in memory of P. W. Nally, the

Mayo athlete who had discussed the foundation of the GAA with Cusack in 1882 but had been in prison when the movement was eventually founded. And in 1959, to celebrate the 75th anniversary of the association, the first Hogan stand was shipped to Limerick and the new Hogan stand became the first cantilevered stand in the country.

• • •

The All-Ireland semi-final at Mullingar saw the debut of an 18-year-old radio commentator. Micheál Ó Hehir was to become 'the voice of the GAA' during a 40-year career relaying games on radio and television.

For 25 years he was their main commentator on a part-time basis, working as a clerk during the week and picking up four guineas for provincial and All-Ireland finals, the only games that were then broadcast.

Ó Hehir prepared for matches with a series of cards which he used to build up a database on the players. When he went on air he would imagine he was telling the story of the game to a close friend.

The opening of the Cusack stand allowed large attendances to watch the games in comfort, and his radio

Victory over Kerry set up Cavan for the final and a breakthrough first title for Ulster. It was a frenetic afternoon which also saw a crowd invasion when a Cavan player was injured. Tim Landers narrowly missed an equaliser for Kerry.

broadcasts helped heighten interest as attendances shot up over a 15-year period from 50,000 to over 80,000.

His most famous commentary of all was in the 1947 All-Ireland final in New York, after the mayor of New York had to use his influence to have lines installed. Ó Hehir appealed on air for extra time from the post office lines people.

From the 1940s right up to 1963, the French-run Radio Brazzaville rebroadcast the All-Ireland and Railway Cup finals to Irish missionaries in Africa.

Opinions vary as to his best commentary of all, but many nominate the 1954 match between Cork and Wexford.

The 1938 football final, the first in front of the Cusack stand, ended in confusion. Galway had just scored an equalising goal, but Kerry came back for what should have been the winning point by John Joe Landers.

Not so. The point was disallowed because the final whistle went early. Kerry complained no time had been added for stoppages, but for the second year in a row the final was declared a draw.

There was an even more chaotic end to the replay when the referee blew twice for a free two minutes from the end and the crowd mistook this for the final whistle.

The free had been awarded to Kerry. A Galway man stood too close to the ball, and when the referee whistled again the crowd swept across the field.

Even the Kerry players were fooled: nine of them went away to tog off at the Central Hotel. Four more had gathered around John Walsh, who was having hip and shoulder injuries dressed in the new Cusack stand dressing room.

Seán Brosnan and Tim O'Leary were still on the field and probably the first to hear loudspeaker pleas for the players to resume. Myers, Casey, Dillon and Paddy Brosnan had gone.

Joe Keohane, who had been watching from the stand dressed in his Sunday suit, togged out for the final two minutes, as did Mort Kelly, Murphy, Ned Walsh and Jack Sheehy as Kerry finished the match without their full complement of 15. Despite this they scored a point in the remaining minutes.

Despite heavy rain, a record crowd showed up to see Cavan take Ulster's first title in 1933. The crowd of 45,188 paid £4,037 in gate receipts and a further 5,000 were locked out. The historic Cavan team was led by the star of the side narrowly beaten in 1928, Jim Smith. Back: J. Gilheaney (chairman), Willie Young, Jack Smallhorn, Donal Morgan, Vincent McGovern, Mick Denneny, J. J. Clarke (secretary). Middle: P. Murphy (manager), Paddy McNamee, P. Brady, Tom O'Reilly, Willie Connolly, 'Big' Tom O'Reilly (Cornafean), Patsy Devlin, Hugh O'Reilly, J. Rahill, M. O'Reilly (trainer). Front: T. Crowe, Louis Blessing, Packie Phair, Jim Smith (captain), Patsy Lynch, T. Coyle, M. J. 'Son' Magee.

Kerry were back in the replay business in 1939, beating Mayo and going on to win the All-Ireland final against a newcomer to the finals, Meath.

Dan Spring, later to become a Labour TD, scored both goals in the final for Kerry. Meath had one of the best goals of the era from Mattie Gilsenan just before half-time.

But fans had their eyes on a new rivalry which exploded into life in the semi-final of that year, the neighbouring counties of Meath and Cavan.

Unusually, Cavan had won the Ulster final in Croke Park. The Ulster final between Cavan and Armagh was unfinished, being fought out on a steadily shrinking pitch in Castleblayney as the crowd advanced further and further beyond the touchlines. They invaded, eventually, when Conaty scored an Armagh goal in the first half.

Armagh captain Jim McCullough, an iconic figure who played for several Ulster counties, was punched by one of the crowd as he was taking a throw-in (under the rules of the time).

A mêlée followed. The referee abandoned the match when the pitch was not cleared. It had been rough going. The match had started at 4.15 and was called off at 6.45. Cavan won the replay by two points.

The first half of that semi-final between Meath and Cavan produced some of the best football seen for many years. Clearly these teams had much more to offer in years to come.

In 1938 the GAA expelled its patron, Dr Douglas Hyde, the man who had delivered the *de-Anglicising Ireland* lecture of 1892, for attending an international soccer match in his new role as president of Ireland.

It was an unpopular move within the association and seems to have been taken after virtually no debate at a central council meeting. It also led to an unwelcome altercation with the Taoiseach Éamon de Valera who successfully demanded a guarantee that similar treatment would not be accorded Hyde's successor in 1945.

Even more disruptive was the case of Jimmy Cooney who was accused of having attended a rugby international and who was inadvertently the cause of Tipperary being thrown out of the Munster championship.

The two incidents reopened the near-forgotten debate on the GAA's ban on foreign games and all who played or supported them.

The 'policy of exclusion' had its origins in the 1885 ban on the IAAA, as both bodies battled for survival. The two had assumed adversarial positions which would largely remain until 1922, defined partly, but not solely, with the nationalist and unionist constituencies of pre-partition Ireland.

In 1887 rugby and soccer were proscribed on the suggestion of Maurice Davin, a former rugby and soccer player who had drawn up the rules of Gaelic football and was worried that some clubs were still playing both.

RIC members were debarred because they had been shadowing GAA members and joining clubs to spy on activities.

When Cork's Tom Irwin, an inter-provincial rugby and cricket player, appealed against a suspension for playing rugby in

1896, the GAA executive ruled that members could play any games they liked.

The brothers Jack and Mick Ryan from Rockwell in Tipperary helped Ireland win successive triple crowns on the rugby field in 1898 and 1899.

In 1902 Dublin called for a rule that players as well as clubs should be prevented from playing rival codes. The rise of soccer clubs had decimated GAA clubs in the city. All-Ireland champions Isles of the Sea, for example, had lost many of its members to the new soccer club Shamrock Rovers. Young Irelands, three times All-Ireland champions, had lost members to St James's Gate.

Val Harris, three times an All-Ireland medallist, became one of the world's best soccer players in the 1900s. Another Dub who became a professional soccer goal-keeper, James 'Ginger' Reilly, used to run down the field on solo runs and eventually got the rules of soccer changed so that the goalie could only handle the ball in the box.

The ban on foreign games was reintroduced in 1905, as Kerryman T. F. O'Sullivan called 'on the young men of Ireland not to identify themselves with rugby or association football or any other form of imported sport but rather play sports which the GAA provides for self-respecting Irishmen who have no desire to ape foreign manners and customs.'

After 1922 many felt that the ban was no longer necessary, but moves to get rid of it were defeated by just

Mick Higgins captained the legendary Galway Sigerson team of 1933, the first year the competition was entered by Queen's University in Belfast. By the 1930s the Sigerson and Fitzgibbon cups had become an established part of the university sports calendar.

nine votes in 1922, and by slightly increased margins, approximately 2:1, every year until 1927.

For 40 more years it came up for discussion every third year with increasingly acrimonious debate until a campaign by Dublin delegate Tom Woulfe eventually proved successful in 1971. At one Kerry convention in the 1960s an anti-ban motion was greeted with such ire that even the proposer and seconder voted against it and it was defeated by 71 votes to nil.

●　　●　　●

An air of uncertainty hung over the morning of 3 September 1939. Britain and France were going to war with Germany. It was the day when a ferocious thunderstorm struck in Dublin. Cork and Kilkenny were playing in the All-Ireland final, and the 'thunder and lightning final' was to be remembered by everyone who was there.

Jimmy Phelan scored two goals to give Kilkenny a seven-point lead at half-time. But Cork came storming back.

The youthful Jack Lynch scored a goal and Willy Campbell landed a long-range free in the net for a dramatic equaliser in the midst of a spectacular thunder and lightning storm and a rainstorm that reduced pressmen's notes to sodden debris.

The match was over, and so was life as all of Europe knew it.

●　　●　　●

Through the emergency, as World War II was known in Ireland, transport was a growing problem. Emergency restrictions affected attendances at all matches.

For the 1941 All-Ireland football final 11,000 fans arrived by turf-fired train and two hardy Kerrymen cycled from Killarney on a tandem.

In the semi-final of that year's championship, half the Dublin team thought it would be a bright idea to overnight in Limerick on Saturday. The players who came directly from Dublin on Sunday morning arrived to discover that the other half of the team had not yet arrived and were still snailing along en route to Tralee by turf-train.

Despite the problems the 1943 and 1944 finals brought new record attendances to see a new county win successive All-Irelands, Roscommon.

Roscommon's 1943 final with Cavan was watched by 68,023 fans including German minister Hempel and British minister John Maffey sitting a few seats apart in the Cusack stand.

It went to a replay before Phelim Murray scored Roscommon's point to the annoyance of the Cavan players who fought back to two points behind.

Some Cavan men tried to prevent the umpire signalling the score. The crowd rushed the field as a Cavan player felled the referee with a blow, and the trouble took several minutes to clear up.

In 1944, 79,245 watched Roscommon beat Kerry, the county that had won nine of the previous 16 All-Ireland titles. Frankie Kinlough's first half goal was enough to win the match.

That year saw Carlow win the Leinster championship for the only time and miss an appearance in the All-Ireland final by just two points.

Clare goalkeeper Tommy Daly chaired off the field after an extraordinary, fluctuating All-Ireland semi-final at Limerick in 1932. Tull Considine scored six Clare goals, all in the second half, as Clare came clambering back from 13 points down (2-0 to 4-7) at half-time to win by five.

Carlow went two points up against Kerry but conceded an unfortunate goal from a free by Murt Kelly just before half-time.

• • •

In normal circumstances the 1941 hurling final would not measure as one of the more memorable events in GAA history.

The score direct from a sideline ball had been legalised in 1931, just in time for Lory Meagher to score one against Clare in the 1932 All-Ireland final. Kilkenny won by three points after Tull Considine was deprived of a certain Clare goal.

Two of the leading counties, Tipperary and Kilkenny, were excluded because of an outbreak of foot and mouth disease. Instead, Cork and Dublin played in the final and few people were surprised when Cork won by 20 points in front of the smallest attendance for 11 years.

This was Cork's twelfth title, the first in ten years. When Tipperary got the all clear from their foot and mouth quarantine, they put four goals past Cork in the first half and eventually won the Munster championship by eight points, but Cork were allowed to keep the Liam McCarthy cup and, more significantly, the first of four titles in a row.

Cork have won 30 All-Irelands but the five in six years they won in the 1940s still stands out as their greatest era.

Cork is the only city where hurling is habitually played. As early as 1894 the *Freeman's Journal* said that Blackrock players were 'living in a district which might be called the home of hurling'.

The county's status within the GAA was proven when it left the association after an argument over an unfinished All-Ireland final in 1894 and attracted affiliations from Waterford and Limerick and almost bankrupted the parent body.

Matches between Cork clubs such as Glen Rovers, St Finbarr's and Blackrock can command as much support as for inter-county games. The record attendance for a county final anywhere, 34,151, was for a hurling final between St Finbarr's and Glen Rovers in Páirc Uí Chaoimh in 1977.

• • •

In winning the four in a row Cork had easy victories over Dublin and Antrim in All-Ireland finals, but fought out some of the most memorable games of the decade against Limerick and Tipperary.

In the 1942 Munster semi-final, Limerick took a three-point lead, Cork went four points up, Limerick equalised, then points from Buckley and Condon gave Cork a two-point victory.

In the Munster final of that year Tipperary took a two-point lead with 15 minutes to go, but Cork won by 14 points. Colm Tobin got two goals for Cork, Mick Kennefick scored another and Christy Ring added five points.

In 1943 Cork had a scare and needed a late comeback against Waterford, who had two clear goal chances to win the game.

But the biggest shock of the 1943 championship was reserved for Kilkenny, who travelled to the tight, sloping Corrigan Park in Belfast. There Antrim first beat Galway and then Kevin Armstrong scored the winning goal against Kilkenny. Antrim were to suffer a heavy defeat in the final.

The 1944 Munster final was drawn before Cork beat Limerick in the replay with two goals in the last three minutes. Because of petrol rationing most of the 19,000 spectators travelled to the match in Thurles by bicycle, giving it the nickname, 'the great bicycle final'.

In 1945 Cork won their first All-Ireland football final in 34 years thanks to goals from Mick Tubridy and Derry Beckett.

The most famous member of that team was Jack Lynch, one of the towering figures in GAA history who picked up the fifth of six successive All-Ireland medals that afternoon.

Jack Lynch was just 22 years old when he captained Cork in the 'thunder and lightning' final against

Richard Blake of Clare gets a block in against Kilkenny in the 1932 All-Ireland final. Clare had come from 13 points down at half-time in the semi-final to win by five.

Kilkenny in 1939, but he was already a veteran of three years of inter-county hurling and winner of county championship medals with Glen Rovers in hurling and St Nicholas in football.

He won four successive All-Ireland medals at midfield on the hurling field, a fifth at corner-forward on the football team in 1945, the year he became a barrister, and a sixth in 1946. When he transferred to the Civil Service club in Dublin in 1944 because of travelling difficulties, he played three matches in one day, the first for Civil Service v Eoghan Ruadh in a Dublin league match and then for the Munster football and hurling teams.

In 1947 he narrowly missed a seventh medal in a row when Kilkenny beat Cork by a single point in the All-Ireland hurling final.

He was always good for three or four points from centre-field, but Jack Lynch's most spectacular performances came in the years when he didn't win All-Ireland medals.

In 1948, when Jack was elected to the Dáil in February, he scored two goals against Limerick in the Munster semi-final and another goal as Cork were beaten by Waterford in the Munster final.

In 1949 he scored a dramatic late goal against Tipperary in the first round of the Munster championship, collecting the ball at midfield and running through the defence, but Tipperary earned a replay with an equalising point and Cork were beaten after half an hour of extra time in the replay. There was controversy over a 'missing' second Cork goal which struck the stanchion and rebounded into play.

'Do that again and there will be a by-election', the legendary Tipperary goalkeeper Tony Reddan is reputed to have said to him after one altercation during the game.

In 1950 he made his last appearance in a Munster final at full-forward against Tipperary, brought to a premature end by a pitch invasion.

He was the most successful of many political figures to have played GAA, becoming Fianna Fáil party leader in 1966 as a compromise candidate in a leadership battle and serving two terms as taoiseach, 1966–73 and 1977–79, after delivering the biggest majority in Fianna Fáil's history.

And just when Munster seemed to have captured the Liam McCarthy cup for keeps, a Leinster victory.

Kilkenny marched with 14 men in the pre-match parade for the 1947 All-Ireland hurling final because of Paddy Grace's knee injury.

They then went on to win what some still describe as the greatest hurling final ever. Cork complained loudly that Terry Leahy was allowed to replace the ball before he took the equalising free.

Leahy scored again to spark off celebrations that are still recalled across Kilkenny. They hadn't won since the 'thunder and lightning' final in 1939. They weren't to win again for ten years.

The rivalry between Roscommon and Kerry resumed in 1946, but first the harvest had to be saved.

The GAA postponed the final from 19 September in support of a national 'save the harvest' campaign to prevent crops being ruined after a bad summer and lost to an economy still curtailed by wartime conditions.

Laois might have been in that final. In the semi-final Tommy Murphy led a storming Laois come-back and went for the winning goal, only to see Roscommon goalkeeper Dolan make one of the most spectacular saves seen at Croke Park. It was to be 58 years before they would win another Leinster title.

Antrim might have been there, but their mobile hand-passing style was short-circuited by Kerry's tactics, hitting the man in position to take the pass.

Two Kerry players were sent off, with the radio commentator diplomatically ignoring the warfare despite a chorus of boohs which almost drowned him out.

Roscommon might have won, and led by six points. The newsreel camera at the game missed what were two of the most dramatic goals in football history, scored by Paddy Burke and Tom 'Gega' O'Connor in the final two minutes of play.

Kerry came from behind to win yet another replay by four points. They led by a point until they got yet another last-minute goal.

Ten years after his famous radio commentary, Michael Hamilton re-emerged on the GAA scene in 1947, this time with a strange proposal for the association.

To celebrate the centenary of the worst year of the Great Famine, he suggested that the 1947 All-Ireland football final should be staged in New York.

Mayor O'Malley would support the venture and the Polo Grounds would be rented for the occasion. Amazingly, the proposal went through and the Kerry and Cavan teams were sent out to fight for All-Ireland honours on American soil.

When GAA officials arrived in New York they discovered that the match was poorly publicised and the pitch bumpy. But 34,491 attended and Cavan's victory was recalled with affection afterwards.

Four points in each half earned Peter Donohue the description of 'the Babe Ruth of Gaelic football' by an American sportswriter.

It was recorded as a momentous event in GAA history, but New York's efforts to bring the 1950 All-Ireland hurling final to the Polo Grounds were unsuccessful.

Cavan retained their title in 1948 on what was to be remembered as the 'day of the big wind'. Cavan went 3-2 to nil up at half-time. Mick Higgins scored a fourth goal early in the second half and after John Joe O'Reilly was carried off with a shoulder injury, Mayo came storming back.

There was just one point in it at the end, 4-5 to 4-4. Mayo's Pádraig Carney scored from a penalty, the first to be awarded in an All-Ireland final.

Limerick attack the Cork goal in the 1934 Munster hurling championship. Limerick's Jackie O'Connell had a late goal against Cork followed by a point from Mick Mackey to send Limerick into the Munster final.

Cavan might have had three in a row, but instead Bill Halfpenny scored a goal that brought Meath their first title. Jim Kearney, who had played in the 1939 All-Ireland final team, was brought out of retirement to help Meath at midfield for this game.

There was a new name on hurling's role of honour. Waterford beat Cork in the 1948 Munster final by two points after goals from Tom Curran and Willie Galvin put them eight points up with 15 minutes to go and just survived goals by Cork's Billy Murphy and Mossie O'Riordan. It set them up for their first All-Ireland, putting six goals past Dublin, winning a medal for Vinny Baston, who had refereed an All-Ireland final three years earlier.

Laois beat Kilkenny in the Leinster semi-final that year and came back to beat Kilkenny again a year later in the Leinster final, with the exotically named Paddy Rustchitzko as team captain. Their lucky break came when the Kilkenny goalkeeper made a mistake pucking out the ball. Having led by ten points at half-time, they won by just two points.

But they lost the All-Ireland final by 17 points and went into rapid decline. They conceded seven goals to Wexford in the following year's championship.

Their conquerors were a Tipperary team that was setting out its stall for the next decade.

Rural Ireland in the 1950s was in crisis. In the years between 1951 and 1961, 409,000 people emigrated, a figure equal to the entire population of Connacht.

They included many of the most prominent GAA players in the country: Tom 'Gega' O'Connor, hero of the 1946 football All-Ireland final, Terry Leahy, hero of the 1947 All-Ireland hurling final, the Morrissey brothers from Wexford and thousands more.

Parishes all over the country were decimated as the young packed their bags and headed for England or America. The 1952 congress report describes how whole parishes could disappear.

And on All-Ireland Saturday, a new ritual emerged, emigrants coming home to watch the All-Ireland final, which had become the central event in the sporting culture of the nation.

One of the worst-affected counties had the most to cheer about at the start of the decade.

Mayo lost a third of its population between 1926 and 1961, but in 1950 it took the All-Ireland football championship with a freak goal five minutes from the end of their final against Louth.

Seán Boyle tried to clear, Seán Flanagan charged the ball down and ran 20 yards to score a goal.

The character of the team was really tested in the All-Ireland semi-final of 1951. Mayo had been trailing by four points as the game entered injury time.

Spectators among the 25,000 attendance at Thurles for the Cork v Limerick Munster championship match in 1934.

Kerry mixed up their kick-out, the ball fell to Éamonn Mongey, who passed to Tom Langan, with the full-back out of position. Langan scored a trademark goal. Paddy Irwin added a point a minute later to earn a replay which Mayo won by two points.

They then beat Meath by five points in the final, Pádraig Carney scoring three points in the closing minutes.

Meath might have won the 1952 All-Ireland but for one of the most bizarre incidents in GAA history. Edwin Carolan chased a ball that appeared to go over the end line, and kicked it across the goalmouth. It hit the far post and rebounded over the bar.

Much to everyone's surprise the umpire signalled a point. Some speculated that Carolan had been merely kicking the ball back for the kick-out.

Cavan could thank a more sure-footed Mick Higgins for a cherished replay victory over their neighbours. He gave an exhibition of free-taking as Cavan won by four points and won the All-Ireland for the fifth and last time.

Although Cavan now had five titles, no other Ulster county had won the All-Ireland. In 1953 it appeared all that was about to change.

The newly opened Casement Park in Andersonstown, west Belfast, was crammed with 30,000 spectators for the Ulster final between Armagh and the reigning champions Cavan. They saw Armagh snatch victory with a famous goal from Art O'Hagan.

Such was the interest in the 1953 All-Ireland final between Armagh and Kerry that 86,155 paid to see the game and an estimated 10,000 more gained admittance when the gates were broken in. Another 5,000 were locked outside listening to the radio.

Safety officers wouldn't have been impressed. That number represents more than the current bigger Croke Park can hold.

With six minutes to go Bill McCorry faced a penalty for Armagh. He missed. And that wasn't all of their bad luck. Armagh lost Seán Quinn from the defence through injury and they had to play with three different goalkeepers at various stages of the game.

It was to be 50 years before Armagh eventually won their All-Ireland. They missed a penalty that day too, for old time's sake.

Gaelic football was never so open as in the mid-1950s. The sport had five different champions in five years.

Limerick defeated Waterford in the Munster final on the way to the All-Ireland championship of 1934. The attendance at the old Athletic Grounds was 15,000, on the site where Páirc Uí Chaoimh was constructed in 1976. A member of the Waterford team, Billy Barron, won an All-Ireland junior hurling medal with London 27 years later, in 1961.

In 1954 a goal from Tom Moriarty gave Meath a surprisingly easy victory over Kerry. Offaly and Wicklow had both threatened to break through that year. Paddy Meegan scored the winning point for Meath against Wicklow in the ninth minute of lost time, Wicklow having led by two points at the end of the 60 minutes. The 'long count' went into Wicklow folklore, especially when Meath won the All-Ireland.

Just when Meath looked set to dominate, a tactically astute Dublin beat them in the Leinster final of 1955. Full-forward Kevin Heffernan roved out of position and took Meath's full-back Paddy O'Brien with him, leaving a gap through the middle through which Dublin scored five goals in the Leinster final.

Kerry then shocked a fancied Dublin side in the All-Ireland final, holding on in the last four minutes in the face of Dublin's final desperate onslaught.

Meanwhile, two of the deadliest forwards in the history of the game emerged together on the same St Jarlath's and Galway teams. Frankie Stockwell scored 2-5 for Galway against Cork in the 1956 final. He had another goal disallowed, and his scoring record was to stand for 20 years.

Stockwell was just half of the story. His 'terrible twin' Seán Purcell sent in the line ball which allowed him

Waterford v Limerick in the 1934 Munster hurling final. Limerick retained their title on a slippery pitch with two goals from Dave Clohessy, a third from Mick Mackey and a fourth direct from a 70 by Paddy Clohessy.

to skip in to sidefoot the first goal. Purcell's punched pass gave him the second.

Meath's big rivals in Leinster football in the early 1950s was Louth. Then in 1957 Ireland's smallest county defeated the biggest county in the All-Ireland final.

Louth had a Seán Cunningham goal just five minutes from the end, sent to the net from a Kevin Beahan line ball. Dermot O'Brien, already a household name as an accordion player and one of the country's best band leaders, missed the pre-match parade as he couldn't get in through the crowds.

Dublin won the 1958 final against an emerging Derry team. Des Ferguson's centre hopped 25 yards from goal, the full-back slipped and Paddy Farnan was left with a clear run for goal. It took Derry 35 years to get over the catastrophe.

In hurling, Tipperary were running up three All-Irelands in a row, followed by Cork with two in a row. That suggested the real action was back in Munster where the famous hurling rivalry between these counties infatuated the province.

The attendance grew with each encounter, 34,702, 39,816, 43,000, 46,265 and 52,449 between 1949 and 1954, until eventually 60,177 crammed into Limerick Gaelic Grounds to see the 1961 final.

Every year there was a new incident to get supporters talking. In 1949 a would-be winning point by Tipperary's Mick Maher was disallowed because the whistle had been blown. A defender had thrown a hurley at him as he raced through for the score. Play was brought back for the free, but Tipperary's chance was gone and the match was drawn.

After that prelude a stormy replay ensued. 'It was pull first — ask questions later', Seán Coughlan reported in the *Irish Press*.

They now had a name for the Tipperary goalmouth, 'hell's kitchen'.

When Mossie O'Riordan scored a goal for Cork in that 1949 replay, it was claimed that the ball had come back, not from the crossbar, but from the wire stanchion behind the goal. The game was played at such a fast pace nobody could be sure.

The design of goal nets was subsequently changed to prevent a recurrence, but it did happen again.

That was just the first round. The following year, 1950, Cork and Tipperary met in the Munster final.

Officially 39,816 paid to see the game, but we will never know how many actually crammed into the Killarney stadium that day, because at least 10,000 more got in when the gates were rushed.

It was a chaotic and incident-packed afternoon. The squashed and excited spectators invaded the pitch within minutes of the start, when Cork's Christy Ring was fouled.

The referee had to stop the match again ten minutes from the end to clear the pitch. Spectators came on to the field in the area around the Tipperary goal-mouth to get a closer look as Cork pressed for the equalising goal.

An umpire was signalling a 70 when the unsighted referee blew the final whistle, and the referee was forced to flee as enraged spectators pursued him to the dressing room.

When the confusion was cleared up, Tipperary had won by three points and went on to win the All-Ireland.

When the teams met again in the 1951 final, gate receipts were £6,207, double the previous record. Tipperary won by two points after the bizarre tactical device of changing their six forwards around every minute between the 12th and 22nd minutes of the second half.

Sportswriter John D. Hickey concluded: 'All the roaming caught Cork out for two golden goals.'

When they met again in the 1952 final the crowd had swelled again to 43,000 in a stadium that was barely able to hold 20,000.

Cork won when Liam Dowling was awarded a goal under the 'advantage rule' 14 minutes into the second half. It prevented Tipperary getting four in a row. The problem was the advantage rule didn't exist. Tipp fans

He connected with a rebound off Tony Reddan's chest after Christy Ring beat three defenders and whipped the ball into the square from 20 yards out. Ring added a point to give Cork a three-point win.

Seán Bannon had a Tipperary goal called back for 'whistle gone' at the beginning of the second half, a decision that rankled with Tipperary fans who remembered Cork's 'advantage' goal of two years before.

There was more controversy two years later in the 1956 Munster semi-final when Tipperary's Paddy Kenny had a goal in the last minute disallowed because a Cork defender had thrown a hurley. Tipperary scored a point from the free but lost the match by one point.

The 1960 final was rated as 'the fastest of them all' by some sportswriters. Though Cork took the lead in the second half, Tipperary surged to take the title in a manner that is still recalled with awe. It swelled the

Limerick against Cork in the 1935 Munster hurling semi-final in Thurles. During the match Cork's Tommy Kelly was injured and given the last rites, while players and spectators knelt. He was discharged from hospital the following day.

remembered how Mick Maher's winning point of 1949 was disallowed in exactly the same circumstances.

The crowd was bigger again, 46,265, when Cork won by five points.

And then in 1954, 52,449 watched Paddy Barry snatch the most famous winning goal in the long series of meetings between these teams.

attendance at the 1961 final to 60,177, still a record for a Munster hurling final nearly 45 years later, all crammed into the Limerick Grounds.

'There is a Leinster championship too', a delegate at the Wexford convention had complained in 1952.

Wexford were the rising stars of the east, emerging to play in the All-Ireland final of 1951. Glamorous in their purple and gold, they had charisma, class and a new hero, the handsome vet with the amazing dead-ball shot, Nicky Rackard.

Amazingly, they had started the season with a draw against Meath, but beat Dublin, Laois and Galway and seemed about to sweep Tipperary aside before Tipp killed them off with three goals in the last 12 minutes.

Mitchel Cogley wrote in the *Irish Independent* that the Wexford v Kilkenny semi-final of 1952 was 'one of the best matches ever seen in Croke Park'.

But it was 1954 before Wexford won another Leinster title and the two great hurling icons of the decade faced each other.

• • •

The contrast could not have been greater in terms of honours won. Christy Ring was seeking an eighth All-Ireland hurling medal; Nicky Rackard was seeking his first. Croke Park couldn't hold the 84,856 crowd that came to watch. Thousands more were left outside when the gates were locked.

Dour-faced Mick Mackey after captaining Limerick to victory in the 1936 All-Ireland final. He became famous for his weaving solo runs, something he later cautioned young players against over-using.

Limerick's Mick Mackey has his supporters, but folklore has accorded Christy Ring of Cloyne the reputation of being the greatest hurler of all time. Monuments have been erected in his honour. A statue of Ring greets passengers at Cork Airport. His skills are still spoken about, as is his passion to share his knowledge. When Louis Marcus made an instructional hurling film about Ring in 1961, Ring insisted that Marcus should learn all the skills he was teaching as the film was being made.

Christy Ring had been a sub in Cork's 1937 minor hurling championship team. He was on the 1938 minor team and a panellist since the 1939 All-Ireland final.

He was good for four points in each of the 1941, 1942 and 1943 finals. But it was emerging that, like Mick Mackey, he liked to take on defences and run at people.

In the 'bicycle final' of 1944 the great Munster rivals faced each other. Both scored uncannily similar goals, soloing through almost to the end line and striking to the net. Mackey's goal was disallowed; Ring's was not; the match was drawn and Cork won the replay.

Ring set the 1946 All-Ireland final alight with a classic solo-run goal to help Cork to a decisive win over Kilkenny. He was captain of the Cork team and at the peak of his career.

• • •

Ring had also developed one of the hardest shots in the game, as Limerick found out in the 1947 Munster final. His display in the 1951 Munster final against Tipperary, when Cork were beaten, is rated by many as his best ever. He was switched back to centre-field in an attempt to counter Tipperary star Phil Shanahan.

It took six more years before he was back in Croke Park, having scored the winning point for Cork in the 1952 All-Ireland semi-final after an incredible nine minutes of injury time, and five points in the final.

He scored a glorious 60-yard goal in the 1953 final in controversial circumstances. Galway, given a bye straight into the final, fancied their chances after their semi-final near miss of twelve months earlier. Micky Burke, who was marking Ring, was the victim of an ugly strike midway through the second half that would have repercussions on Ring's record. The blow was captured on newsreel. Ring was struck in retaliation, and a vitriolic post-match newspaper campaign resulted.

Christy Ring and Mick Mackey toss a coin before the 1946 Munster hurling final, one of the few encounters between two players who have long disputed the title of greatest hurler of all time. Ring's career was on an upward path, and was perhaps ten years before his peak; Mackey's was by this time in decline. In this match Mackey was successfully 'tamed' for the second time in three years by Din Joe Buckley.

By the time the 1954 final came round, Ring and Rackard were the biggest names in hurling and a record 84,856 spectators came to see them in action. Ring scored five points.

The family home of Nicky Rackard of Rathnure was reputedly the home of 1798 hero, 'Kelly, the boy from Killane'.

An uncle, John Doran, won an All-Ireland football medal in 1918. Two of his brothers, Bobby and Billy, played with him on the Wexford hurling team, and another brother, Jimmy, played on the 1951 All-Ireland final team.

But it was Nicky who was most associated with Wexford's hurling revival, shattering scoring records every step of the way. As early as 1941 as a lanky schoolboy he had scored two of Wexford's goals as they led Kilkenny until 15 minutes from the end of the first round tie at Nowlan Park.

In 1950 he scored two goals again when Wexford had their nearest miss ever, losing the Leinster final by three points to Kilkenny, thanks to a crucial goal-keeping error at the start of the second half.

Nicky was a renowned dual star. He played with Wexford footballers in the 1953 Leinster final and he

had played in two Railway Cup finals on the same afternoon in 1950 for the Leinster football and hurling teams.

The Nicky Rackard 'special', a soon-to-become-familiar 21-yard free propelled to the net with all the force of a Killane musket, was unveiled to the public in the 1951 Leinster final.

Legendary Tipperary goalkeeper Tony Reddan was up to the Rackard challenge in the All-Ireland final, defying Rackard on three separate occasions. Nicky had started by getting the ball in the Tipp net after just two minutes, scored one of the best goals of his career eight minutes later, and finished with 3-2. But wily Tipp won by ten points.

The turning point in the 1953 Leinster final was when he failed to lift one of his frees at a crucial point, and a demoralised Wexford lost by four points.

In 1954 Rackard proved unstoppable. In the Leinster final he scored a highest ever 6-4 and having another goal disallowed as Wexford beat Dublin by 22 points. Wexford also beat Kilkenny by 19 points.

In the All-Ireland semi-final he scored a record 7-7 against Antrim. Newspapers said he could have got more as he 'did not seek any more scores than came his way'. One Rackard 'special' scraped the crossbar and sent spectators scattering to avoid decapitation in the Nally stand behind.

But Wexford lost their full-back Nick O'Donnell through injury in the final and were defeated by Cork by three points.

He got his All-Ireland medal at last in 1955. It was inevitably Rackard who landed a 60-yard free into the net to secure Wexford another Leinster title, and who scored the first goal as Wexford went on to beat Galway in the final.

But there was unfinished business to be dealt with, and in 1956 Wexford got to meet Cork again.

In a magnificent semi-final display against Galway in 1956, Rackard scored four goals: two in the first half and two near the end, and he added three points as well.

In 1956 Rackard secured his immortality by landing the winning goal against Cork with two minutes to go. A save by Wexford goalkeeper Art Foley had deprived Christy Ring of his ninth All-Ireland medal just a few seconds earlier.

Ring continued his run in as far as the goalkeeper, to congratulate or damn him, according to different accounts.

● ● ●

Christy Ring, at the peak of his career, scored six points and was deprived of a goal by another equally magnificent but less famous save by Art Foley in that match. He never won an All-Ireland, but one of his most spectacular achievements was still in the future.

Earlier that summer he had performed one of the most amazing feats in an extraordinary career when he scored 3-1 in a four-minute spell, bringing Cork from six points down to victory in the Munster final.

He rattled in goals for seven more years until a hip injury in the 1963 Railway Cup competition forced him out of Cork's championship team after 24 years.

In 1961 at the age of 40 he scored 3-4 against Waterford in the semi-final, including a classic goal in the first minute of the second half, rated by many as his best ever when it was said 'no one saw his hurley touch the ball'.

Indelibly associated with the glory period of the Railway Cup, he won 18 Railway Cup medals with Munster, playing in 22 successive finals.

● ● ●

Introduced in a flush of enthusiasm after the Tailteann experiment in 1927, the Railway Cup peaked in the 1950s as one of the country's most popular sporting events.

It was a straightforward formula. The four provincial teams played semi-finals in February and the finals in Croke Park on St Patrick's Day.

Fans flocked to see players who normally did not feature in the All-Ireland series such as Niall Crowley of Clare, who scored three goals to give Munster victory in the

1949 football final replay, Georgie O'Reilly of Wicklow, a goalscorer in the 1952 final, Clare hurler Jimmy Smyth, who scored three goals in the 1960 final, and Packie McGarty of Leitrim, who scored the winning goal for Connacht in the 1957 football final.

The attendance had climbed to 30,000 by the mid-1930s. It reached 40,000 by 1949 and peaked at 49,023 in 1954.

But it was mainly Christy Ring they came to see. Because of the reputation the hurling final was gaining, the new Hogan stand was opened in July 1959 with the delayed Railway Cup final, and Ring put in a virtuoso performance for the 23,258 attendance, scoring four goals including a superb palmed effort. By now he was balding and some of his team mates had not been born when he started hurling.

● ● ●

It may be a coincidence, but when Christy Ring retired, the Railway Cup went into terminal decline.

Live television arrived in 1962. In 1968, five years after a crowd of 30,000 had cheered their way through Christy Ring's last hurling final, attendance figures had crashed to 11,000, and the competition was described as being 'on its last legs'.

The Liam McCarthy cup is presented to Mick Mackey (1912–1982), one of the handful of players regarded as the greatest hurlers of all time. He scored 5-3 in the 1936 Munster senior hurling final against Tipperary. He also won eight Railway Cup medals and 20 Limerick senior hurling medals with his club Ahane.

Ten years later 1,900 turned out to watch a final on St Patrick's Day.

A 1980 hurling semi-final between Munster and Ulster drew an attendance of 94 to Croke Park.

When Ulster met the Combined Universities in 1973 there was a bigger attendance for the curtain-raiser, a Dublin primary schools under-12 final, than for the Railway Cup quarter-final.

The GAA was left with the question of what to do with a competition with a great tradition but no following.

It is a question it still hasn't answered.

Christy Ring was probably the greatest hurler of all time. He was the nation's top scorer in 1959, 1961 and 1962, and the only player ever to average more than ten points per match in the 1959 season. In 1964 he starred in the GAA's first coaching film, made by film maker Louis Marcus, later to win two Oscar nominations for his documentaries.

In the 1957 Munster semi-final against Tipperary, Ring scored the turning point goal to bring Cork right back into the match and then went off injured, stopping for a chat with an umpire on the way.

That umpire was Mick Mackey and his smiling word with Christy Ring became one of the most famous GAA photographs of its time. Mackey had tried to flag a Tipperary goal in the first half. The Cork goalkeeper was bundled over the line but he had already steered the ball around the post.

Ring is reputed to have said: 'You never lost it', and Mackey replied 'Neither did you.'

Mick Mackey had another statement to make. He trained the 1955 Limerick team that snatched a famous Munster final victory, the famous 'Mackey greyhounds'.

Clare hadn't won a Munster title for 41 years and, after beating Cork and Tipperary, felt their hour had come.

Two years earlier they had beaten Limerick by 34 points in the first round. Their star forward, one of the

greats of the game, Jimmy Smyth, scored 6-4, all in the first half. In 1954 while Clare tested Tipp in the Munster championship and Wexford in the Oireachtas competition, Limerick gave what was probably their worst display ever, scoring just one point in their match against Waterford.

But Limerick brought five juniors into their team and 21-year-old Vivian Cobbe scored 2-3 in their first round win over Waterford.

Goals from Cobbe and Dermot Kelly broke Clare hearts in the Munster final and Clare had to wait 40 more years for their breakthrough.

Mick Mackey waits for the break from the throw-in for Limerick v Cork.

In the end Limerick too ran out of steam. Galway, who had been given a bye to the final, also had a new star in 18-year-old schoolboy Paddy Egan. He scored two goals in a four-minute spell, but Wexford were unphased and collected their first All-Ireland title in 45 years.

Across the Barrow things were stirring as well. Phil Grimes was Waterford's man of the match as they recaptured the Munster title in 1957.

Kilkenny were re-emerging after one of the most barren decades in their history.

In 1955 Kilkenny and Wexford drew when the highlight of the game was an acute-angled goal from Wexford's Tim Flood, scored almost from the end line.

In 1956 Wexford won by one point.

Finally, in 1957 Kilkenny goalkeeper Ollie Walsh defied Tim Flood and Nicky Rackard early in the game, and Kilkenny ran out winners by 19 points.

Walsh was the star of the final as well, saving a last dramatic free from Waterford's Phil Grimes, having already made three point-blank saves earlier on in the game.

Film star John Gregson lined up with the Kilkenny team in the parade as part of the shooting of *Rooney*, a film about an Irish sanitation worker with an eye for the girls and a talent for hurling, trying to avoid marriage. Scenes from the final were used in the movie.

Kilkenny came storming back from six points down to win by a point.

By the end of the decade Dublin were emerging, squeezing Wexford out of the 1959 Leinster final and coming within 45 seconds of beating Kilkenny, only to lose when Johnny McGovern struck a line ball to the net.

That set up another Kilkenny–Waterford final. The fans wondered if it would be as exciting as 1957 and they were not disappointed.

Séamus Power scored an equalising goal for Waterford with 90 seconds to go. Waterford then won the replay.

Kilkenny had a new name to remember. Minor star Eddie Keher was barely on the field when he scored a lovely lift-and-strike point.

It was a new name for a new hurling generation.

Football too had a new name. Kerry outmanoeuvred Galway with a series of tactical switches to win the 1959 final, but it was a young midfielder from Valentia Island whose name was on everyone's lips.

Mick O'Connell may have been the greatest footballer of all time. Born on Beginish Island in Valentia harbour, he came to prominence for his display in the semi-final against Dublin, excelling in the first half when Dan McAuliffe got the vital goal.

After the match, the ice cool O'Connell left the cup in the dressing room in the excitement. He needn't have worried. He and Kerry would be back for more.

Opposite:
Mick Mackey limbering up for the All-Ireland semi-final against Galway. The 1936 encounter was one of the worst tempered ever seen. After Limerick's fourth goal a row erupted at centre-field, blows were struck, the crowd invaded the pitch and it was some time before the Gardaí cleared it again. Galway withdrew from the pitch when they found that one of their players had been beaten in a melée.

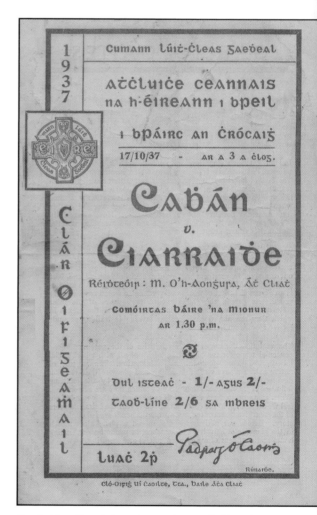

The fact that Cavan's last-minute point was disallowed gave Kerry a replay in the 1937 All-Ireland final they scarcely deserved. Many of the spectators and radio commentator Michael Hamilton thought the point had been allowed and that Cavan had won. Kerry won the replay, as they had in the semi-final against Laois.

A plan of the field published in the newspapers giving zones to assist radio listeners during the 1933 All-Ireland football final commentary. The listeners had an unexpected interruption when commentator Éamonn de Barra was surrounded by gunmen who ordered him to read out a demand for the release of political prisoners.

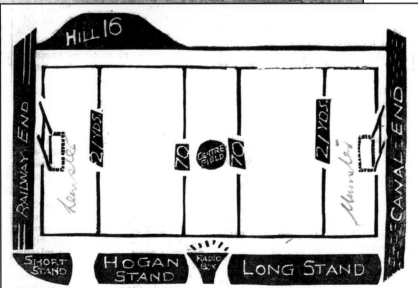

Every vantage point is taken for a Munster hurling
championship match at the Cork Sports Grounds
in 1936. For 70 years Cork were unbeaten on their
home ground in a championship match.

J. J. Landers runs past Cavan goalkeeper Willie Young after a short-range hand-pass goal in the drawn 1937 All-Ireland final. Landers had the ball in the Cavan net twice in the first 13 minutes, but Kerry were lucky to get a replay.

The old Cusack stand at Croke Park is under construction in the background as Dan O'Keeffe of Kerry and 'Son' Magee of Cavan contest a ball during the drawn 1937 All-Ireland final.

Look, no floodlights! A futuristic Croke Park as visualised by an architect in 1941.

Galway goalkeeper Jimmy McGauran is beaten by Kerry's
Tim O'Leary in the 1938 All-Ireland final after a fine move
involving Mike Doyle and J. J. Landers. Kerry's replay luck
ran out. Not only that, but the final whistle was blown early
and their would-be winning point disallowed.

Croke Park on the day the first Cusack stand was opened
in 1938.

Jack Lynch leads the Cork team in the parade before the 1942 Munster hurling final. Even though Cork were All-Ireland champions for 1941, Tipperary had beaten them in a delayed Munster final which had been postponed because of an outbreak of foot and mouth disease. Cork's 14-point victory margin in 1942 was misleading, for Tipperary led by two points entering the last quarter of the game.

Cork captain Seán Condon celebrates with the Liam McCarthy cup after Cork's fourth successive title in 1944.

Cork completed four All-Ireland hurling titles in a row in 1944, a feat that has never been equalled. Corner-forward Joe Kelly, who scored two goals against Dublin in the final, was also a national sprint silver medallist.

Barrister and Glen Rovers player Jack Lynch won four All-Ireland hurling medals between 1941 and 1944, a football medal in 1945 and a hurling medal in 1946, thus earning a unique six in a row. It might have been seven had not Kilkenny denied Cork with a late point in 1947.

Jack Lynch sans hurley in the 1948 National Hurling League final against Tipperary. He had been elected to the Dáil in the general election of February 1948 and was one of a handful of sitting TDs to have ever appeared on the field after their election. He would go on to serve as taoiseach in 1966–73 and 1977–79. Tipperary goalkeeper Tony Reddan is said to have told Lynch after one encounter: 'Do that again, Lynch, and there will be a by-election.'

Cork against Tipperary in the 1945 Munster hurling championship.

Legendary trainer Jim 'Tough' Barry gives a fiery half-time speech during the 1946 Munster hurling final between Cork and Limerick. 'Tough' trained every Cork team from 1912 to 1966. 'Cork are like mushrooms: they can come overnight', he once said.

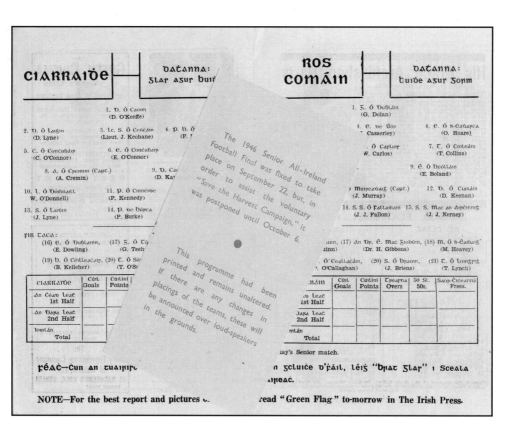

The 1946 All-Ireland football final was postponed to allow would-be spectators to participate in a national emergency save-the-harvest campaign, as an unusually wet summer meant that crops were still in the fields. A slip was inserted in the match programme noting the change of date.

Eddie Walsh tussles for the ball with a Roscommon forward in the 1946 All-Ireland final. Kerry forced a draw with two dramatic late goals.

Tipperary goalkeeper Tony Reddan in action against Clare.

Regarded by some as the greatest hurling final ever, this point from a sideline ball by Christy Ring in the second half set up a cracking finish for the 1947 All-Ireland hurling final. While Mossie O'Riordan and Joe Kelly rattled in Cork goals, Kilkenny patiently picked off their points, including four at the end by Terry Leahy for a one-point victory.

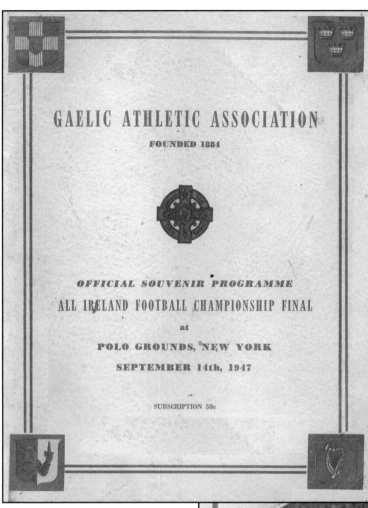

GAELIC ATHLETIC ASSOCIATION

FOUNDED 1884

OFFICIAL SOUVENIR PROGRAMME

ALL IRELAND FOOTBALL CHAMPIONSHIP FINAL

at

POLO GROUNDS, NEW YORK

SEPTEMBER 14th, 1947

SUBSCRIPTION 50c

The prospect of playing the 1947 All-Ireland final at the Polo Grounds in New York was first floated by Michael Hamilton. It commemorated the centenary of the worst year of the Great Famine and injected immense interest into the 1947 championship and Gaelic football in general. The teams travelled by the new transatlantic air service to New York. Substitutes had to travel by ship.

The renowned fielding skills of the Kerry team of the 1940s, seen here in the 1947 semi-final against Meath, served them well in traditional zoned catch and kick games. Against Antrim in 1946 and Cavan in 1947, however, their tactics were less successful.

The organising committee for the 1947 All-Ireland final included the 1913 Tipperary hurling captain 'Wedger' Meagher and the acting Irish consul general in New York. Back: Patrick C. Downey, Joe Casey, Peter Toal, Joseph F. McLoughlin, James Cotter, Frank McArdle, Martin O'Neill, Stephen O'Connor, James J. Comerford, Patrick J. Grimes, Patrick J. Linehan, 'Wedger' Meagher. Front: Edward Martin, Seán Keating, Col Martin Meaney, Commr James B. Nolan, P. J. O'Keeffe, acting consul general Matthew Murphy, James J. O'Brien, Thomas MacNamara, Dr Thomas Dougherty, John 'Kerry' O'Donnell.

One of four second half goals for Mayo in the dramatic 1948 All-Ireland final. Cavan allowed Mayo to come back from 12 points down to equalise, then won with a late point.

Cavan against Roscommon in the 1947 football semi-final.

The Polo Grounds in New York during the 1951 National Hurling League final. After the success of the 1947 Polo Grounds final, New York teams were invited to play against the visiting National League champions.

Louth against Mayo in the 1950 All-Ireland final.

Cork defend their lines against Tipperary in the 1951 Munster hurling final, one of the best of a legendary series of clashes between the counties at the time. Christy Ring, switched back to midfield, may have had his best ever performance that day. Tipperary changed the six forwards around every minute between the 12th and 22nd minutes of the second half.

Seán Purcell of Tuam Stars and Galway, one of half a dozen contenders for the title of the greatest footballer of all time. When the *Sunday Independent* ran a team of the century poll in 1984, he was the most decisive winner in any position.

Phil 'Gunner' Brady in action for Cavan. His distinctive nickname made him a household name when he played at midfield on the winning 1947–48 All-Ireland teams and at full-back in 1952. He was also the inspiration of Mullahoran teams that dominated football within the county, winning five county championships in uncompromising fashion over a six-year period, 1945–50.

Kilkenny on the attack during the 1950 All-Ireland hurling final. An exchange of goals near the end injected life into the game before Tipperary won by a point.

The throw-in for the best-attended
hurling final of them all, as 84,856
crammed in to see Cork play Wexford
in 1954.

Of the hundreds of ballads written in honour of Gaelic footballers and hurlers, 20 are in honour of Christy Ring, the iconic hurler from Cloyne who spent most of his career with Glen Rovers.

An aerial shot of the Limerick Gaelic Grounds on the day of the 1951 Munster hurling final between Cork and Tipperary. Gate receipts that day, at £6,207, were double the previous record. The attendance was 42,337. Ten years later 60,177 crammed into Limerick for a Munster championship record.

Christy Ring captained Cork to victory in 1953, retrieving his acceptance speech in a slip of paper from inside the Liam McCarthy cup. Ring scored one of his best goals in the match but controversially struck Galway captain Mick Burke off the ball during the game and was in turn struck by a Galway player.

Willie Rackard of Wexford blocks off Cork's Paddy Barry as Nick O'Donnell (Wexford), Bobby Rackard (Wexford) and Éamonn Goulding (Cork) bear down on goal in the 1954 All-Ireland hurling final.

A young Wexford supporter at the 1956 final. Wexford's appeal went beyond the traditional hurling fan base.

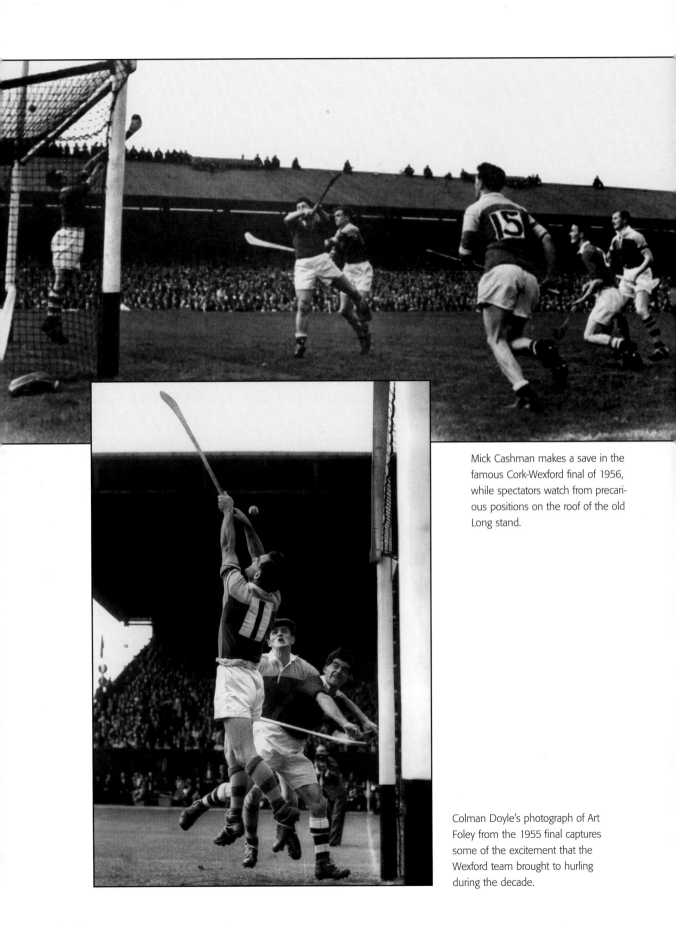

Mick Cashman makes a save in the famous Cork-Wexford final of 1956, while spectators watch from precarious positions on the roof of the old Long stand.

Colman Doyle's photograph of Art Foley from the 1955 final captures some of the excitement that the Wexford team brought to hurling during the decade.

Nicky Rackard as a schoolboy with St Kieran's in Kilkenny. He was as adept at football as at hurling in his younger days.

Wexford eventually won the All-Ireland title for the first time in 45 years with an eight-point win over Galway in 1955. While the teams parade, dozens of spectators are perched precariously on the stand roof.

Despite a heavy defeat against Tipperary in the 1951 All-Ireland final, the emergence of Wexford was creating a stir. Here Nicky Rackard has the ball in the net after only two minutes, and his second goal after ten was a marvellous spectacle.

Ned Wheeler scores a goal for Wexford against Galway in the 1955 final.

Nicky, Bobby and Billy Rackard prior to the 1955 All-Ireland final
with Tom Ryan, Paddy Kehoe, Ned Wheeler and Padge Kehoe.

Art Foley of Wexford clears in the 1956 All-Ireland final against Cork. Despite not being captured on newsreel film, his save from Ring towards the end of the game, and the exchange of words that followed, have both entered GAA folklore.

Christy Ring and Nicky Rackard. Confrontations between the two greatest players of their era brought record crowds to Croke Park for the 1954 and 1956 hurling finals.

Folklore records the conversation between Christy Ring and Mick Mackey for this famous photograph as 'You never lost it', with Mackey replying, 'Neither did you.' Ring was referring to Mackey's attempt to flag a Tipp goal which was not allowed in the first half of a 1957 championship match against Cork. Mackey reached for the green flag when the Cork goalkeeper was bundled over the line in the first half but he had steered the ball around the post before he crossed the line.

Opposite:
Neighbouring counties Kilkenny and Waterford played
a magnificent draw and replay in the 1959 final.

Waterford's Séamus Power is confronted by Cork corner-back
Jim Brohan. Waterford astonished the hurling world with a
17-point rout of All-Ireland champions Tipperary in 1959.

Ned Power of Waterford emerges
with the ball despite the close
attention of Christy Ring in the
1959 Munster final.

Seán Power of Tipperary tussles with Ned Power of Waterford in the 1962 Oireachtas competition. Crowds at this autumn competition peaked at 37,227 for the Wexford-Kilkenny final of 1956.

Kieran Carey of Tipperary holds off Phil Grimes of Waterford as Tipperary goalkeeper Donal O'Brien makes a clearance. The Oireachtas tournament gave a rare opportunity for Dublin audiences to see matches between Munster teams.

Tipperary pressurise Waterford in
the 1960 National Hurling League
final.

Paddy Meegan grabs the ball (the
'man in the cap' as radio commentator Micheál Ó Hehir called him),
and Peter McDermott awaits the
outcome, as Meath defeat Laois in
the 1951 Leinster final. Two Meath
goals before Laois had scored
ensured it was a one-sided contest.

Meath pile pressure on the
Kerry goal in the 1954 All-
Ireland final. Eventually Tom
Moriarty's 50th minute goal
sealed victory for Kerry.

Brian Smyth in
possession for
Meath against
Kerry in 1954.

Paddy O'Brien's performance at full-back laid the foundation for the 1954 All-Ireland victory over Kerry. When Dublin's Kevin Heffernan worked a way round him in the 1955 Leinster final, it was the first indication of the tactical nous of the future team manager.

Meath against Kerry in the 1954 All-Ireland football
final. A great second half performance brought Meath
a six-point victory.

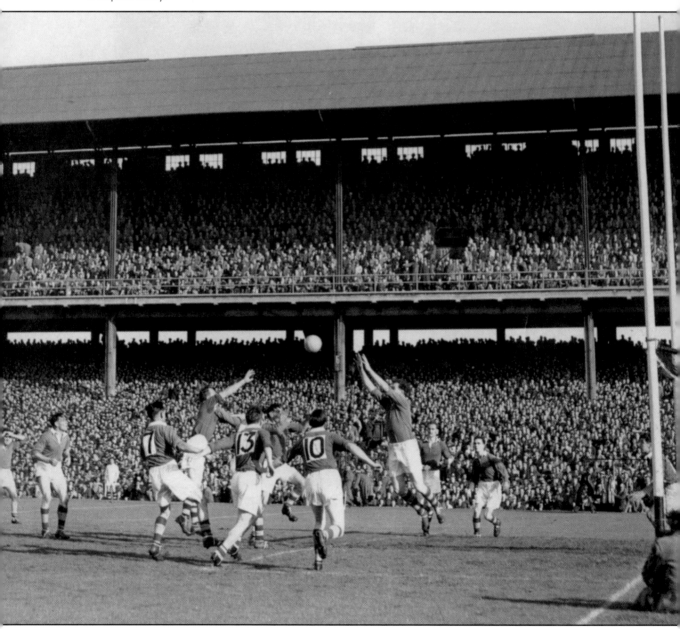

The GAA launched its first youth annual in 1958, interspersing instructional articles by past stars such as Mick Mackey with articles on the development of jet flight and discourses in Irish.

The terrible twins, Frankie Stockwell and Seán Purcell, inspired Galway's 1956 football final victory over Cork. Here Jack Mangan is presented with the Sam Maguire cup in chaotic scenes under the old Hogan stand.

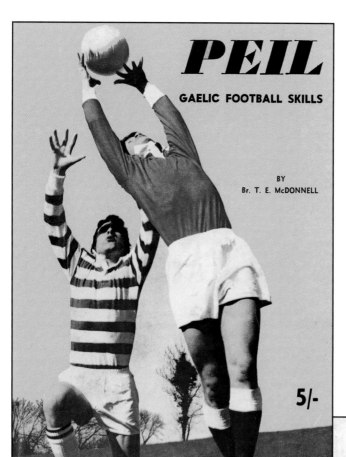

Peil, by Brother T. E. McDonnell, was part of the first coaching initiative in the early 1960s which included two films.

A press photographer gets scattered by a hurler in a 1957 championship match.

The radio 'voice of the GAA' in a pre-television age, Micheál Ó Hehir was the son of the coach to Clare's 1917 All-Ireland team. A civil servant by profession, he started his broadcasting career at the 1938 All-Ireland semi-final.

Corkman Pádraig Ó Caoimh was the GAA secretary general from 1929, having defeated Frank Burke in a contest for the position.

Shifting seats into position before the opening of the second Hogan stand in 1959.

Pádraig Ó Caoimh, Seán Ó Síocháin and other members of the staff of Croke Park in 1958.

The reconstruction of the Hogan stand was
one of the major construction projects in
Dublin during the recessionary 1950s.

Testing the Hogan stand before it was
opened for the 1959 Railway Cup finals.

chapter five

New Colours, New Thoughts

In 1956 the polemicist and future politician Conor Cruise O'Brien wrote that the GAA was 'one of the most important mass movements in European history'. Significantly, he added that 'its importance hadn't been understood yet'.

In the 35 years since Ireland's partial independence the association had asserted its place at the heart of Irish social and cultural life. Attendances at matches dwarfed those of other sports. Its parish network of 2,815 clubs was impenetrable.

Even a British-induced ban on international competition had made little impact on its sister athletics body, the NACA, who continued to organise popular athletics while the eight Dublin-based clubs recognised by England's AAA selected the Olympic team from among their members. When American-based athletes like Ronnie Delany and Noel Carroll were enabled to participate, Ireland started winning athletics medals in international arenas once more.

At a time of economic decline, the Gaelic Athletic Association was planning a new Hogan stand, the first cantilevered structure in the country.

In contrast with the problematic Cusack stand development of two decades earlier, it was opened on schedule in 1959 to commemorate the 75th anniversary of the association.

It was the only major construction project in Dublin that year and made Croke Park by far the biggest sports venue in the country. Work was about to begin also on another large GAA stadium in Belfast.

The new stadium provided a home, not just for All-Ireland finals, but for the huge pageants to commemorate Ireland's historical, spiritual and cultural occasions. Over 90,000 gathered for the anniversary of the Pioneer Total Abstinence Association.

Another massive crowd gathered for Mass to celebrate the 1,500th anniversary of St Patrick's assumed death-date, celebrated by Dublin's famously rigorist Catholic Archbishop, John Charles McQuaid.

The pageantry of sport, Church and state were virtually indistinguishable. Until 1963 the crowd at Croke Park joined in a rousing chorus of 'Faith of Our Fathers' before the All-Ireland final, an unconscious (or maybe not) echo of the 'Abide With Me' sung at English FA Cup finals in Wembley.

The patron of the association, the Archbishop of Cashel, or a bishop from one of the competing counties, was invited to throw in the ball for matches until the mid-1960s, leading to a few chaotic scenes at the start of big matches, including at least one collision between a player and a bewildered bishop.

In 1966, Croke Park was again chosen for a major pageant commemorating the 50th anniversary of the Easter Rebellion of 1916, the revolution in which so many GAA members had fought.

But the years since 1916 had been fraught with difficulties. Ireland was still partitioned. The GAA's progress was made against a background of national stagnation. The 1950s had been a bad decade for Ireland and the high ideals of the founders of the Irish state hadn't been delivered.

The country was running a trade deficit and emigration was at the highest levels since before the British left.

Entire football teams were known to leave at this time. The decision of five of the Ballyduff hurling team to emigrate together on 2 February 1958 inspired John B. Keane to write the play *Many Young Men of Twenty*.

Even as the seats at the new Hogan stand were put in place for an inter-provincial match on opening day, T. K. Whitaker was drawing up a new economic policy for the new government led by Seán Lemass. It included a provision that Ireland should apply to join the infant European Economic Community.

In Whitaker's home county of Down something else was stirring. A group of young footballers were getting together to rethink the game of Gaelic football and how it should be played.

By the start of the 1960s Ulster had just five All-Ireland titles, all of them won by Cavan. None of them had been won by footballers from the six counties that had found themselves under the Stormont regime after 1922.

It was a political climate where Catholics were not welcome, and especially those Catholics (and a small but significant number of their Protestant colleagues) who played Gaelic football.

Within these communities the playing of GAA was an issue of identity as well as sport. Their efforts had brought precious little success at national level.

Antrim had come close. They had qualified for finals in 1911 and 1912. They were deprived of what might have been an All-Ireland success in 1946 by a Kerry team who roughed them up and disrupted the classical hand-passing style devised by Alf Murray, who had backboned the success of the Ulster team in the 1943 Railway Cup.

In 1951 they had come closer still to a final, losing by a mere two points and having a goal disallowed.

Armagh in 1953 had failed in the final against Kerry, due to a series of injuries to key players and also, and less significantly, a missed penalty for which Bill McCorry was blamed for decades afterwards.

Derry had been deprived of an All-Ireland by an uncharacteristic defensive lapse in 1958.

When Down succeeded in 1960, a strange symbolism became attached to the taking of the Sam Maguire cup across a border which the GAA, in common with the vast majority of Irish sports bodies, did not recognise.

One of the important influences which came to shape the Down team was the successful Queen's University team of 1958, which had captured the university's first Sigerson cup.

Players like Seán O'Neill brought a new approach to the game. In the year Queen's won the Sigerson, Éamonn O'Sullivan, the son of the 1891 Laune Rangers captain, had produced his classic *The Art and Science of Gaelic Football*. It laid down the key to football success: zoned line-outs, man marking, and the delivery of the ball into space where a successful fielder could outjump a back.

Down were not the first to attempt to introduce new concepts. Kildare in the 1920s, Antrim in the 1940s and Dublin in the 1950s had all challenged the Kerry system without enjoying lasting success.

This Down team played with six interchangeable forwards and introduced off-the-ball running. They worked to create space in front of their opponent's goal. And they brought in an outsider to coach the team, Peter McDermott of Meath.

Even such oddities as track suits were hardly ever seen at GAA grounds until Down arrived. In Kerry they joked about the boy who wanted to know when the Down players would take their pyjamas off.

Down won the 1959 Ulster title but lost the All-Ireland semi-final when Paddy Doherty missed a penalty. They then beat Cavan in the National League final of 1960 in front of a record 49,451 spectators in Croke Park in May.

The following September they won the Sam Maguire cup with two quick-fire goals against Kerry, from Dan McCartan and a Paddy Doherty penalty.

It was one of the biggest home-comings in Gaelic history, with a special stop on the border to reflect on the symbolic value of it all.

Offaly felt they should have beaten Down in the 1960 All-Ireland semi-final, but they got their chance a year later.

The prospect brought a record 90,556 spectators to the final of 1961, crammed into Croke Park with little regard for the comfort of those squashed on the terraces.

Down goalkeeper Éamon McKay punches clear under pressure from Donie O'Hanlon and Tommy Greene. A record 90,556 attended the 1961 All-Ireland final between Down and Offaly.

Down fell six points behind but scored three goals before half-time and went on to win the match.

Offaly had a famous penalty request turned down, when Harry Green was apparently dragged to the ground by two Down defenders.

Television had been around for over 20 years, but the GAA could count the number of games that had been televised on one hand.

In 1950 a Birmingham television crew recorded a match between John Mitchel's of Birmingham and Naomh Mhuire of London for broadcast the following weekend. A hurling match in Gaelic Park, New York, in 1951 was televised.

Television had arrived in Ireland with the introduction of an hour of programming a week from Belfast in 1952. Highlights of the 1953 Fitzgibbon final in Belfast were recorded for broadcast on the BBC the following evening, the first time GAA had ever been seen on television in Ireland.

The popularity of the Belfast programme and the emergence of an independent provincial station, Ulster TV, in October 1959 caused the Irish government to re-examine its attitude to television, one minister having declared it 'a luxury we can well do without' as late as 1955.

When Ireland's first indigenous television station, the government-owned Telefís Éireann was eventually set up in 1961, Raidió Éireann's GAA commentator Micheál Ó Hehir was appointed head of sport.

Keen to become involved, the GAA granted live television rights for the All-Ireland finals, semi-finals and Railway Cup finals at a nominal cost of £10. The first RTÉ broadcast of Gaelic games, the 1962 All-Ireland semi-final between Dublin and Kerry, became almost a national event in itself, attracting a then record 100,000 viewers, neighbours and friends gathering in the comparatively few households which had televisions amid scenes that recalled the early days of radio.

They saw a great performance from the Valentia Island midfielder Mick O'Connell and a Kerry victory thanks to first half goals from Tom Long and Garry McMahon.

The first televised hurling final saw one of the most explosive starts to a game ever, when Tipperary's Tom Moloughney had the ball in the Wexford net in the first minute and Moloughney scored a second direct from the puck-out. It helped inspire Tipperary to a two-point victory. By way of contrast, the first televised All-Ireland final may have been the worst of all time. 'Undistinguished, unexciting, cheerless and insipid' was sportswriter John D. Hickey's verdict of Kerry's victory over Roscommon.

Dublin brought Des Ferguson back from retirement and won another title in 1963. The game produced 52 frees, and at one stage the referee appeared to award a penalty to Galway then changed his mind, before Dublin won by two points. When Dublin went on to play Down in the 1964 National Football League final, a record 70,125 turned up to watch.

Galway returned to win three in a row, with Mattie McDonagh martialling the attack that beat Kerry twice and then Meath, with Cyril and John Dunne popping over the points.

Live television was here to stay. The BBC in Belfast also saw potential in the huge interest that Gaelic games generated and broadcast the Ulster championship 1966 final between Down and Donegal.

It was a bad choice, a ragged 57-free match won with a penalty goal from Seán O'Neill after the Donegal full-back picked the ball up in the square three minutes from the end.

Popular telecasting was still a long way away and was severely limited in the scope of the games and the quality of the coverage until the arrival of an outside broadcast unit in 1976 and the introduction of RTÉ's *Sunday Game* highlights programme in 1979. As in radio broadcasting, the GAA was the first Irish sporting body to embrace the new medium.

● ● ●

Transatlantic links were strengthened by new airline connections between Ireland and its diaspora. In June 1960 the first direct passenger flight left Shannon for New York.

In the days before low-cost airlines and mass international tourism, GAA players loved the glamour of being able to play their games abroad.

Famous tours were widely reported on both sides of the Atlantic, such as that of the Tipperary hurlers in 1926 and the Kerry footballers in 1927, when New York won the 'World Championship' by 3-11 to 1-7 before 30,000 spectators in the New York Giants baseball stadium, and in 1931 when they played before a crowd of 60,000.

After 1958 London county board staged an annual Whit weekend challenge in Wembley Stadium which attracted large attendances of immigrants, peaking at 42,500 for games between Kerry and Cavan (football) and Kilkenny and Tipperary (hurling) in 1963.

But it was the prospect of playing in the slightly dishevelled surroundings of Gaelic Park in New York's Bronx district that excited Irish players the most. The owners of the lease seemed more interested in the upkeep of the bar facilities than the upkeep of the ground, but for the largely rural hurlers and footballers of Ireland it was a chance for free travel and international competition.

Between 1954 and 1960 annual matches between National League champions and New York were played for the St Brendan's cup, won twice by the Americans, the footballers in 1954 and the hurlers in 1958.

Then between 1963 and 1970 the National League winners were sent out to play New York in Gaelic Park.

Jim McCartan scores a goal for Down against Offaly in the 1961 All-Ireland final.

For the teams who won the honour, Cork, Kilkenny, Tipperary and Waterford hurlers, and Dublin, Galway and Kerry footballers, it was largely a recreational exercise, a small reward for sportsmen who were amateurs.

But the appetite for international travel among GAA teams was growing. Kerry and Meath even arranged world tours that brought them to Australia at the end of the decade. An Australian team came to Ireland in 1968, a taste of what might happen if real international links could be established with Australian Rules football in Melbourne, the first cousin of Gaelic football.

It was not until the All Stars awards were introduced that the American tour was regularised on an official basis by the GAA. By the mid-1970s even that arrangement was running out of options.

Transatlantic arrangements were not always cordial. The Americans insisted on their own rules, including the use of a hooter to call the end of the game, and occasionally blackballed referees of whom they did not approve.

The New York board was not even affiliated to the GAA central council between 1975 and 1988.

These annual matches in New York created a new unforeseen problem for successful GAA teams — jet-lag. Galway players still wonder whether their American trip in May of 1967 led to their surprise exit in the Connacht semi-final as they were chasing four All-Irelands in a row.

Mayo were convincing winners after P. J. and Willie Loftus dominated the midfield, and then beat Leitrim in the most one-sided Connacht final of all time.

A shot from Down's Jim McCartan on the Offaly goal during the five-goal first half in the 1961 All-Ireland final.

It paved the way for new All-Ireland champions. Cork trailed Cavan through most of the All-Ireland semi-final before winning with a late penalty.

Meath might have reached the 1964 All-Ireland final had not Jack Quinn's goal been controversially disallowed. They were beaten in the 1966 final, but Terry Kearns secured the Sam Maguire when he managed to sneak unnoticed behind the backline to punch the ball to the net from five yards out on the right-hand side.

All of Dublin's six All-Ireland hurling championships had been won by migrant hurlers from Cork, Tipperary, Kilkenny and other counties, men like Tommy Daly, Mick Gill, Pat 'Fowler' McInerney, Garret Howard, Mattie Power and Jim 'Builder' Walsh.

Only one Dublin-born player has ever won an All-Ireland hurling medal, 1938 star Jim Byrne of Eoghan Ruadh.

But in 1961 they won the Leinster championship with a home-grown team based around the northern suburb of Marino and the St Vincent's club.

Their four previous campaigns had brought three defeats in semi-final replays and another by a last-minute goal in the Leinster final.

In 1961 they devised a roving full-forward on the lines of their 1955 football colleagues. Liam Shannon took out Wexford full-back Nick O'Donnell, the hero of Wexford's 1960 All-Ireland victory over Tipperary. The result was a seven-goal spree in the Leinster final and a place for Dublin in the All-Ireland final against Tipperary.

Dublin came desperately close to winning, losing by a point after leading by four points and missing an equalising chance in the last minute. It was to be their last Leinster title. Des Foley often pondered afterwards how different the profile of hurling in the city might have been, had they won that day.

Tipperary now seemed unstoppable. With midfield hero Jimmy Doyle as team captain, they defeated Wexford in that 1962 two-goals-in-the-first-minute final.

They had a goal disallowed and missed two spectacular chances in the 1963 Munster final when they were beaten by Waterford. That may have cost them five in a row.

It set up another All-Ireland between neighbours Waterford and Kilkenny, victors over Dublin in the Leinster final, thanks to a little dog which interrupted play in injury time in the first half, and directly caused a goal for Johnny McGovern.

The neighbours served up another memorable final. Waterford scored six goals, came back from 11 points down and still lost.

Offaly goalkeeper and captain Willie Nolan punches clear against Down.

It was just an aberration in the Tipperary story. In 1964 and 1965 they demolished all comers with six of the most decisive championship displays in hurling history, beating Clare by 20 points in the 1964 Munster championship, Cork by 14 points in the Munster final, Kilkenny by 11 points in the 1964 All-Ireland final, Clare by 11 points in the 1965 Munster championship, Cork by 18 points in the Munster final, and Wexford by 12 points in the 1965 All-Ireland final.

Then when all seemed set for another Tipp spree, up popped 21-year-old Éamonn Cregan from Limerick. He scored 3-5 as Limerick dumped Tipp out of the first round of the 1966 championship.

Cork beat Limerick and went on to the Munster final of 1966, which will be remembered for one of the greatest goals of the era. With ten minutes to go Waterford's Larry Guinan travelled 80 yards with the ball on his hurley and crashed it to the Cork net. Cork were underdogs in the All-Ireland final. It was even rumoured they would bring Christy Ring out of retirement for the game. When they beat Kilkenny with an overwhelming second half display Jim 'Tough' Barry, trainer since the 1920s, wept on the field.

Tipperary were back in the All-Ireland finals of 1967 and 1968, but lost to Kilkenny and Wexford, who were building up a nice rivalry of their own.

● ● ●

For 19 of the 20 years between 1960 and 1980, Kilkenny and Wexford met in every final of the Leinster hurling championship.

Honours were almost even, 11 wins for Kilkenny, eight for Wexford, and one draw.

Players got to mark each other year after year, to know their strengths and weaknesses and their pet likes and dislikes. And the public got to see some spectacular hurling and thrilling finishes. Ten of the matches finished with a winning margin of less than four points. On 12 occasions the team who led at half-time were beaten.

Passions ran high. The referee had to be escorted to the dressing room after the 1966 final when aggrieved Wexford supporters surrounded him.

In 1968 Wexford won by a point after Kilkenny's Eddie Keher missed a chance from the left sideline 40 yards out in the last minute.

In 1972 fortunes fluctuated so wildly that Kilkenny led by eight points, then Wexford led by ten, before the match finished even.

In 1973 it was Kilkenny's turn to protest. The ball seemed to cross the sideline, Jack Berry got his stick to it, the umpire signalled wide, and whilst some Wexford players protested, the referee saw the ball in the net and the other umpire signalling a goal.

In 1978, just the thickness of the post prevented Wexford from beating Kilkenny for the third year in succession.

The best final of all was reckoned to be 1974, when 14-man Wexford stormed back into the game before Kilkenny won by a single point, 6-13 to 2-24, thanks to Eddie Keher's winning point from an acute angle.

These Barrow-bank battles were to be fondly recalled for decades.

● ● ●

Out of such a tumultuous Leinster final Kilkenny emerged in 1967, coming back from eight points down against Wexford to win by seven points. They then laid a 45-year Tipperary bogey with the help of three goals at vital stages of the All-Ireland final.

The sides met again in a bad-tempered National League final. When Ollie Walsh was suspended for six months after an incident with John Flanagan, Kilkenny threatened to pull out of the 1968 championship altogether.

Instead, a new red-haired Wexford hero called Tony Doran put them out of the championship, scoring a goal in the Leinster final which Wexford won by a single point, and two more goals in the All-Ireland final when they beat Tipperary with a blistering second half display.

Those Wexford players didn't have any organised training until the championship began, but things were changing.

The GAA was organising coaching courses for the first time. Two films, *Peil* and *Christy Ring*, were produced in 1964 to demonstrate the skills of the game.

The top stars of the time were unwilling to settle for the standards of a previous generation and wanted more. The training camps that had been a feature of GAA preparations for All-Ireland finals in the 1930s and 1940s had been abandoned. Better transport meant that county players could get together more often in the run-up to big matches.

The proponents of skills coaching and high levels of fitness included players like Justin McCarthy of Cork, Éamonn Cregan of Limerick, Michael 'Babs' Keating of Tipperary, Kevin Heffernan of Dublin, Eugene McGee of Longford and Mick O'Dwyer of Kerry.

Down star footballer and Gormanstown College teacher Joe Lennon was the author of two books on GAA coaching in the 1960s, and became a vociferous campaigner for changes in the playing rules.

In 1968 the Dublin government's Minister for Education Donogh O'Malley introduced free education at secondary level. The numbers of students from rural Ireland qualifying for a university education swelled fivefold in as many years.

They brought a desire for better organised sport and higher coaching standards. The GAA set up its first coaching division and organised its first coaches.

By the end of the decade the first Gaelic players were attending physical education colleges in England such as Strawberry Hill.

A little county from Leinster was winning the hearts of football followers in 1968. Longford won their first

Dublin against Galway in the 1963 All-Ireland final. Dublin got their winning goal from Gerry Davey nine minutes into the second half.

Leinster title by beating Laois. Longford even led Kerry by a point in the All-Ireland semi-final, when Jackie Devine scored a goal from a penalty, before Kerry moved up a gear and put paid to their dreams.

The Sam Maguire Cup ended up in Ulster. Down kept their 100 per cent record in finals, thanks to a dramatic two-goal start to their 1968 final against Kerry. After six minutes Seán O'Neill got the inside of his boot to a rebounding ball after Rooney hit the post. Two minutes later John Murphy got another goal, following confusion in the Kerry goalmouth.

Down's Brian Morgan played with a fractured jaw. The teams were accorded a civic reception by the Lord Mayor of Belfast, despite unionist protests.

The GAA congress of 1971 did not debate the most important business it had on hand. The debate was already over. The ban on any members playing rival games was to go.

The ban on players of rival sports, association and rugby football, hockey, tennis, but not equestrian sports, rowing, squash, boxing or basketball, was the subject of 70 years of vehement internal debate within the GAA.

A campaign by Dublin delegate Tom Woulfe kept it on the agenda.

What sports counted as rivals? What sports didn't? Should it apply just to sports of foreign origin, those that impinged on the Irish national ideal? The debate looks awkward and ill conceived to anyone looking back on it now.

John D. Hickey wrote in 1962: 'In many places, and they are not all in Dublin, the rule is more honoured in the breach than in the observance. As matters stand, the rule is a mockery rather than the cornerstone of the association. All over the country the rules are openly flouted.'

The suspension of Waterford hurler Tom Cheasty for attending a dance sponsored by the local soccer club further discredited the ban in 1963. It cost him a National League medal which was eventually awarded retrospectively in 1996. When Mick O'Connell was photographed by the *Irish Independent* newspaper attending a soccer match in 1969, there was no attempt to cite him.

A commission was set up to report to the 1971 congress on the question as to whether the ban should be retained in the 1970s. Amazingly, it found no reasons for keeping the ban.

As GAA president Pat Fanning mentioned in his speech to the congress, 'Not a funeral note was sounded.'

Within two months of the ban's removal, Gerry Mitchell and David Pugh of Sligo Rovers became the first soccer players to play inter-county GAA.

Seven years later Dublin footballer Kevin Moran became the first to play championship GAA at inter-county level and top-flight football for a major English soccer club, Manchester United, in the same season.

In 1988 Moran played for Ireland in the finals of the European championship. A former All-Ireland minor hurling medallist, Niall Quinn, and another Gaelic footballer, Stephen Staunton, played for Ireland at the 1990, 1994 and 2002 World Cup finals.

As a result of the removal of the ban, GAA schools embraced rugby and soccer. So far no traditional rugby school has started playing GAA.

● ● ●

A year later camogie dropped its own foreign games rule, which had banned players of hockey. Nancy O'Driscoll of Cork represented Munster at both hockey and camogie in 1974. Mary Geaney, goalkeeper of the Irish hockey team that won the Inter-Continental cup in Kuala Lumpur in 1983, was later secretary of the Kerry camogie board.

The 1972 convention also traded the black stockings and gym slips of the previous generation for more modern gear.

Competitive camogie was expanding fast. The All-Ireland club championship was introduced in 1964, the junior championship followed in 1968, the colleges championship started in 1969–70, the minor championship, the junior colleges championship and Féile na nGael in 1974, the National League in 1977, and the National Junior League in 1980.

Crucially, the championship was changed from the old provincial system to an open draw in 1973, the year after colleges star Angela Downey made her inter-county debut for Kilkenny.

Galway's 1964 team and subs which won the first leg of three in a row.

It was Downey who came to dominate the decade as Kilkenny emerged from the shadow of Cork's four-in-a-row team to win three All-Irelands in a row of their own, then embarked on a seven in a row from 1985.

Helena O'Neill's spectacular angled equalising point in 1973, when Kilkenny thwarted Cork's bid for five in a row, was compared with Terry Leahy's equalising point in 1947. Camogie had a folklore of its own at last.

● ● ●

Women were playing football at All-Ireland level for the first time. Representatives from Galway, Kerry, Offaly and Tipperary created Cumann Peile Gael na mBan at a consciously footstepped foundation meeting at Hayes's Hotel in Thurles in 1974.

Offaly, south Tipperary, north Cork and west Waterford were the early strongholds of the game. As well as the four founders, Cork, Laois, Roscommon and Waterford also entered the first championship.

Tournaments in Ballycommon, Tullamore, Clonmel and Dungarvan in 1968 led to the new game's biggest

Mattie McDonagh played hurling for Roscommon and football for Galway as a minor. He was one of the outstanding players in Galway's three-in-a-row team of 1964–66.

innovation, when women were permitted to lift the ball directly off the ground. Unlike camogie, a full-sized pitch was used.

A well-organised Tipperary team, trained at Rockwell College by John O'Donovan, won the first two All-Irelands in 1974 and 1975.

But it was football powerhouse Kerry which dominated women's football in the 1980s, winning nine consecutive All-Ireland championships with star players such as nine-times All Star Mary Jo Curran, the unrelated goalkeeper Kathleen Curran, and Annette Walsh.

Not everyone was anxious to embrace change. Events in Northern Ireland took an ugly turn in July 1970 when British forces turned their guns on the people they had come to protect. After the Falls Road curfew, Northern Ireland's political impasse turned violent.

The GAA found itself being targeted by British and loyalist paramilitary forces who were moving against the nationalist community and their civil rights movement.

Stories of harassment emerged from each of the six counties. British forces forcibly occupied GAA grounds across the province, including the major stadium which had staged the 1970 Ulster final, Casement Park in Belfast. A young man protesting the occupation of McCrory Park in Derry, Edward Doherty, was shot dead.

In May 1972 during a match between Crossmaglen and Silverbridge, a helicopter landed in the middle of the pitch, a young British soldier dismounted and pushed his rifle butt into the face of Silverbridge player Patrick Tenyson. Worse was to follow. The spectator area was occupied in 1974 and much of the remaining land in 1976.

The GAA grounds in Crossmaglen were to remain occupied for 37 years.

Soldiers intervened to prevent games taking place and stopped teams on their way to training.

In July 1972 Frank Corr, a leading referee, Antrim hurling selector and secretary of the south Antrim board, was shot dead.

He was the first of over 40 people to die in Northern Ireland because of their involvement with the GAA.

The GAA had another problem to solve — at 60 minutes matches were regarded as too short. They decided to add 20 minutes on to the length of provincial finals, All-Ireland semi-finals and finals. That meant that for five years, until matches were standardised at 70 minutes, teams got to play for 20 minutes more in big matches.

It led to enormous scoring sprees. Cork beat Wexford in the 1970 All-Ireland hurling final by 6-21 to 5-10. Meath beat Offaly in the Leinster football final by 2-22 to 5-12.

Kerry too were enjoying the extra 20 minutes of play, claiming it suited their principle of allowing the ball to do all the work.

'The catch and kick game that Kerry play is ten years out of date', Down schoolteacher Joe Lennon had written in 1968. When Kerry beat Meath to take the All-Ireland of 1970, Tadhgie Lyne, selector and uncle of Pat Spillane, retorted that the result was 'our answer to the Gormanstown professors and their blackboard tactics'.

Kerry outstayed Meath in the All-Ireland final, but Offaly proved an even more successful 80-minute football team, winning All-Ireland finals in 1971 and 1972 thanks to the free-taking of Tony McTeague from Ferbane and the defensive obtuseness of Paddy McCormack, proclaimed in the county's tribute song as 'the iron man from Rhode'.

A young Cork team, which had been cleaning up almost all the available minor and under-21 All-Ireland titles, re-emerged to win the All-Ireland with one of the classiest displays of all time.

Their teenage hero, Jimmy Barry Murphy, who scored two goals, had already a hatful of medals and was equally dextrous at football and hurling. Brian Murphy too was to win medals at minor, under-21 and senior level at both hurling and football.

It appeared that the prevailing colour of the new decade, in football and hurling, would be red.

Not so. Fr Tommy Maher of St Kieran's College took charge of the Kilkenny hurling team in 1971 and immediately set about eroding the narrow lead of its more resourceful rivals, Cork and Tipperary, on hurling's honours list.

He fashioned a championship team around one of the finest sharpshooters in the history of the game, Eddie Keher, with the commanding figures of Pat Henderson and Pat Delaney in key positions. True, Kilkenny lost two All-Ireland finals to Tipperary in 1971, victims of two freakish goals on a day Babs Keating discarded his boots, and to Limerick in 1973 on a rainy day when they were decimated by injury. But they will be remembered for their three All-Irelands over a five-year period.

Elegant and majestic, shy perfectionist Mick O'Connell from Valentia Island emerged as the outstanding footballer of the 1960s. The legend that he rowed to training from his island home in the early days added a mystical dimension to his personality. O'Connell's generation was succeeded by an even more talented Kerry team.

The day before they beat Galway in 1975, Liam 'Chunky' O'Brien had two teeth extracted and had to call a doctor at 1 o'clock on Sunday morning to stop a gum haemorrhage. He scored five points in the final.

It was Galway's first return to a hurling final after an unhappy ten years in the Munster championship. It had taken ten years for them to be admitted, but when they were there they won just one match in ten years. Now, inspired by Maynooth Fitzgibbon cup medallists Iggy Clarke and Seán Silke, they reached the All-Ireland finals of 1975 and 1979, only to lose heavily on each occasion.

Clarke, the hurling priest, was particularly interested in laying one shibboleth. The story went that a priest noticed that some of the Galway hurling team were skiving off early from Mass on Sunday morning, on their way to Dublin to play a big match. He put a curse on them, that they would never win another All-Ireland (they were champions in 1923). The curse became part of Galway folklore.

Like Galway, Clare were showing promise but delivering only in the less exalted circumstances of the National League. With players like Ger Loughnane on board, they suffered heartbreak in the Munster finals of 1976 and 1977 at the hands of Cork.

GAA officials were always uncomfortable with the cult of the individual star. The fans did not concur.

In 1963 a weekly newspaper, the *Gaelic Weekly*, had suggested that 15 players, one in each position, should be given an award at the end of the year to acknowledge their high standards of play.

The All Star scheme, as it became known, was put on a regular footing in 1970 when Mick Dunne, a former *Irish Press* and RTÉ journalist, arranged a selection panel of national sportswriters and a sponsor.

The teams were also rewarded with a promotional tour of the US during which they played exhibition matches against the All-Ireland champions from the 1970s until the 1990s, when the tour petered out after two visits to the Toronto Skydome. In later years an All Star tour travelled to Argentina, Dubai and Hong Kong.

The all-time All Star awards were first presented in 1980 to hurler Mick Mackey and footballer Larry Stanley.

Since then the All Star awards have passed through four separate sponsors. The scheme has unfailingly generated debate and occasional controversy and their presentation each November is a highlight of the GAA's social calendar.

The introduction of televised handball in 1973 introduced many Irish people to the country's most successful sporting export and a new set of handballing heroes, Pat Kirby, Dick Lyng and Joey Maher among them.

Down came back to win a third All-Ireland title in 1968. This is the aftermath of Seán O'Neill's goal in the final.

The Irish Amateur Handball Association affiliated with the American AAU which revived the world championship and invited teams from Ireland, Mexico, Canada, Australia and the US to New York in 1964. Subsequent championships were staged in Toronto in 1967 and in 1970 in Croke Park's new 1,800-capacity glass-walled alley, but the championship lapsed for 14 years.

While team handball is recognised as an Olympic sport, an attempt to introduce court handball in 1932 did not succeed and has not been tried since.

Clare man Pat Kirby won the world championship representing Canada in 1970 and later returned to become Irish handballer of the year in 1975, 1976 and 1977.

When the RTÉ Top Ace television tournament began in 1973 and was extended to American and Mexican players in 1980, the rules were altered specially to allow fixed-time games for television.

After 1974 handballers from Canada, Ireland and Mexico competed in the US Handball Association open championships.

The traditional Irish court size was 60 x 30 feet, and the ball a hard leather one, but by the 1940s a soft ball had become more popular. In the 1973–83 period 152 new courts were built in the American size 40 x 20 alongside just nine new 60 x 30 courts.

The GAA was also strengthening its contribution to other areas of Irish culture.

From its early days the association was run by Irish language enthusiasts, and meetings of some bodies such as the Ulster council were held exclusively in Irish. But like the language revival itself, the language was used more for artistic purposes in writing and commentary than for the interpretations of the rule book. Some found the requirement that team lists be filed in Irish an encumbrance.

'Hurling identifies my Irishness,' champion hurler and later coach Justin McCarthy told an interviewer. 'I'm not an Irish speaker, so the game portrays my national spirit, it's so Irish, so unique.'

But unexpectedly at the beginning of the 1970s the GAA made a real contribution to off-field culture, the revival of the traditional set dance.

Gael Linn (since 1954), Cómhaltas Ceoltóirí Éireann (since 1955) and bodies such as the Pipers Club (intermittently since 1900) had been successfully promoting Irish music, song and dance for over a decade when the GAA introduced the Scór competition in 1970.

Scór was devised as a winter activity to broaden the appeal of GAA clubs and bring people into the clubhouses being built throughout the country, an unsophisticated and accessible talent competition.

By picking set dancing among the categories, the GAA sparked off a new movement and touched a vibrant tradition that had been ignored by other organisations which were concerned with the more spectacular Irish step-dancing. By the middle of the 1970s set dancing was enjoying an explosion in interest in areas where it hadn't existed for decades.

At the same time a summer camp movement for primary schoolchildren was established. Féile na nGael is

part competition, part social occasion, involving hundreds of children and their families travelling to different parts of the country to compete in hurling. It was an instant success and was replicated in football.

Defeat by Galway in 1975 helped steady the nerves of Cork hurlers. In the 1976 All-Ireland final they were two points down against Wexford with ten minutes to go, but Jimmy Barry Murphy scored three points as they came through to win by four points.

Wexford had been fortunate to make it at all. Even John Quigley was surprised that a Wexford goal was allowed. He had scored after the referee had blown for a foul.

In the Leinster semi-final they had trailed unfancied Kildare with ten minutes to go, Kildare's attack led by Wexford native Johnny Walsh and the defence manned by the implacable Richie Cullen. It was the high point of Kildare's hurling history. Walsh and Cullen featured on an Ardclough side that defeated Tony Doran's Buffer's Alley in the Leinster club championship later that year.

In 1977 Cork triumphed again. Cork goalkeeper Martin Coleman brought off a match-clinching save from Christy Keogh late in the game and they won by three points.

Galway deprived Sligo of a would-be Connacht championship with a burst in the last eight minutes. It was another ten years before Sligo's outstanding Michael Kerins was to get his provincial medal.

In 1978 they completed three in a row thanks to Jimmy Barry Murphy's goal 13 minutes from the end.

Jack Quinn and Bertie Cunningham of Meath, and Jody Guinning and Matt Connor of Offaly in action in the 1970 Leinster final. When the GAA extended the length of provincial finals to 80 minutes they hardly expected anything as explosive as this match and its record combined score of 7-34.

Galway hadn't gone away, and Cork's four in a row came to grief when Finbarr Gantley and Bernie Forde scored Galway goals in the 1979 semi-final. Galway lost the final by a massive 15 points, losing direction after Liam 'Chunky' O'Brien scored direct from a 70 which spun in off the goalkeeper's chest.

Hurling's profile was in decline. Only 53,535 attended that 1979 final, the lowest in 21 years. By contrast, football's profile could not have been higher, thanks to a renewed rivalry between Dublin and Kerry.

Three titles in four years achieved by Dublin's footballers between 1974 and 1977 has come to be regarded since as a sort of golden age of the cultural life of the capital. It happened somewhat by accident.

The closing sequence of the 1977 semi-final against Kerry, especially the sequence leading to Bernard Brogan's winning goal with three minutes to go, is one of the best-known Gaelic football televised recordings. Nine Dubs won All Star awards after the side won that 1977 All-Ireland, beating Armagh by a record 5-12 to 3-6 on a day when Jimmy Keaveney's personal tally was also a record, 2-6.

The story of Dublin's success pre-dates 1974. Like most of Dublin football since 1949, the 1970s team was formed around the northside suburb of Marino, St Joseph's CBS and St Vincent's club.

Free-taker Jimmy Keaveney, manager Kevin Heffernan and captain (and player-manager in 1977) Tony Hanahoe were all St Vincent's members and the team won the 1977 All-Ireland club title.

After their first county title in 1949, St Vincent's won five Dublin titles and boosted interest in Gaelic football in the capital. Their drawn and replayed county finals with Garda attracted crowds of over 30,000.

Dublin won the 1953 National League with a team of natives for the first time, 14 of them from St Vincent's. The policy yielded a football All-Ireland in 1958 (after a near-miss in 1955, when St Vincent's had 12 on the team) and almost won a hurling All-Ireland in 1961.

The footballers beat Galway in 1963 for their fifteenth title, but ten years later the GAA's profile in the city was in decline despite the fact that the population was bigger. At the time the GAA was founded, Dublin city's population was 245,000; the county had 419,000.

In 1971 it was 852,000, one-sixth of the population of the island, with no enduring sporting culture to embrace.

One man was determined to change that. After Dublin were beaten by Louth in the 1973 championship, the full-forward of 20 years earlier, Kevin Heffernan, came into the dressing room in Navan, stood up on a timber bench and said he would get a team that was going to win

Jimmy Grey, the then chairman of the Dublin board, felt there was no future for the old, unwieldy five-man selection committee and persuaded his board to agree to the appointment of just three selectors, Kevin Heffernan, Donal Colfer and Lorcan Redmond.

Heffernan became identified with a new movement in the city, as motivator and manager. He recalls: 'We wanted to create in the players a sense that they had an asset which nobody else had. We were going to make them the fittest team in the country. Winning itself would be a boost but it was more important in justifying our emphasis on the fitness. Loyalty to each other was hugely important in our approach.'

Dublin's first match was against Wexford, the curtain-raiser for the 1974 National League final between Kerry and Roscommon.

One of the players, David Hickey, recalled: 'It seemed to me that we were the comedy sketch going on before the main act.'

Dublin scraped through, thanks to a goal by Leslie Deegan. Leslie who? Yes, the forgotten hero, another GAA character, the player who intervenes, changes the course of sporting history and disappears again into the background while others share the bounty of his intervention.

It was clear from the Wexford match that Dublin needed a free-taker. Heffernan thought of 1965 Leinster final hero, Jimmy Keaveney, but Keaveney had watched the match from Hill 16, was overweight and out of shape.

Heffernan decided that even if Keaveney only stood and kicked the frees it might be worth having him in the team. He brought Keaveney back, legend has it, on the suggestion of a 7-year-old boy who travelled home from the match with him, Terry Jennings.

● ● ●

Dublin's force gathered momentum, beating Meath by five points in the Leinster final and Cork by six in the All-Ireland semi-final. Paddy Cullen became the

first goalkeeper to save a penalty in an All-Ireland final when he turned Liam Sammon's 52nd minute penalty around the post.

The Dublin team went straight to the heart of the city's culture very quickly with their team of doctors, engineers, a solicitor, an economist, executives and entrepreneurs, a schoolteacher and a publican.

It was also essentially suburban. An old man at the 1974 match derided them as 'a team of culchies from Whitehall and Terenure'.

Dublin fans flocked to Hill 16 with denim shirts and blue scarves and started singing supporters' songs with simple lyrics: 'Come on you boys in blue' or 'We are Dubs'.

It was the first manifestation of GAA fashion at a time when most GAA followers' idea of supporting their team was wearing a crepe cap dyed with colours that ran across your face when it rained.

● ● ●

Down in Kerry, where the rigorous 15-a-side game had been formulated by Dick Fitzgerald and Éamonn O'Sullivan, they watched with interest.

Kerry's under-21 team had been beaten by Cork at Skibbereen in 1973. It led to a rethink about Gaelic football tactics in the county, especially in the wake of Kerry's replay defeat by Offaly in the 1972 All-Ireland.

Like Dublin, the team Kerry fielded in 1975 was the fruit of the Donogh O'Malley secondary education generation. Like Dublin, it was a team of doctors, engineers, solicitors, entrepreneurs, schoolteachers and a publican.

Asked about how the social profile of the game had changed, 1940s hero Paddy Bawn Brosnan from Dingle told an interviewer: 'In our day we had a few farmers, a few fishermen and a college boy to take the frees.'

Their manager was another entrepreneur, Mick O'Dwyer, a teetotaller, non-smoker and fitness fanatic. He was a veteran of four All-Ireland victories and, as he was to point out, much more importantly, of several big match defeats.

O'Dwyer's team was beaten by Meath in the quarter-finals of the National League in 1975. Some Kerry GAA followers wanted him replaced before he embarrassed the county in the championship.

Meath captain Jack Quinn with the cup after the 1970 Leinster football final, one of the highest scoring of all.

Instead, O'Dwyer's Kerry teams went on to win eight All-Ireland titles in 12 years and established themselves as the greatest in the history of the game. In 1981 nine of the team won All Star awards.

'You'll see great individual players,' O'Dwyer says, 'but you won't see a team of that quality again. I don't believe you will anyway.'

The Kerry and Dublin saga inspired mass interest in the game over a five-year period. Their superior fitness resulted in some huge victories over other counties.

Martin Furlong under pressure from Eoin Liston and Pat Spillane during the 1982 All-Ireland final. Furlong's penalty save was as big a contributory factor as Séamus Darby's late goal in unhinging Kerry's bid for five in a row.

Kerry won the 1979 All-Ireland semi-final by 22 points, and semi-finals in 1975 and 1976 by 18 and 19 points.

They beat Clare by 9-21 to 1-9 in the 1979 championship and Laois by 6-11 to nil in a 1978 National League match.

But not everyone was being left behind. Cork might have beaten Kerry in a dramatic Munster final in 1976, had their goal from Colman Corrigan been allowed, or another by Seánie Walsh not counted. Cork opened their new stadium for those matches, but Páirc Uí Chaoimh was unable to handle the huge throng of supporters who came to watch.

Galway in 1976 and Roscommon in 1979 might have denied Dublin their place in the final. Offaly too almost caught Dublin in 1979.

The sides met in four finals and a semi-final in five successive years. Kerry won the first round, beating Dublin with two goals from John Egan on a rainy day in 1975. 'Kerry's attacks were fashioned in the style that Dublin had patented — the ball put in the path of a colleague coming forward at full speed', sportswriter Con Houlihan noted.

Dublin got revenge in 1976, winning by seven points with goals from John McCarthy, Jimmy Keaveney and Brian Mullins.

In 1977 they met in the semi-final. The sides were level five times before the game reached its climax when Tony Hanahoe conjured up victory with his deft distribution to David Hickey and substitute Bernard Brogan for match-winning goals. Con Houlihan described it as 'the best thirty minutes of Gaelic football since you could buy the pint for ninepence'.

In 1978 Dublin took a five-point lead before Kerry barged them aside with five goals, three of them from their bearded new full-forward, Eoin 'Bomber' Liston.

It was Mikey Sheehy who scored what must be the most famous goal in GAA history. Paddy Cullen maintains he was unfairly penalised for his brush with Ger Power. He was protesting the decision when Sheehy sent the ball into the unguarded net.

Con Houlihan, the greatest sportswriter of the generation, described the incident:

Mike Sheehy came running up to take the kick — and suddenly Paddy dashes back like a woman who smells a cake burning. The ball won the race and it curled inside the near post as Paddy crashed into the outside of the net and lay against it like a fireman who had returned to find his station ablaze.

And that was the end of poor Molly Malone. So it was. The champions looked like men who had worked hard and seen their savings plundered by bandits. The great rain robbers were out onto the field for Act Two.

Mike Sheehy scored two goals and six points as Kerry beat Dublin in 1979, and it was four years before Dublin re-emerged from Leinster.

• • •

Kerry had answered the Dublin question. Now they longed to do something that had never been done before, to win five All-Ireland championships in a row.

They came within two minutes of doing so.

Roscommon might have stopped the run in 1980 if they had found a free-taker, having taken an early lead of five points.

Seven players combined for the goal that saw off Offaly in 1981 before Jack O'Shea eventually shot from 14 yards to the net. It was a classic Kerry combination.

Folk group Galleon released a record commemorating Kerry's prospective five in a row in 1982 to go on sale immediately after the match. Offaly manager Eugene McGee got hold of the words and used them in his pre-match pep talk.

The phrase 'impact sub' hadn't been invented at the time, but Offaly substitute Séamus Darby had scored a last-minute goal in a local match for Rhode a few weeks earlier, and when he was slipped on to the field almost unnoticed with two minutes to go, it was clear what Offaly had in mind. The TV commentator didn't know he was on the field.

Darby replaced a half-forward but moved to the full-forward line. Kerry's wing-back fell back into an unfamiliar corner-back position to mark him. The Kerry defender advanced too far to meet an incoming ball and appeared to be nudged as he prepared to collect.

Darby gathered, unmolested, ran five yards and blasted a goal past stranded goalkeeper Charlie Nelligan. Kerry in disarray could not organise their counter-attack. Offaly won their third title with the most famous finishing goal in football history.

• • •

This is what Kerry had done to their opponents in the 1926 and 1946 All-Ireland finals; now it was done to them. And it happened again in the Munster final the following year against Cork. This time Tadhgie Murphy gathered a high free which was bustled into the net off the post two minutes from the end.

'I concentrated on sending it low into the corner of the goal,' Murphy recalled. 'That's where it went, only into the wrong corner.' It hit the post and rebounded into the far corner of the net.

Kerry came back to win three in a row, beating Dublin in 1984 and 1985, and Tyrone in 1986 in a final that was regarded as the finest hour for one of

The outstanding teenager Jimmy Barry Murphy scored two goals for Cork in the 1973 All-Ireland football final. Cork's seven-point win over Galway suggested a new red tide was coming in, but by 1974 it was going out again. Also included are Galway's goal-scorer Johnny Hughes, Tommy Joe Gilmore, Declan Barron and Jack Cosgrove.

the best of that team, Pat Spillane, a notoriously one-footed footballer who won a record nine All Star awards and became a respected TV analyst after his retirement from the game.

Tyrone had won the hearts of the crowd with their attractive style and charismatic players such as Plunkett Donaghy. 'We had to beat 31 and a half counties', Mick O'Dwyer said afterwards.

Dublin's native-born hurling team came close to winning the 1961 All-Ireland final against Tipperary.

Munster. A motion to set up a club championship was rejected by the 1948 congress for the same reason: the calendar was too overcrowded.

The first All-Ireland finals were played in 1971. East Kerry footballers defeated Bryansford of Down before a handful of supporters on a Friday evening in Croke Park. Roscrea beat St Rynagh's of Offaly in the hurling final in Birr, the venue for the first inter-county hurling final, on the Sunday before Christmas.

Cork clubs dominated both competitions through the first decade. Blackrock won three hurling titles and Glen Rovers and St Finbarr's two each.

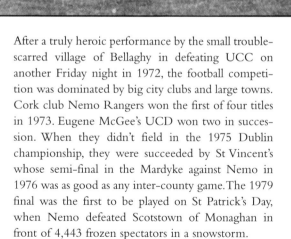

Kerry's sense of self-assurance was restored. But at the back of Kerry minds was the regret that without those interventions by Darby and Murphy they might have won nine All-Ireland championships in a row.

In a replayed Munster final in 1987, Cork brought Kerry's greatest era crashing to an end. 'The circus is over. It's time for a new act', Kerry full-forward Eoin Liston declared. Mick O'Dwyer gave all the impressions that this was a swan-song for the old 1975 boys, even calling up Vincent O'Connor to rejoin the panel after four years and sending him on for the last two minutes of the replay. The greatest team in football history went down together.

Where camogie led, hurling and football followed and established a club championship. Almost unnoticed and in the face of official apathy or even opposition, what was to become arguably the GAA's most important competition had come into existence.

The unwanted club championships grew out of unofficial club championships in Connacht and

After a truly heroic performance by the small trouble-scarred village of Bellaghy in defeating UCC on another Friday night in 1972, the football competition was dominated by big city clubs and large towns. Cork club Nemo Rangers won the first of four titles in 1973. Eugene McGee's UCD won two in succession. When they didn't field in the 1975 Dublin championship, they were succeeded by St Vincent's whose semi-final in the Mardyke against Nemo in 1976 was as good as any inter-county game. The 1979 final was the first to be played on St Patrick's Day, when Nemo defeated Scotstown of Monaghan in front of 4,443 frozen spectators in a snowstorm.

The potential of the club championship was slowly being realised. In 1980 Castlegar from Galway won the hurling championship. Aidan McCarry's winning goal gave the title to Loughgiel Shamrocks from the Glens of Antrim at Casement Park in April 1983.

'The club championships are a breath of fresh air', Meath footballer Colm O'Rourke wrote in 2003. 'New teams and games are played between sides with no history. The supporters get to travel and players must be able to combat conditions of winter which demand as much bravery as skill. At the same time prince and pauper stand together on the terrace and face slanting sun and cutting wind — the real opium of the masses.'

• ● •

In Ulster the action was still well off-field as the GAA nearly cleaved in two over politics. At half-time during the 1981 Ulster final, the Clones playing field was filled with people carrying black flags, supporting prisoners who were on hunger strike for political status in Long Kesh Prison.

Ten of the hunger strikers died including, on 1 August 1981, Kevin Lynch, the captain of the Derry hurling team which won an under-16 championship for developing hurling counties in 1970. The GAA in the province came under pressure to support the campaign.

Clubs came down on one side or the other, while others were split down the middle. Individual GAA officials had allegiance to the SDLP which opposed the hunger strike, and Sinn Féin which supported it. One Down official was a councillor with the Alliance Party, a proto-Unionist party which encouraged dialogue between the communities.

Derry-born president Paddy McFlynn made a series of careful statements expressing concern about the situation, but stopped short of supporting the demands.

As during the Civil War 60 years earlier, the GAA provided a place for people to find common cause as the crisis passed.

But it also realised that it was struggling to keep the games functioning in the north of Ireland in the face of ongoing violence.

Harassment from British forces interrupted preparations for All-Ireland quarter-finals and semi-finals. The entire Antrim team was detained on its way to training for the 1989 All-Ireland final. The Tyrone team of 1986 faced similar difficulties.

Dozens of club houses were firebombed across the province on an annual basis. Keeping the games going was something about which GAA members, whatever their political allegiance, could find common cause.

The enormously gifted Din Joe McGrogan, scorer of the goals that put Antrim in the All-Ireland under-21 final of 1969, was killed in a 1976 bomb attack.

The troubles were to continue until 1995. And amid the continued trauma, Ulster had found a cause to celebrate its deeds on the football field.

Ollie Walsh of Kilkenny in action in 1963. The outstanding goalkeeper of the 1960s was eventually succeeded in the Kilkenny goal by his nephew, Noel Skehan.

John O'Donoghue in action for Tipperary against Cork
in the 1964 Munster hurling championship. Cork were
flattered by their 14-point winning margin.

Tipperary goalkeeper John O'Donoghue saves
against Cork. By 1965 Tipperary had established
itself as Munster's leading hurling power. Cork's
re-emergence in 1966 was to rejuvenate interest
in the Munster championship.

Tipperary captain Jimmy Doyle of Thurles Sarsfields scored six points in his side's
defeat of Wexford in the 1965 All-Ireland hurling final, the second time
in four years he had captained Tipperary to victory over Wexford.

OFFICIAL PROGRAMME

5 Meán Fómair
1965

Cluící Ceannais Iomána na hÉireann

SINSIR 3.15 p.m

loc Jarman v. Tiobraid Árann

MIONÚIR 1.45 p.m

Át Cliat v. Luimneac

luac 1/-

Seán Ó Síocháin
Árd-Rúnaí.

Tipperary's victory over Wexford brought an eighth All-Ireland medal for John Doyle of Holycross, equalling Christy Ring's record.

The programme for the 1966
Railway Cup finals. Breandán Mac
Lua's revamp of the Railway Cup
match programme in 1966 came
as the competition was in decline.
In the cover photograph Ollie
Walsh of Kilkenny faces Jimmy
Doyle of Tipperary with Seán
McLoughlin and Tom Neville
also in action.

Jim 'Tough' Barry with the Cork
hurling team of 1966. It was to
be the last year of Tough's fabled
involvement with Cork hurling,
and one of the sweetest.

Unlikely champions at the start of the season when they played in the curtain-raiser for the league final, Dublin's 1974 team was to grip popular imagination like no other. Back: Steve Rooney, Anton O'Toole, Robbie Kelleher, Jimmy Keaveney, Tony Hanahoe, Paddy Cullen, John McCarthy, Alan Larkin, Bobby Doyle. Front: Brian Mullins, George Wilson, Paddy Reilly, Seán Doherty, Dave Hickey, Gay O'Driscoll.

Paddy Cullen saves a Galway penalty in the 1974 final, confirming the belief among Dubliners that their time had come.

Dublin's defeat of Galway in the 1974 All-Ireland final coincided with the decline of League of Ireland soccer and gave new focus to sporting culture in the capital.

Kerry were worried about facing Tipperary after a bad 1975 National League quarter-final defeat; instead they won the All-Ireland and dominated football for 12 years. Back: Paudie Lynch, Paudie O'Mahoney, Pat Spillane, Tim Kennelly, John O'Keeffe, John Egan, Brendan Lynch, Ger Power. Front: Denis 'Ogie' Moran, Páidí Ó Sé, Michael Sheehy, Jim Deenihan, Michael O'Sullivan (captain), Pat McCarthy, Ger O'Keeffe, Leo Griffin (masseur).

Video evidence hasn't quite backed up the claim that the Dublin-Kerry matches of the 1970s were the greatest of all time, but their five successive championship clashes brought an exciting rivalry to a new generation of football fans.

Dublin corner-forward Bobby Doyle in 1975. Dublin's teams reinstated Gaelic football in urban culture. 'Basically everything associated with a Dublin gurrier at the time, I had it. I had long hair, a dark complexion, I wore my football socks down around my ankles.'

Sligo's celebrations after winning the Connacht title in 1975 were curtailed by a heavy defeat in the All-Ireland semi-final, suggesting their breakthrough had come ten years too late. Back: Des Kerins, Mick Laffey, Mickey Kearins, Mattie Hoey, Thomas Cummins, Francis Henry, John Brennan, Fr Tom Colleary, Johnny Stenson. Front: Paddy Henry, Robert Lipsett, Barnes Murphy (captain), Aidan Caffrey, James Kearins, Mattie Brennan. Mascot: John Clifford.

Jimmy Keaveney was coaxed out of retirement in 1977. Three years later he was to establish an individual scoring record in the All-Ireland final, beating Frankie Stockwell's 21-year-old record with 2-6. His scoring tally for the year of 1975 is still a Dublin record.

The Kerry and Austin Stacks corner-forward Mikey Sheehy equalled Keaveney's scoring record for an All-Ireland final in 1979 with a total of 2-6.

Robbie Kelleher, Brian Mullins, Seán Walsh, Eoin Liston, Seán Doherty, Kevin Moran and Tommy Drumm in action in the 1978 All-Ireland final, a match of such drama it was discussed for decades afterwards.

The sequence of events that led to the turning-point goal in the 1978 All-Ireland football final between Dublin and Kerry. Dublin goalkeeper Paddy Cullen was arguing referee Séamus Aldridge's decision to award a Kerry free when Mikey Sheehy noticed he was out of position and sent the ball into the net.

Dermot Earley scores a goal against Armagh in the 1977 All-Ireland semi-final. One of the outstanding players produced by the introduction of the under-21 grade, Earley won an All-Ireland under-21 medal in 1966, and in common with the entire team was almost immediately promoted to senior. Roscommon won four successive Connacht titles, a National League in 1979, and gave Kerry a scare in the 1980 All-Ireland final.

Opposite:
Eoin Liston contests a high ball with Dublin's Mick Holden in 1979. Liston earned the nickname 'Bomber' playing beach soccer in 1974, when Germany's Gerd 'Bomber' Muller was the star of the World Cup in soccer.

Dublin goalkeeper Paddy Cullen gets the ball away under pressure from Mikey Sheehy, John Egan and Pat Spillane.

Opposite:
Brian Mullins fields the ball against Offaly in the 1979 Leinster championship. Mullins's ability to impose himself on the opposition turned the 1979 Leinster final in Dublin's favour.

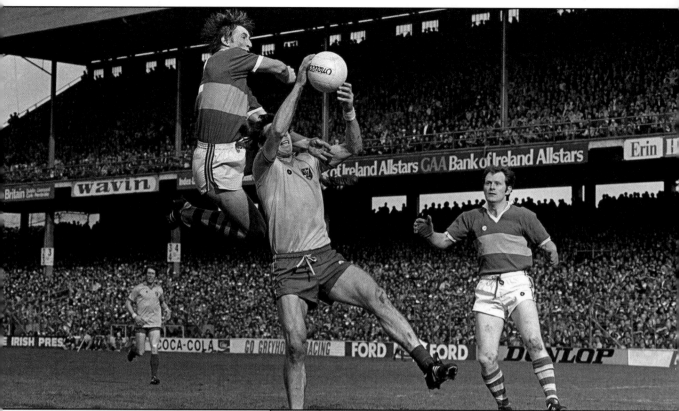

Pat Spillane in the air
against Roscommon in
1980. Kerry's first final
against opposition other
than Dublin, they fell five
points behind Roscommon
but won by three.

Pat Spillane canters past
Mick Holden with a characteristic jinking run. The
most honoured footballer
in All Star history was one
of three brothers on the
greatest of all Kerry teams,
all nephews of three
brothers who had played
in the 1950s.

Tim Kennelly with the Sam Maguire cup after Kerry's victory over Dublin in 1979. Starting without Ger Power, losing John O'Keeffe and having Páidí Ó Sé sent off did not deter Kerry, who won by 11 points.

Son of Limerick All-Ireland hurling medallist Jackie, Ger
Power was one of five Kerrymen to win eight All-Ireland
medals between 1975 and 1986.

One of the greatest players of the 1980s, Offaly forward Matt Connor (on right) had his career tragically cut short by a motor accident.

Eoin Liston gathers for Kerry against Offaly in the 1982 final.

Colman Doyle's sequence of photographs capturing Séamus Darby's winning goal in the 1982 All-Ireland final. Darby had just been sent on to the field, bringing the Kerry wing-back back to the corner position, and was on hand to accept a pass from Liam Connor, run five yards and blast a goal past stranded goalkeeper Charlie Nelligan. Just as in the 1933 semi-final, Kerry had a chance to score an equaliser, but failed.

Dublin fans in Páirc Uí Chaoimh when the All-Ireland semi-final between Dublin and Cork was replayed. Dublin won decisively on a sweltering day. The atmosphere was such that players could not hear each other's calls on the playing field. The tumultuous gathering of Hill 16 regulars was nicknamed 'Hill 17'.

Denis 'Ogie' Moran lets loose a shot against Dublin goalkeeper John O'Leary in the 1985 final, the last encounter in a ten-year rivalry.

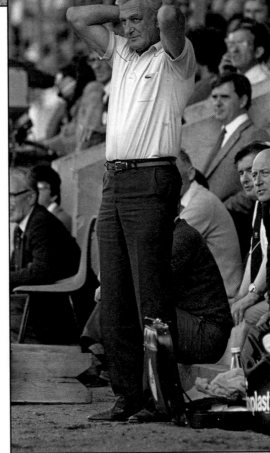

Dublin's manager restored his reputation as a master tactician by returning to win the All-Ireland of 1983 with what was effectively a new team.

Gaeltacht captain Páidí Ó Sé is chaired off the field after the 1985 All-Ireland final. He conceded only one point to immediate opponents in All-Ireland finals, against David Hickey in 1976.

John Kennedy and Brian Mullins in action in the 1985
All-Ireland final.

Opposite:
Kerry, having been foiled of five in a row, embarked on
a new three in a row in 1984. Back: Jack O'Shea, Tom
Spillane, Ger Lynch, Charlie Nelligan, Ogie Moran, Pat
Spillane and Seán Walsh. Front: John Egan, Eoin Liston,
Tommy Doyle, Páidí Ó Sé, Ambrose O'Donovan, Mick
Spillane, Ger Power, John Kennedy.

Jack O'Shea was the
outstanding midfielder
of the Kerry team of
the 1980s, inviting
comparisons with
predecessors Paddy
Kennedy and Mick
O'Connell. When Kerry
decided to pick a team
of the century, they
had to opt for two.

Frank McGuigan, scorer of 11 points for Tyrone against Armagh in the 1984 Ulster final. His career was cut short by injury and Tyrone had to wait 20 years for their All-Ireland title.

Pat Spillane in action against Joe McNally of Dublin in the 1985 All-Ireland final. He recovered from a cruciate ligament injury to win more awards

Colm O'Rourke and Finian Murtagh in action in the Leinster football final of 1986.

Mikey Sheehy kicking for goal for Kerry in the 1986 All-Ireland semi-final against Meath's Martin O'Connell (left) and goalkeeper Mickey McQuillan. It was Seán Boylan's Meath who were to take over the mantle as the dominant team from Mick O'Dwyer's Kerry.

Martin O'Connell, David de Lappe, Liam Harnan and Robbie O'Malley in action in the 1987 Leinster football final.

Ger Henderson of Kilkenny against Ray Cummins of Cork in the 1978 All-Ireland final. Cork completed three in a row with a victory over their old rivals.

After disappointment in 1975 and 1979, Galway supporters' celebrations surpassed anything ever seen in Croke Park after 58 years of waiting. It took captain Joe Connolly ten minutes to reach the podium. Back: Conor Hayes, Steve Mahon, John Connolly, Michael Connolly, Michael Conneely, Frank Burke, Noel Lane, Seán Silke. Front: Niall McInerney, Séamus Coen, Jimmy Cooney, Joe Connolly (captain), Sylvie Linnane, P. J. Molloy, Bernie Forde.

Jim Connolly's photograph of Ray Cummins rising highest to retrieve the ball in a 1977 championship match with Galway. Full-forward on the Cork hurling teams that won three in a row between 1976 and 1977, Ray Cummins won an All-Ireland football medal in 1973 and Railway Cup medals in both codes.

Opposite:
Dramatic scenes as Offaly captain Pádraig Horan lifts the
Liam McCarthy cup after victory over Galway.

John, the elder of the Connolly brothers from Castlegar,
who served as an inspiration to Galway hurling at the time
of their 1980 breakthrough.

Opposite:
Offaly's team came from one of the smallest playing bases
in the country and were surprise All-Ireland champions
when veteran corner-forward Johnny Flaherty hand-passed
a goal with three minutes of the 1981 All-Ireland final to go.
Back: Pat Kirwan, Pat Fleury, Joachim Kelly, Liam Currams,
Pat Delaney, Eugene Coughlan, Aidan Fogarty. Front: Tom
Donoghue, Johnny Flaherty, Damien Martin, Pádraig Horan
(captain), Ger Coughlan, Pat Carroll, Mark Corrigan,
Brendan Bermingham.

Offaly's goal-scorer Johnny Flaherty in action against Galway's Séamus Coen and Niall McInerney in the 1980 All-Ireland hurling final.

Cork goalkeeper Ger Cunningham in action against Offaly in the centenary final of 1984. Cork prepared for the match in the Ursuline convent in Thurles.

Clare's mini breakthrough of the mid-1970s yielded two National League titles, but the hurlers from Cusack's birthplace like Ger Loughnane thirsted for something more.

Two goals from Pat Cleary helped Offaly win another All-Ireland title by two points in 1985. Back row: Pat Fleury, Joachim Kelly, Tom Conneely, Eugene Coughlan, Pat Delaney, Joe Dooley, Pádraig Horan, Aidan Fogarty. Front row: Danny Owens, Brendan Bermingham, Pat Cleary, Ger Coughlan, Jim Troy, Mark Corrigan, Paddy Corrigan.

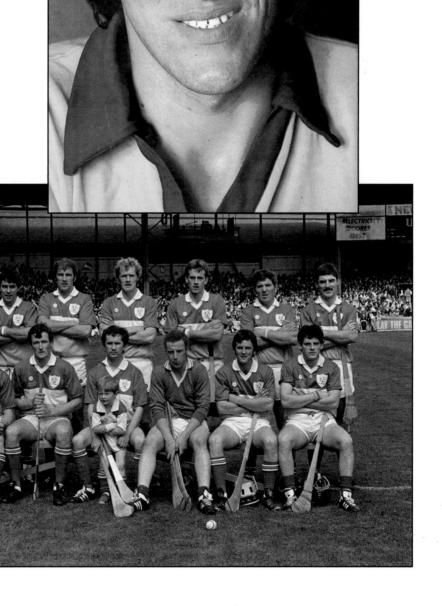

Wrap of the ash as Cork meet Limerick in the 1985
Munster hurling championship.

Nicholas English, one of Tipperary's greatest hurlers, helped bring the county out of a barren period to victory in the All-Ireland championships of 1989 and 1991. He later managed the team.

Joy on the face of Jimmy Barry Murphy as he scores against Tipperary in 1985 in a thundering final that produced a score for every two minutes of heart-stopping play in the Cork sunshine.

Galway manager Cyril Farrell before the 1988 All-Ireland hurling final between Galway and Tipperary.

Offaly players and officials form a guard of honour for the winning Antrim team after Antrim's unexpected 4-15 to 1-15 victory in the 1989 All-Ireland hurling semi-final.

Croke Park was used for Aiséirí,
a 1916 Rising golden anniversary
pageant staged on the anniversary
of the date of the rebellion.

The sizeable border town of Crossmaglen had its pitch
occupied by the British Army for over 30 years, but it was
on the sportsfield that Crossmaglen made headlines at the
turn of the twenty-first century as one of the strongest club
sides in football history.

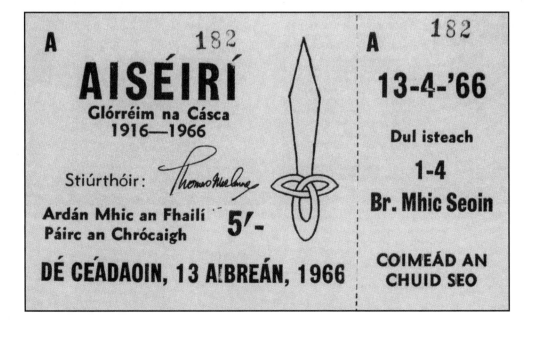

The place of Gaelic games in the culture of the North is reflected by this wall mural in the north Belfast Catholic enclave of Ardoyne.

A hurling field prepared by the Irish
Army for a game in the Congo.

A new generation of Gaelic footballers were
looking beyond the Polo Grounds and New
York to forge links with the oval ball Australian
Rules code. Meath's Peter McDermott, a
veteran of US tours, was one of the driving
forces behind a tour to Australia with Meath
footballers in 1968 that produced the first
attempt at compromise rules games.
Australian promoter Ron Barassi was
enthusiastic about the tour, but it took
another 20 years before an official
international series would be attempted.

Outstanding player on the Wexford camogie team of 1968, Margaret O'Leary was carried from the field by their supporters.

The Wexford camogie team's victory in the 1968 All-Ireland championship ended a long period of Dublin domination and was the first indication of a shift in power back towards the traditional hurling counties.

Angela Downey came to personify Kilkenny's domination of the camogie championship in the 1970s and 80s.

Oranges at half-time for the Dublin camogie team, who overwhelmingly dominated women's hurling from the inception of the All-Ireland championship in 1934. They were unbeaten in the Leinster championship between 26 July 1936 and 2 June 1968.

chapter six

Faster, Higher, Fitter

A handful of matches have been nominated as the greatest played in the history of the game.

P. D. Mehigan, a leading GAA writer of his day, nominated the second of the three matches between Kilkenny and Cork in the 1931 All-Ireland hurling final. John D. Hickey nominated the 1958 National Hurling League final between Wexford and Limerick. Pádraig Puirséal, with a hint of partiality, nominated Kilkenny's victory over Cork in 1947.

In football, Paddy Foley said, without fear of contradiction nowadays at least, that the first 15-a-side match between Kerry and Louth back in 1913 was the greatest ever. Kerry's come-backs in the 1926 and 1946 All-Ireland finals were fondly recalled in later years. An entire generation of fans will claim that the 1977 semi-final between Dublin and Kerry was the greatest.

Then, a revolution. Higher fitness levels in hurling and changes to the rules of football in the 1990s, combined with a levelling out of both championships, nearly put the nostalgia industry out of business.

An increasing number of matches in both codes were being nominated as the greatest ever. Future generations will espouse the virtues of the 1991 Meath-Dublin and 1997 Meath-Kildare marathons in football, the Down-Derry match of 1994, the dramatic Armagh-Dublin finish of 2002, the Dublin-Tyrone drawn game of 2005, each of the hurling All-Irelands between 1994 and 1997, and the hurling semi-finals of 2002, 2003, 2004 and Galway's dramatic defeat of Kilkenny in 2005.

There are those who say that sheer speed is interfering with skill levels. Younger players 'cannot hit a decent ball on the sod, cannot double with direction on the ground or overhead, cannot strike a flying drop with any reasonable degree of accuracy', one critic complained.

'Perhaps it is for want of a sound tutor. Perhaps it is that the age of speed at all costs, allied to the current craze for the spectacular, has left its mark on our ancient game.'

If it sounds familiar, it is because it was written by P. D. Mehigan in the GAA's short-lived cultural journal, *An Ráitheachán*, in June 1936.

The past is another playing field.

When the GAA celebrated its centenary in 1984, one of its more ambitious projects was to stage a full series of matches against a team of Australian Rules footballers under specially devised international rules. There had been tentative contacts in 1967 and 1968, but this was the first attempt by Gaelic football to embrace its first cousin.

How close a cousin was the subject of controversy. In Canberra in 1984, Australian sports historians Bill Mandle, Rob Hess and Geoffrey Blainey claimed that the games were unrelated, as undue Irish influence would have led to the new game being shunned by English immigrants in Melbourne. The debate continues.

The Canberra trio argue that the four men who drew up the rules in 1857 were English public schoolboy types, including a graduate of

Trinity College in Dublin, not caid-playing gold miners, and there are few Irish names among the early team lists.

The point went largely unanswered, but similarities with Gaelic football persist. Unlike the English public school codes, the founding father of Aussie Rules did not introduce an off-side law and ruled that a player running with the ball must bounce it along the way. The scoring posts closely resembled Gaelic football, which was not codified until 27 years later.

Vast numbers of Irish who arrived in Victoria during the gold rush in the 1850s were already playing football, and the earliest recorded football match in Australia was between two Irish regiments in Sydney in 1829.

A series of matches under shared rules against a Scottish shinty team also resumed in 1988.

In football, Australia won the first international series in 1984, and when an Irish team travelled to Perth, Melbourne and Adelaide in 1986 the series was re-established on an annual basis. Canberra was added to the venues in 1990. In 1998 the number of matches was reduced to two. A pattern emerged that the visiting team usually won the series. Public interest remained high, driving attendances past the 60,000 mark in both countries.

Rule-makers were impressed by the fluidity and skill of the Australian high-marking game and wondered what they could borrow for themselves.

When former Dublin captain and manager Tony Hanahoe was given the brief of cleaning up the playing rules of Gaelic football, bedevilled since the 1940s with problems concerning the tackle and the hand-pass, he made one major recommendation.

All free kicks and line balls in future were to be taken from the hand.

Simply and effectively, he transformed Gaelic football. The future was a faster, more fluid game.

Connacht had had very little to celebrate since the heyday of the Galway footballers in the mid-1960s, but the 1980s were to change all that.

The celebrations of Galway hurling supporters surpassed anything ever seen in Croke Park when they recaptured the All-Ireland hurling championship after 58 years.

It took captain Joe Connolly ten minutes to reach the rostrum, and several hours for the team bus to reach home the following night.

A flying start did the trick. Galway went 2-1 to nil up with goals from Bernie Forde and P. J. Molloy, led 2-7 to 1-5 at half-time and survived Joe McKenna and Éamonn Cregan's second half goals to win.

Galway faced Limerick again in 1981 when Galway won an enthralling replayed semi-final with the help of a doubtful penalty and the fact that Limerick had a goal disallowed. Galway trailed by a point at half-time. Then they came through with second half goals from John Connolly, P. J. Molloy and Joe Connolly, who scored 2-7 in all. Earlier the teams served up a controversial drawn match when Galway finished with 14 men and Limerick with 13. The referee was attacked by an angry supporter as he left the field.

The Galway people who returned for the 1981 All-Ireland hurling final saw another breakthrough.

Offaly veteran Johnny Flaherty hand-passed the goal that won the match with three minutes to go. At the other end goalkeeper Damien Martin batted out an almost certain Galway goal at a crucial stage early in the second half.

Although Offaly swept from six points behind and Galway failed to score in the final 23 minutes, it was nevertheless a famous victory.

The old inscription over the medieval city of Galway had borne the inscription: 'From the fury of the O'Flahertys, Good Lord Preserve Us.'

Flaherty was Offaly's man for the tight spot. He had also scored goals in the Leinster finals of 1980 and 1981 as the county emerged from one of the smallest hurling bases to win the All-Ireland championship.

The eight hurling parishes around Birr and Banagher have supplied all but one of the stars which have won the four All-Irelands. Local championships are hard-fought, with the small clubs jostling for honours with the two big towns, and they steeled both St Rynagh's and Birr to win provincial club titles, Birr going on to All-Ireland success in 1995 and 1998. Many attribute the rise of Offaly hurling to the arrival of Corkman Brother Denis Rice in Birr Presentation College in the 1960s.

In 1982 Offaly lost the Leinster title after a dispute over a ball that appeared to roll over the line before Liam Fennelly flicked it out to Matt Ruth for Kilkenny's winning goal.

Kilkenny came back for successive All-Irelands. In 1982 they brought Christy Heffernan in at full-forward to score two goals in a 40-second spell two minutes before half-time.

Clare's Seán MacMahon outjumps Kilkenny's John Hoyne. The re-emergence of Clare, Limerick and Wexford to dominate hurling against the three traditional powers, Cork, Kilkenny and Tipperary, rejuvenated the game in the mid-1990s.

In 1983 they used the strong wind to dominate the first half. Richie Power added a vital goal 18 seconds into the second half and they defeated Cork by two points in the end.

There were some familiar faces on the Dublin team that returned to win the All-Ireland championship of 1983. Tommy Drumm and Brian Mullins had been there before. But it was up to the best known of the newcomers, Barney Rock, to snatch as dramatic an equaliser as Croke Park had ever seen, when he got a goal with 30 seconds to spare in the All-Ireland semifinal against Cork.

The match was replayed in bright sunshine in Páirc Uí Chaoimh, a tumultuous and celebratory occasion where players could not hear each other's calls because of the noise of the crowd, but fears of a riot proved without foundation.

Instead, it was a riot of colour and excitement.

Barney Rock secured Dublin's All Ireland with an opportunist 11th minute goal, sent back into the net over the goalkeeper's head after a fluffed kick-out, while team manager Kevin Heffernan was tending to an injured Dublin player in the square in front of the goalkeeper.

After outbreaks of fisticuffs and a kicking incident diminished Dublin's numbers, their remaining 12 men fought a rearguard action in the second half and received a mixed reaction from an astonished public and officialdom.

Brian Mullins, Ray Hazley and Ciarán Duff of Dublin and Tomás Tierney of Galway were all sent off, a record for an All-Ireland final, and bitterness remained for months afterwards throughout a long sequel of disciplinary hearings which never established exactly who had given Galway midfielder Brian Talty a black eye in the tunnel on the way to the dressing room.

Emigration returned to stalk the communities of the west of Ireland. By the mid-1980s entire townlands were disappearing.

An entire football team from Mayo emigrated together and re-emerged to play in New York.

In 1986, the last year that Ireland ran a trade deficit,

one of the best players in the country was based in America. Kildare's Larry Tompkins went to New York to play for one of the clubs there, stayed 18 months and returned to Castlehaven to play and win two All-Ireland medals for Cork.

The New York championship became a who's who of famous Irish players who took the plane to America as soon as their counties were eliminated from the inter-county championship at home.

The allegiance of the player at home had no bearing on their choice of team in New York. Donegal and Leitrim dominated the New York championship in the 1980s. They happened to be the best funded of the New York teams, paying the plane fares and allowances for footballers to come over. The situation became more regularised when New York reaffiliated to the GAA in 1988.

New York always stayed separate from North America where a high level of organisation was achieved. By 2004 the number of affiliated clubs reached 111 adult and 12 youth clubs in 30 cities. A well-supported American championship is staged in all four major sports, 26 grades in all.

In Australia, GAA became an officially accredited sport of the Australian Sports Commission, giving it better access to the school PE curriculum. Playing numbers rose spectacularly. In Adelaide they rose from 40 to 750. Hurling was revived in New South Wales and Victoria. Two New Zealand international rugby players, Zin Zan Brooke and Bernie McCahill, were among the diverse participants in a well-supported Australasian championship first played in 1971 and rotated between the Australian states and New Zealand. Restrictions on visa players were introduced to help bring more native players. Australia won the women's football World Cup in 2002 and 2004 against teams from Canada, Europe, North America, Britain and London.

Gaelic games were now played in South-East Asia, which stages its own seven-a-side championship, contested by 30 teams from 12 Asian countries. The annual Dubai Sevens tournament was launched in 1994 and is played in March.

A European county board was established in 1998 after the game had developed primarily in the Hague, Luxembourg and Paris. Tournaments were hosted in the 1990s. The European Gaelic Football League was established in 2000, involving eight of the continent's 16 teams. Women's football is played in six cities. An interesting side effect of the GAA's international series against Australia is the growth of 'compromise' rules matches between GAA and Australian Rules clubs in cities such as Munich.

The largest and oldest GAA organisation abroad is in Britain. As early as March 1885 a club in Wallsend, Newcastle-upon-Tyne, affiliated, and London won an All-Ireland senior hurling title in 1901.

There are affiliated boards in Gloucestershire, Hertfordshire, Lancashire, London, Warwickshire and Yorkshire, and the Scottish county board was revived

The 1994 hurling final was winding down when Johnny Dooley, one of three hurling brothers from Ireland's smallest parish, lined up to take this free with four minutes to go. He defied instructions from the sideline to go for a point, banged it into the Limerick net and presaged a historic whirlwind finish in which Offaly came from five points down to win by six.

in 1975. British universities have well-supported competitions, and GAA is now played in British schools for the first time.

Galway hurlers were rekindling the bonfires. The youth and skill of the team which won All-Irelands in 1987 (adding the League and Railway Cup as well) and 1988 was suggestive of more to come.

A new trend: goalkeeper John Commins scored from a penalty and had to scamper back to his goal. That team was beaten by goal-hungry Cork.

Mixed emotions for the Offaly manager Éamonn Cregan after his side's victory over Limerick in the 1994 All-Ireland hurling final. It was the first time a team manager had guided his adopted county to victory over his home county.

Substitute Noel Lane, a veteran of 1980, scored the winning goals in 1987 and 1988. His 1987 shot hit off Kilkenny goalkeeper Kevin Fennelly on the way to the net.

A hasty charge upon the Galway goalkeeper as Tipperary's Nicholas English was scoring a point in Croke Park helped send Galway into the final. The referee awarded a free out and in a twinkling Éanna Ryan had the ball in the Tipperary net.

Galway faced Tipp in the 1988 final, and Lane did it again, although Galway looked doomed at half-time when they led by just four points and faced a strong wind in the second half. Cormac Bonner's goal shot was parried by goalkeeper John Commins and sent out for a 70 with two minutes to go.

Galway were narrowly beaten by Tipperary in a controversial 1989 semi-final and by Cork in the final of 1990.

Meath footballers were left wondering what might have happened had not a series of goalkeeping errors put paid to their ambitions in 1983. Meath looked far from All-Ireland championship material when they lost to Wexford in 1981 and Longford in 1982, but they then asked the hurling team's masseur, Seán Boylan, to manage the team. He stayed for two decades.

In 1984 they were without Mick Lyons when they lost to Dublin again, slipped up against Laois in 1985 and were beaten in the 1986 All-Ireland semi-final when a defensive mistake let Ger Power through for Kerry's first goal.

When Meath finally made the breakthrough in 1987, long-serving Colm O'Rourke deservedly got the winning goal ten minutes before half-time. Seven minutes earlier Cork had their goal attempt blocked by Mick Lyons when Jimmy Kerrigan seemed clear through. The goal would have put Cork seven points ahead. Instead it was Meath who led 1-6 to 0-8 at half-time, and they went eight points ahead as Larry Tompkins, the Cork super-shooter, uncharacteristically sent six of his eight free kicks wide in the second half. Meath midfielder Liam Hayes was awarded man of the match.

Tompkins scored the equalising points from frees in the Munster final and All-Ireland final, earning him the nickname 'equaliser' after a popular television show.

The nickname was also accorded to Monaghan player Éamonn McEneaney for a dramatic equalising point from the sideline in the 1985 All-Ireland semi-final.

When Meath retained their All-Ireland in 1988 it was in much more controversial circumstances. Cork scored the only goal after three minutes of the drawn final, when Teddy McCarthy finished a Dinny Allen-Paul McGrath move by sending to the net through the goalkeeper's legs. Cork failed to convert their second half domination into scores, ending up

Clare had suffered Munster final defeats when they re-emerged for a surprise All-Ireland victory in 1995. Nobody in the county could remember the previous success 81 years earlier, and the 'bachelor boys' (they were all unmarried) earned a place in 1990s popular culture for themselves and their heroics. Back: Brian Lohan, Michael O'Halloran, Frank Lohan, Conor Clancy, Davy Fitzgerald, Seán McMahon, Gerard O'Loughlin. Front: Liam Doyle, P. J. O'Connell, Ollie Baker, Anthony Daly, James O'Connor, Fergal Hegarty, Fergus Tuohy, Stephen McNamara.

with 15 wides as against Meath's seven. The Cork backs insisted that David Beggy took a dive when a 14-yard free was awarded against them 30 seconds from the end.

Meath were down to 14 men after just seven minutes of the replay. After midfielder Gerry McEntee was sent off, P. J. Gillic switched to midfield. Meath crowded and fouled the Cork forwards. They kept the score down to 0-5 to 0-6 at half-time, and eventually pushed themselves into a three-point lead at the three-quarter stage. Two great blocks by Liam Hayes and some cool defending by Robbie O'Malley and man of the match, Martin O'Connell, secured their victory.

Afterwards Colm O'Rourke explained Meath's tactics of controlled aggression in a controversial newspaper article headlined, 'In the Heat of Battle — Nice Guys Finish Last.' The recriminations continued for years.

● ● ●

Tipperary have won an All-Ireland senior title in every decade of hurling history — but it was a close-run thing in the years between 1971 and 1989.

From 1974 to 1983, Tipperary did not win a single championship match — a distinction shared only by Kilkenny footballers. They even managed to lose in 1981 in a replay after they went 14 points up against Limerick, thanks to four goals from Joe McKenna.

When they finally emerged from Munster after a pulsating replayed final with Cork in 1987, captain Richard Stakelum declared, 'The famine is over.'

Substitute Michael Doyle scored two goals in extra time, and the jubilation was matched by scenes around the stand afterwards and a triumphal home-coming to Nenagh.

When the famine really did end in 1989, the All-Ireland was a poor one as Antrim suffered from stage fright. Antrim's progress had begun with Loughgiel's success at club level in 1983 with players like 15-stone goalkeeper Niall Patterson.

Antrim's first All Star, Ciarán Barr, helped Belfast club Rossa reach the 1989 club hurling final and after a great show against Buffer's Alley, Barr then starred in a 4-15 to 1-15 All-Ireland semi-final win over Offaly. After the game the Offaly players applauded Antrim off the field.

Antrim failed by just two points against Kilkenny in 1991 but never made it back to the final.

Tipperary won another All-Ireland in 1991. They beat Cork in a replay, coming back from seven points down in the first game and nine points down in the second, before Michael Cleary's goal defeated Kilkenny in the final.

● ● ●

In 1988 Cork brought 35-year-old Denis Allen and soccer exile Dave Barry back for the Munster championship, and Allen ended up scoring the goal that beat Kerry. The match erupted into a fracas near the end, and although only four players were booked by referee Pat Lane, eight were further disciplined after the game by the Munster council.

In a 15-day period in 1990, Cork rewrote the history books by winning All-Ireland titles in both hurling and football. Teddy McCarthy played in both teams, making even more history. The hurling/football double had been achieved before at under-21 level in 1970 and 1971, at minor in 1967, 1969 and 1974, and even at senior level in 1893 (when three counties contested the hurling and four the football).

But when it was finally achieved in modern competition it was, deservedly, the GAA's largest playing community who achieved it.

● ● ●

The 1983 All-Ireland football final between Galway and Dublin took place on a damp blustery day. It was a last hurrah for Kevin Heffernan's Dublin heroes of the 1970s, but suddenly from an unpromising beginning they grew in confidence and strength to reach the All-Ireland final after a dramatic replayed semi-final against Cork. Dubs wanted to see what this new team was about, and they came in their thousands to seek admission to the GAA's biggest stadium.

What followed was nearly a disaster, the sort of disaster that occurred six years later at a stadium in Sheffield in England at an FA Cup semi-final.

Unknown to the public at large there was serious crowding and crushing on Hill 16. A gate was forced and people were squashed.

The day after the match, the GAA went into emergency session. Six years before the same conclusion was forced on the soccer world, they decided a nineteenth-century stadium design couldn't stage a modern sporting occasion. Croke Park would have to come down.

The first part to be replaced was Hill 16,

which had been rebuilt in 1988. But in the course of that exercise the GAA looked at American stadiums, especially Giants Stadium in New York and a stadium in Miami, and began to rethink the landscape of their home.

They devised plans for a three-tier horseshoe stadium, with Hill 16 retained as a standing area. Two tiers of corporate boxes, the first at an Irish sports facility, would be sold to corporate clients. Progress would

Clare's Davy Fitzgerald jumps for joy after Clare had won the All-Ireland hurling championship for the first time in 81 years. Described by D. J. Carey as the best goalkeeper of his era, Fitzgerald had gifted Offaly a goal, but true to the new spirit of the Clare team, they had recovered two points in as many minutes.

depend on financing, and was not dependent on government grants although three tranches of aid were later made available by successive Irish governments.

The old Cusack stand was demolished after the 1993 All-Ireland and the new stand finished for the 1996 All-Ireland. By 2000 the Canal end had been completed and by 2003 the Hogan stand.

The whole exercise cost in the region of €250 m and included escalators, new players' lounges, first aid and security facilities, an executive level and a museum where the story of the ancient games could be told.

'Another ding-dong battle in Jones's Road, but this one was a little different, a struggle for people's attention, between venue and event', Diarmuid Murphy wrote in the *Irish Examiner*.

•   •   •

The rebirth of Croke Park was a personal triumph for the GAA's low-profile general secretary Liam Ó Maolmhichil.

Ó Maolmhichil succeeded three exceptionally long-serving secretaries, one from Wicklow and two from Cork.

In both cases the GAA had chosen a conservative option, when an apparently less conservative alternative was available. The two men had served the association well, but created the sense of a paternalistic association that was entrenched in tradition.

Luke O'Toole served for 28 years, Pádraig Ó Caoimh served for 35 and Seán Ó Siocháin for 15.

Pádraig Ó Caoimh, Roscommon born but Cork reared and ten years secretary of the board there, had been appointed in 1929 ahead of Frank Bourke, the dual All-Ireland medallist from Dublin and Pádraig Pearse's successor as headmaster of St Enda's.

He administered the GAA through the rebuilding of the Cusack stand in 1938, which came in two and a half years late and £10,000 over budget due to a strike and other unexpected problems, but Ó Caoimh had cleared the debt by 1945. When he died in office after 35 years, the then GAA president Alf Murray said: 'He gave this association a place in the life of the country that no other national body could aspire to.'

Seán Ó Síocháin, a champion ballad singer, had been appointed in 1964 ahead of Maurice Hayes, a Down

man who was to fill several roles in the resolution of the Northern Ireland conflict as an establishment-leaning Catholic.

An association founded by a schoolteacher and perceived to have been run by schoolteachers (14 of the first 27 presidents were schoolteachers), eventually appointed Ó Maolmhichil, who had been appointed one of the youngest school inspectors in the history of the Department of Education, as director general in 1979.

Quiet and unassuming, he established a reputation as a safe pair of hands and the leading sport official in a

Clare manager Ger Loughnane with the McCarthy cup after Clare had won the All-Ireland hurling championship for the first time in 81 years. Changing demographics had, for a change, helped hurling in the county as rapid urbanisation and development was concentrated in the hurling-playing east of the county — Ennis, Shannon, Sixmilebridge and Clarecastle. The goalscorer in the final, Éamonn Taaffe from Tubber, Fergal Hegarty of Kilnamona and later Colin Lynch of Lissycasey were the west Clare players on the teams of the 1990s. Previously only one west Clareman had ever played for the county. Jim Carney, a native of Dunbeg, featured on the great Clare team of 1952–56 and played in the Railway Cup semi-final and final of 1956. Even he played his hurling with Sixmilebridge.

period of rapid change which sent several major well-funded sporting organisations into tailspins over professionalism, finance, government, sports restructuring, media rights, merchandising and facilities.

Much of the GAA's energy, even before his arrival, had been put into construction projects at club and county level, over 1,000 in the 1970–2000 period.

Ó Maolmhichíl took a deep personal interest in the Croke Park project, busying himself with construction details in his dealings with contractors.

The sports columnist in the *Sunday Business Post* (and author of this book) called it the 'Taj Ó Maolmhichíl' in 1999.

•　　•　　•

While bricks and mortar were being constructed in north Dublin, mortars and bricks were still flying in Northern Ireland. An attack on O'Toole's public house in June 1994 left six people dead while watching Ireland play a soccer match. A similar attack in Annalong followed a few weeks later on a group of people watching a GAA match.

In 1996 it was suggested by Protestant supremacists marching at Drumcree, Co. Armagh, that they might launch a paramilitary attack on the Ulster final.

'When it comes to the GAA one lot genuinely doesn't know what makes the other lot tick', commentator Fionnuala O'Connor wrote in 1993. 'A sport that crosses all classes, drawn on local talent with the strongest local support, is enviable in Protestant eyes. Theirs is a thinner sense of community, the Orange hall a local hub for only one section; the fierce allegiance of GAA fans is a major mystification for Protestant onlookers.'

The shooting of Aidan McAnaspie by a British soldier in 1988 was a watershed for the GAA, according to Desmond Fahy in his study, 'How the GAA Survived the Troubles'.

Whether the GAA liked it or not, and all the signs indicated significant unease, it was now a player in the wider political process in Northern Ireland. The shooting dead of one of its members by the British Army could hardly have produced a different result. It had become an organisation with an unavoidable political dimension and there was no turning back.

The antagonism, harassment and physical abuse directed to GAA members in Northern Ireland could never again be casually explained away by the security forces responsible.

The shooting dead of one of its own members by a British soldier forced the powers that be within the GAA to confront some difficult truths about the political and cultural life of Northern Ireland. Men and women were being repeatedly singled out for adverse treatment simply because of their GAA membership.

Between 1994 and 2002 there were 594 attacks on symbolic properties such as churches, Orange halls and GAA clubs, an average of five attacks a month over a nine-year period.

Bellaghy in Co. Derry had been burned and rebuilt twice. In May 1997 Seán Brown, chairman of the

Chaotic scenes in Croke Park as Offaly supporters sit on the field to protest the fact that the 1998 All-Ireland semi-final against Clare was ended two minutes prematurely. Offaly were granted a replay and went on to win the All-Ireland championship.

Bellaghy club, was locking up the Wolfe Tone GAA club after attending a meeting. Local people heard a shot. His body was dumped ten miles away in Co. Antrim.

Seamus Heaney wrote to the family.

> *I heard the news in Olympia, shortly after visiting the ancient Olympic stadium. I could not but help thinking of his death as a crime against the Olympic spirit.*
>
> *The Greeks recognised that there was something sacrosanct about the athletic ideal and regarded any violence during the period of the games as sacrilegious. He represented something better than we have grown used to, something not quite covered by the word reconciliation because that word has become a policy word — official and public. This was more like purification, a release from what the Greeks call the miasma, the stain of spilled blood. It is a terrible irony that the man should die at the hands of a sectarian killer.*

The GAA delegates who gathered for Seán Brown's funeral could see for themselves the treatment mourners received at the hands of the British armed forces and the police force that had been established by the Stormont regime, the RUC.

It took two more attempts before the ban on British armed forces joining the GAA was removed shortly after the RUC was abolished and replaced by the new Police Service of Northern Ireland.

The Ulster Defence Regiment of the British Army, which had been responsible for the destruction of some of the GAA clubhouses such as Glenullin in Derry, was also abolished.

And finally, the British Army agreed to pull out of their occupation of the GAA grounds at Crossmaglen in July 1999.

Peace, in the words of W. B. Yeats, was coming dropping slow to the north of Ireland, although ten years after the 1995 ceasefires, pipe bomb attacks were still being reported on GAA premises.

A dried-out sod has never had such an impact on the history of any sports organisation as that under the Cusack stand of Croke Park on Gaelic football events during the summer of 1991.

A speculative ball by Colm Coyle bounced over the bar because the ground was hard. If it had been wet and soft it would have landed in the unguarded Dublin net and we would not have had four famous matches between the Leinster rivals.

The four matches had a pattern. Dublin kept going into the lead and Meath kept coming back. They lost a lead of five points on each of the first and third days.

A role reversal in 1998 as goalkeeper Davy Fitzgerald of Clare has his penalty saved by wing-back Brian Whelehan of Offaly. Fitzgerald scored a famous goal from a penalty in the 1995 Munster final. The gamekeeper turned poacher trend first emerged in the late 1980s, with big-hitting goalkeepers such as Cork's Ger Cunningham and Galway's John Commins scoring high-profile penalties. The goalkeeper has to be wary of being caught out of position by a quick puck-out.

Brian Lohan and Davy Fitzgerald lead the Clare team around Croke Park. Ger Loughnane's team raised their standards of fitness in the mid-1990s and were rewarded with two All-Irelands in three years.

In the fourth match they led by five points midway through the second half and by three points with five minutes remaining. To add to their woes Keith Barr missed a penalty. Then Kevin Foley, who had never taken a shot at goal before in his playing career, turned up at the end of a Meath attacking move to score a famous winning goal.

Meath were favourites to win the All-Ireland, but Down built up an 11-point lead by the 50th minute with a Barry Breen goal. Liam Hayes got a consolation goal for Meath as they came storming back, but still lost by two points.

● ● ●

Ulster football, for long the poor relation, was now brimming with confidence and passion, and came back to collect four All-Ireland championships in a row from three different counties. In 1992 Donegal's running game made history as Tony Boyle popped over the points for victory over Dublin, their first ever title. Dublin's Charlie Redmond missed a penalty and Gary Walsh had a great save from Vinny Murphy at the end. Inspirational captain Anthony Molloy

brought the cup back on an emotional journey home that took 11 hours.

Donegal contested five successive Ulster finals, one of them replayed, a unique achievement in the province which was dominating the All-Ireland championship at the time. They then proceeded to contest the National League final three times in a four-year period without success, playing another replay against Dublin in the process.

In 1993 it was Derry's turn. They defeated Dublin in a frenetic semi-final.

'The old Croke Park had more atmosphere', Joe Brolly recalled afterwards. 'The place was heaving. In the second half you couldn't hear anything. Just roaring and screaming.'

Derry beat Cork in the final. Damien Cassidy left the ball hanging in the air just long enough for Séamus Downey to fist the clinching goal. It was a match memorable for Damien McCusker's saves and Enda Gormley's curling free for the last point of the match. Cork's Tony Davis was harshly sent off.

Derry won three National League titles in a five-year period, but that was to be their only All-Ireland as they bowed out in the first round of the following year's championship to Down after as gripping an encounter as Ulster had ever seen.

Down went on to win the All-Ireland in 1994 when Mickey Linden fed James MacCartan for a winning goal under Hill 16, which silenced the Dublin fans.

Many fans remember Dublin's football story of the decade as a puzzlement of missed penalties. In the 1988 Leinster final Charlie Redmond put the last kick of the match over the bar when a goal was needed to draw with Meath; Keith Barr missed in the third replay against Meath in 1991 when Dublin were leading; Charlie Redmond again missed early in the 1992 All-Ireland final against Donegal when Dublin were leading; Redmond missed yet again in the final quarter of the 1994 All-Ireland final against Down; and Paul Bealin hit the bar with the last kick of the 1997 Leinster championship tie with Meath when Dublin trailed by three points.

By then Dublin had at last returned to the podium, preventing an Ulster five in a row and beating Tyrone by a point in the 1995 All-Ireland final.

Jason Sherlock was the hero for the teenagers on the terraces, but it was Charlie Redmond who scored the winning goal, and then created another storm when he failed to leave the field for a minute after he was sent off. The incident led to the introduction of a system of red and yellow cards to prevent further confusion.

At the end of the 70 minutes Peter Canavan, scorer of 11 points for Tyrone, might have won a free to equalise. 'Peter the Great' would be back, but it would take him eight years to get the All-Ireland medal he nearly had in his grasp.

Another Ulster team missed the party as well. When Damian O'Reilly fed Jason Reilly for a goal in the 1997 Ulster final, it restored Cavan to the Ulster title they once expected as a matter of routine.

Cavan provided most of the 60,072 attendance who came to see the semi-final, where they succumbed to Kerry by seven points after a Michael Francis Russell goal with four minutes to go.

● ● ●

Cork's hurling and football double in 1990 was followed by an unexpected hiatus. They lost a replayed 1991 Munster final to Tipperary and an All-Ireland final to Kilkenny in 1992, then went into a sharp decline and lost to Limerick in 1996 by an unprecedented 15 points. More than pride was at stake here.

Cork also lost their undefeated record at home in championship matches that extended back 74 years. It took them nine years to win a championship match again.

In football, Cork's 15-point win over Kerry in 1990 was followed by a defeat in the following year's Munster semi-final against Kerry. The two powers were no longer seeded in Munster, and it presented an opportunity for a David to emerge.

From a marshy, stoney and poorly populated territory west of Ennis came Clare's footballers to fill the role. Mayo-born manager John Maughan provided the inspiration, Colm Clancy and Martin Daly the goals, and Tom Morrissey the heroics to pull off victory over Kerry in the 1992 Munster final that shook football's traditional order.

Clare might have gone further. A disallowed goal from Pádraig Conway unnerved them in the All-Ireland semi-final against Dublin and they lost by five points.

'Conway picked John O'Leary's pocket', sportswriter Con Houlihan wrote. Houlihan was one of the many who thought the goal should have been allowed.

● ● ●

Connacht's old order was also due a shake. In 1994 Leitrim beat Roscommon by a point, Galway by a point in a replay, and Mayo by two points to win their

Outstanding Offaly half-back and the only current player selected on the team of the millennium, Brian Whelehan in action on his home ground at Birr, venue for the first All-Ireland hurling championship final staged in 1888 (in the adjoining field to the current playing pitch) and the first All-Ireland club hurling final in 1971.

first Connacht championship since 1927. They too lost to Dublin, by just two points.

Leitrim was the first county to benefit under the GAA's parentage rule but also the first to lose their big catch, as Declan Darcy came back to his ancestral home in 1994, only to dramatically declare once more for Dublin in 1998.

Sligo were edging closer too, drawing with Mayo in 1992, with Galway in 1995 and 1996 with superb equalising points by Declan McGoldrick and Paul

the last 20 minutes. Maurice Fitzgerald's nine points qualified him for the player of the year award.

Before the end of May 1998, Mayo were out of the championship, having collapsed in the second half against a revitalised Galway team managed by Mayo-born John O'Mahony.

Galway went on to win the All-Ireland, playing a direct kicking game that pleased traditionalists. The TV audience of 603,000 was the highest for an All-Ireland final and the most viewed sports event of the year, ahead of the soccer World Cup.

With outstanding performances from Ja Fallon and Michael Donnellan and a superbly taken goal from Pádraig Joyce, Galway defeated a Kildare team that carried the weight of 70 years without success on their backs. Kildare had beaten the previous three All-Ireland champions, Dublin, Meath and Kerry, in their run-up to the final.

'The GAA should get down on their knees and give thanks for John O'Mahony and his gallant Galway players', sportswriter and former Offaly team manager Eugene McGee wrote. 'They re-invented the great old game of Gaelic football. After years of the short-game mania by many other counties they reverted to the game's original great skills and triumphed with marvellous high catching, brilliant long-range points and, above all, moving the ball with the foot rather than the hand.'

Teen icon of a new generation when Dublin captured a much-needed All-Ireland, Jason Sherlock blasts the ball past Cork goalkeeper Kevin O'Dwyer for his side's goal in the 1995 All-Ireland football semi-final.

Taylor respectively, and losing a controversial Connacht final in 1997 to Mayo by a single point. Meath returned to contest another All-Ireland against Mayo in 1996, snatching a draw with a Colm Coyle equaliser after Mayo had led by six points.

Set-piece goals from a Trevor Giles penalty and Tommy Dowd's quick free won the replay after a chaotic punch-up which resulted in Liam McHale and Colm Coyle being sent off. Mayo might have escaped again. James Horan scored a 66th minute equaliser but Brendan Reilly replied with a point that precipitated another long gloomy journey home for Mayo.

Mayo returned for another big match disappointment in 1997 when Kerry beat them by three points. Mayo scored 1-2 in a two-minute spell but failed to score in

Armagh were also building up to an All-Ireland. Crossmaglen Rangers had to overcome the unique problem of having part of their playing grounds occupied by the British Army. It partly explains the acclaim that greeted their 1997 club football win with goals from man of the match Oisin McConville and his brother Jim.

The club championship had established its place on the calendar as crowds of more than 40,000 turned out for the hurling and football finals played together on St Patrick's Day.

Controversy dogged the women's Gaelic football final of 1997 over the 12 minutes of injury time allowed in the All-Ireland final. The unwanted publicity boosted the profile of the game enormously. An experimental clock was introduced in 1998, just as the rivalry between Monaghan and Waterford, which had captivated the nation, was coming to an end.

The Monaghan-Waterford sparring match drove attendances up from 13,551 to 16,421. The attendance reached 23,358 to see Cork complete a camogie-football double against Galway in 2005 and remains among the highest for any female-only team sports event in the world.

It gave a higher profile to new stars like Cora Staunton of Mayo and helped boost the game in new counties.

Mayo and Galway played an epic All-Ireland semi-final in 2004 before Galway won in extra time by a single point, thanks to a Niamh Duggan goal. Galway completed their remarkable advance from junior to senior champions, beating Dublin 'Jackies' in the final.

Women's football claimed to be Ireland's fastest growing participation sport from the early 1990s on, when membership rose to 27,000. Croke Park staged the finals from 1986 on. Thousands of girls play in primary school leagues organised by Cumann na mBunscoil throughout the country and games are played in Britain, mainland Europe, Australia, Canada, and the US where it has a wider following among non-Irish American players than men's football.

Crucially, the women's football final was televised live after 1997, bringing stars like Jenny Greenan of Monaghan, Sue Ramsbottom of Laois and Diane O'Hora of Mayo to national prominence. The television audience reached 531,000 in 2005 and regularly exceeds the viewing figures for three of Ireland's Six Nations rugby internationals, as does the camogie final.

One by-product of the great series of replays between Dublin and Meath in 1991 was the inauguration of a full-time GAA coaching scheme.

After decades of successful investment in bricks and mortar, the GAA started concentrating more on developing their players. The extra money generated by Meath and Dublin meant full-time coaches could be hired and put on the ground for the first time.

The introduction of a transition year into secondary schools meant that young coaches could be trained.

The movement grew through the decade in tandem with a successful summer-camp movement and the increased profile of the Cumann na mBunscoil primary schools movement through awards, competition finals, and especially through the use of half-time kick-abouts at major matches which allowed promising 10-year olds to savour the atmosphere of playing in Croke Park in front of 80,000 people.

Hurling was about to enter a new exciting era. It all started with an unlikely turnaround at the end of the 1994 All-Ireland hurling final.

With Limerick five points ahead, Johnny Dooley was instructed from the sideline to go for a point but

Keith Barr's ill-fated penalty against Meath during the third replay of the 1991 Leinster championship series between Dublin and Meath.

instead drove the ball straight to the net and Offaly devastated the Limerick team with 2-5 in a frantic spell of four minutes and 14 seconds.

Iconic 1970s Clare hurler Ger Loughnane finally brought Michael Cusack's county to the heart of Gaelic matters in 1995. Building on the 1989 minors and a wealth of talent from St Flannan's College teams, a miraculous come-back in the Munster semi-final against Cork in 1995, inspired by Seánie MacMahon who played on despite a broken collar-bone, was turned into the springboard for two All-Ireland successes.

Unlikely match-winner Kevin Foley had never scored a goal, even in training, when he emerged at the end of a seven-man move to kick the equalising goal at the end of the fourth match of the 1991 series against Dublin. Colleague Mattie McCabe had suggested the wing-back should stray forward to confuse the tight-marking Dublin defence. Some grateful Meath parents named their sons Kevin in his honour after the historic goal. David Beggy added a point to win. Foley is photographed in action in the All-Ireland final against James McCartan of Down, where the epic had a sad ending — Meath were beaten by two points.

Éamonn Taaffe came on to score the winning goal against Offaly in 1995 and was promptly substituted again, and a powerful display by Jamesie O'Connor secured the championship against the first back door finalists, Tipperary, in 1997.

Limerick had come back from nine points behind at half-time against Tipperary in the 1996 Munster final, and then won the replay with a succession of killer goals. But in the final they lost to another county reacquainting itself with the winner's podium.

In 1996 Wexford manager Liam Griffin took his team off their Dublin-bound bus to show them the county boundary. It succeeded in inspiring them to victory in the All-Ireland final against Limerick. Wexford's victory song, recorded by the Wild Swans, managed to name all the Wexford heroes in a breathless last verse.

When Griffin described hurling as 'the Riverdance of sport', his phrase became the catch-cry of a new era for the game.

Even the National League was enjoying a revolution, when winter hurling was brought to an end and Saturday evening matches were introduced. Attendances and interest soared. The erection of floodlights enabled matches to be played on Friday nights as well, and four grounds a year were upgraded to boost the game's television profile.

We will never know whether Clare would have had another All-Ireland in 1998, had their three-point victory over Offaly not been rendered null and void by a refereeing error. Jimmy Cooney blew the final whistle two minutes early and angry Offaly fans occupied the field in protest. Clare lost a second replay by three points when the Offaly goalkeeper Stephen Byrnes made a series of stunning saves. 'It had to be done', he stoically declared afterwards.

Offaly went on to capture the All-Ireland, the first county to use the back door to do so. In 1999 Waterford had re-emerged to win the Munster title after 39 years.

Clare goalkeeper David Fitzgerald acquired a name as a penalty-taker, scoring the winning goal in the tumultuous 1995 Munster final, missing in the first of the three 1998 encounters with Offaly, and scoring again with the last puck of a drawn match with Tipperary in 1999.

It was back to the traditional counties after that, and the incredible genius of D. J. Carey, winner of a record nine All Star awards in hurling.

Carey shot to prominence in 1988 when he won both colleges and minor All-Irelands. By 1993, when he won his first hurler of the year award, Diarmuid Healy claimed he was as good as Christy Ring.

Having announced his premature retirement at the age of 27 in 1998, he reconsidered and was soon resuming the trademark run on goal that brought comparisons with Ring and, from the few who could remember, Mick Mackey.

Even with Carey relatively muted, by his own standards, Kilkenny went on to win further All-Irelands in 2002 and 2003.

'Hurling should thank God for him', Brian Cody said after the 2000 All-Ireland hurling final. 'What would be the point of building a cathedral like Croke Park if D. J. Carey were not to soar within it', Tom Humphries wrote after the 2002 All-Ireland final.

Was he as good as the greats? It is too early to say.

Where hurling went, camogie followed. The game clung to its smaller pitch, goal and team size until 1999. There was trepidation among some of the game's supporters that change would lead to lower standards, but the opposite happened.

By the start of the 1990s only five counties had won the All-Ireland camogie championship. Three years afterwards, Galway won their first title with goals from 18-year-old Denise Gilligan.

In 1999 a Tipperary team inspired by Deirdre Hughes and Eimear McDonnell won their first title on the new-sized field, with a dramatic winner from Caitriona Hennessy. They went on to win three in a row and five out of the next six titles, stopped only by Cork in 2002 (with three goals from Fiona O'Driscoll) and again in 2005.

Television audiences averaged 250,000. The new names and the Cork-Tipp rivalry after 2000 pushed up the attendance record to 10,235 in 1996, 10,436 in 1998, and after the adoption of the larger pitch 15,084 in 1999, 16,354 in 2001, and 24,567 in 2004.

Camogie still differs from hurling in minor ways. The sliotar is slightly lighter, the hand-passed goal is allowed, the hurley may be dropped to hand-pass, the sliotar may be taken in the hand, shouldering is not allowed, and the opponent's hurley may be flicked.

The Camogie Association celebrated its centenary in 2004. It has a membership of 84,000 in 500 clubs. The

It took four matches before Meath eventually overcame Dublin in the 1991 Leinster football championship. It was Down, however, who were to snatch the All-Ireland championship from Meath in the final.

association is due to be integrated fully into the GAA by 2007 under restructuring proposals.

Cavan's Paul Brady became the first World Handball open singles champion to have represented Ireland when he beat Dave Chapman of the US in the 2003 World Championships. Brady was also the first Irishman to win professional tournaments in the US.

World championships were revived as part of the GAA centenary celebrations in Dublin and Clare in 1984, and further championships staged in Canada in 1986, Australia in 1988, Phoenix, Arizona, in 1991, and at venues in Clare, Dublin, Kildare and Meath in 1994, attracting 650 players from Australia, Britain, Canada, Japan, Mexico and the US. Two entrants from Finland joined the competitors in a record 41 categories for men and women of all ages from mid-teens to 75 years old and over. The tenth World Championships were held in Chicago in 1999.

As the sport placed greater emphasis on participation, it expanded into different age categories for both men and women and the number of national championships was increased from three to 168.

After the 1980s, the sport was dominated by Kilkenny's Michael 'Ducksy' Walsh (often called Duxie), undefeated from 1985 to 1998 in senior singles, and he also won eight All-Ireland titles in the American-sized court, 40 x 20 feet. Walter O'Connor of Meath, Tony Healy of Cork and Eoin Kennedy of Dublin also emerged to win titles in the post-Ducksy era.

Football tactics had fallen into two spheres, partitioning the country more effectively than the politicians ever did. Ulster and Leinster were playing their championships with scarcely any elbow room as defenders marked tightly and often brutally. In Munster and Connacht there was room for a more expansive game. In 2000 the free footballers won out. Galway and Kerry met twice in the All-Ireland final, Kerry winning despite a sublime Declan Meehan goal that was one of the best in the history of the competition.

In 2001 Galway introduced an even more radical approach, calling in extra defenders to shore up the weaknesses of the free game, and overwhelmed Meath by nine points. The team was commended by an

Dublin's All-Ireland of 1995 was their reward for nearly a decade of toil. Their chief marksman, Charlie Redmond, was sent off by referee Paddy Russell but misunderstood the sanction and remained on the field for another minute. Dublin corner-forward Jason Sherlock, who scored a goal against Laois after losing his boot, was to become the teenage icon of the decade.

admiring Eugene McGee for their 'mixture of class, hunger, composure on the field and very sound tactical nous on the sideline'.

The euphoria that accompanied the emergence of the new names to challenge the traditional counties and the transformation of the GAA's home stadium gave the association the courage to do something really radical: to tackle the 'one strike and you're out' nature of the championship.

A second chance was granted to beaten provincial finalists in hurling in 1997, and the description 'back door' by radio commentator Micheál Ó Muircheartaigh quickly passed into popular culture.

In 2001 a qualifier competition in football, not on a provincial basis, was introduced to give defeated counties a chance to come back into the All-Ireland quarter-finals.

The proposal drew some opposition because it threatened the provincial structure which had served the GAA well, but in the first years the run of Westmeath to the quarter-final and the fact that two of the quarter-finals went to replays caught the imagination, including a match between Meath and Westmeath in which Meath came back from nine points down. 'Westmeath's progress has shown the travesty that was the old-style championship for over 100 years. Thankfully, things will never be the same again', Eugene McGee wrote.

A replayed quarter-final in Thurles between Dublin and Kerry, marked with a sublime point from the sideline by Maurice Fitzgerald, was the highlight of the championship.

The expanded hurling stage of the 1990s needed a new star to fill it. D. J. Carey exploded on the scene with a spectacular goal in the final minute of the 1991 Leinster hurling final against Wexford. He became the undisputed master cat for the next 15 years with his stickwork, occasional overhead flicks and, a terrifying sight for any goalkeeper, his distinctive solo runs bearing down on goal with ball on stick.

There was more match-end drama in 2002 as Dublin's Ray Cosgrove hit the post with a would-be equalising point against Armagh that caused 79,386 spectators to miss a heartbeat.

Where Westmeath went in the 2001 qualifiers, Sligo followed in 2002, reaching the quarter-final with a victory over Kildare. The attendance at Sligo's qualifier with Dublin, 60,720, was exceeded only by the All-Ireland final, semi-final and Leinster final.

Fermanagh went even further. In 2003 they beat Donegal in the Ulster championship, then Meath and Mayo in the qualifiers to reach the quarter-final. They went one better, to a semi-final replay in 2004, beating Meath, Cork and Donegal before losing to Mayo.

There were fears for the traditional provincial championships, but here again attendances and viewing figures held up. In Leinster Laois were inspired in turn to win their first Leinster championship since 1946 and Westmeath triggered off wild celebrations in 2004, beating Laois in a replay to win their first ever Leinster title. In Munster Limerick took Kerry to a replay in the 2004 Munster final, then inexplicably opted out of the following week's championship qualifier.

And in keeping with the mood of change, two new All-Ireland champions emerged. Armagh were outsiders in the 2003 final against Kerry, despite the evidence of Kerry's vulnerability, apparent in a record 15-point defeat by Meath in the 2001 semi-final.

Oisin McConville revisited the mythology of 1953 by missing an Armagh penalty but then scored an inspirational second half goal to allow Armagh crank up the pent-up frustration of years of near misses.

'Helicopters landing', said Kerry manager Páidí Ó Sé, describing the force that had overwhelmed them. The reference was to the British Army's 30-year occupation of the GAA grounds in Crossmaglen, and he didn't need to explain.

Armagh's northerly neighbours were also overdue an All-Ireland. Where Armagh had gone, Tyrone followed. This time Kerry were the victims in the semi-final, Tyrone's massed defence smothering their attacks. Tyrone outplayed Armagh in the final, won by three points, but within months of the victory their new captain for 2004, Cormac MacAnallen, had fallen victim to sudden adult death syndrome.

Kerry followed Tyrone to the podium by crushing Mayo in 2004 and when the two clashed in the 2005 final it was Mickey Harte's durable Tyrone team which won, relinquishing Ulster's reputation for dour football in a sparkling ten-match run to the championship. It included a pulsating draw with Dublin, distinguished by a fine individual goal from Owen Mulligan. Peter Canavan saw off their Ulster final conquerors, Armagh, with a late semi-final point.

When they beat Kerry in the final, as one banner put it 'with the help of God and the Sacred Harte', Tyrone recovered from Daire Ó Cinnéide's 6th minute goal to get one of their own from Peter Canavan just before half–time. Kerry's comeback, inspired by Tomás Ó Sé's 57th minute goal, enlivened the best final for a decade. Brian Dooher's emotional eight-minute victory speech paid tribute to his predecessor, Cormac MacAnallen, a tragic victim of Sudden Arrhythmia Death Syndrome 18 months earlier.

The explosion of live sport that followed Rubert Murdoch's entry into the media marketplace changed the GAA's relationship with its broadcasters. In 1991, the BBC and UTV had bid against each other for rights to the Ulster championship and it immediately boosted the profile of the games in the North. When the BBC brought 17 cameras to the Ulster final it was the most extensive coverage ever accorded to a GAA match to that date.

A full calendar of live matches was devised by the GAA and negotiated with the Irish state broadcaster, Radio Telefís Éireann.

After 1996 there was a new indigenous channel with an interest in Gaelic games. Telefís na Gaeltachta, later TG4, started by negotiating rights for inter-Gaeltacht football matches and club games. This was later extended to the club championships and the winter-time National League.

TG4 pioneered the coverage of floodlit League football and hurling in February and March. The advent of Saturday night League matches in 1996 was followed by the introduction of floodlit facilities, first in Cork's Páirc Uí Rinn, Tralee's Austin Stack Park and Dublin's Parnell Park, and extended by four grounds a year to other venues.

The 2004 and 2005 finals attracted some of the biggest sporting TV audiences of all time, 743,000 in 2004 and a record 887,000 in 2005 for the football, and 717,000 and 726,000 for the hurling finals in which Cork surprised Kilkenny and defied a Galway comeback to retain the title.

The GAA touched many people in its 120-year history. How did those it touched respond?

President Mary McAleese spoke of her emotions as she watched a seven-a-side tournament in Asia.

Sportswriter Tom Humphries wrote of the GAA as a national trust, 'an entity which we feel we hold in common ownership. It is there to administer to our shared passion.'

Juan Antonio Samaranch tried the lift and strike with a camán outside an EU meeting in Brussels.

Visiting soccer managers have marvelled at a sport which attracts an average attendance of 52,000 to Croke Park during a championship season and yet has no transfer system, no overt pay-for-play, and which insists its heroes return to play club matches for the villages and townlands from whence they came; and many, many more deeply personal experiences and assessments, because the Gaelic Athletic Association has been many things to many people, often at the same time.

Some historians have been unkind, commenting on it in terms of insularism (Roy Foster) or Anglophobia (David Fitzpatrick), while Diarmaid Ferriter described it as a 'haven of drunkenness and injury'.

It is an association of 2,000 clubs, 300,000 members and over a million followers — all with their own ideas of what the GAA means to them.

One of the GAA's presidents described the reaction of GAA followers when they arrived at the newly reconstructed Croke Park in 1996. In every case it was with a sense of pride, as if they were showing someone around their new house.

They had a sense of ownership.

Croke Park is everyone's.

We all own the GAA.

The emergence of astonishingly talented Henry Shefflin, pictured with the McCarthy cup, led to the Kilkenny team of the turn of the twentieth century being compared with their predecessors of the 1970s.

Small boy, big goal, long tradition. A shinty hurling match was first proposed (and a Scottish team selected) in 1888. Here Nicky Quaid, son of former Limerick goalkeeper Tommy, awaits developments in the cold before the under-12 international challenge match in Inverness. Shinty followed hurling precedent and changed to a summer season in 2004.

The moment Armagh has waited for, their first All-Ireland championship in 2002. Supporters defied Croke Park officials' attempts to prevent them coming on to the field. Invading the pitch at the end of a match was regarded as part of the All-Ireland ceremonial. The closing minutes of games such as the 1980 and 1981 hurling finals were played with expectant supporters crowding closer and closer to the sidelines.

Derry minors celebrate in 2002. The under-18 (minor) final serves as a curtain-raiser to the All-Ireland final. In the 1940s the minor hurling final was played before the senior football final.

History in the making in 2003 as Ulster teams Tyrone and Armagh parade before the All-Ireland final. The introduction of a second-chance All-Ireland series in 2001, the 'back door' as commentator Micheál Ó Muircheartaigh called it, ended 114 years in which provincial champions played off for the All-Ireland in semi-finals which had been strictly rotated in three-year cycles since 1928, a practice initially introduced to prevent dominance by Munster and Leinster teams. The experiment was enormously successful and Ulster unexpectedly provided five of the eight quarter-finalists and three of the four semi-finalists in 2003. The increased interest in the Ulster championship meant that the final for 2004 was switched to Croke Park.

Armagh manager Joe Kernan after victory over Kerry in the 2003 All-Ireland final. Kerry manager Páidí Ó Sé described what happened in the second half as 'helicopters landing', a release of the pent-up frustration of 35 years of suffering under the Northern Ireland troubles. Kernan showed the team his losers' medal from 1977 at half-time, asking 'Which do you want — one of these, or a winner's medal?'

Joe Kernan's son Ross with the Sam Maguire cup on the road home to Armagh. The homecoming ceremonial with the cup on Monday night has become a major part of All-Ireland ritual, followed by a tour of clubs and schools across the county that extends until the following year's championship.

Edel Byrne of Monaghan scores a goal despite the attention of Mayo's Clare O'Hara and Yvonne Byrne in the 2002 All-Ireland football final. All-Ireland women's football finals are among the best supported women's team sports events in Europe.

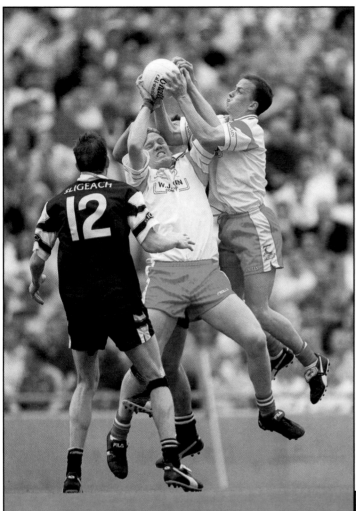

The shocking and unexpected death of Tyrone's outstanding captain Cormac MacAnallen sparked a nationwide investigation into sudden deaths among young sportsmen. GAA culture has cherished the memory of its finest sportsmen who died before their playing career was over. Famous ballads commemorated the deeds of Tommy Daly of Clare, P. J. Duke and John Joe O'Reilly of Cavan.

Therese Brophy of Tipperary in action against Linda Mellerick of Cork. Since 1968 traditional hurling counties have dominated the All-Ireland camogie championship.

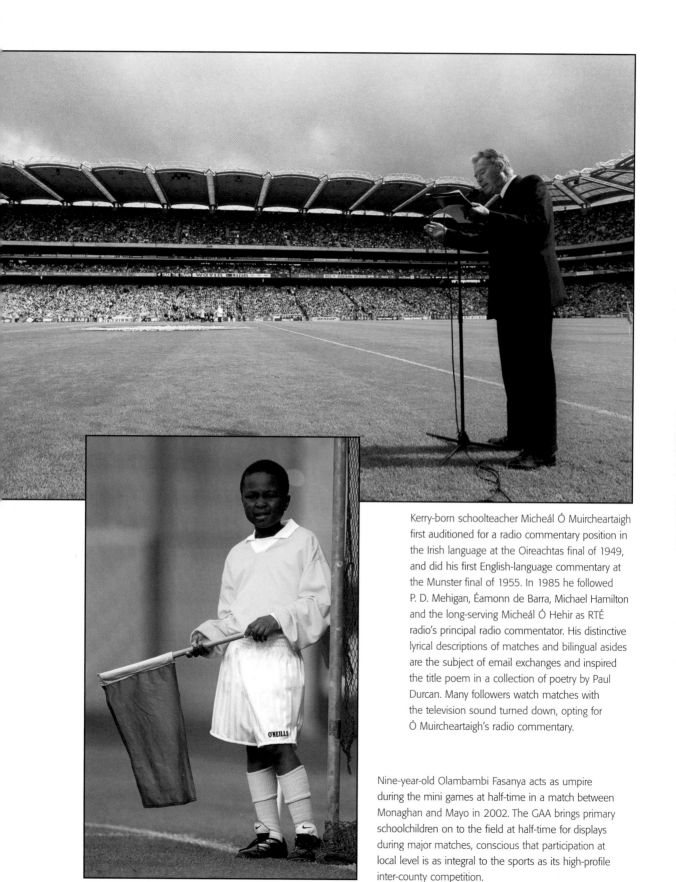

Kerry-born schoolteacher Micheál Ó Muircheartaigh
first auditioned for a radio commentary position in
the Irish language at the Oireachtas final of 1949,
and did his first English-language commentary at
the Munster final of 1955. In 1985 he followed
P. D. Mehigan, Éamonn de Barra, Michael Hamilton
and the long-serving Micheál Ó Hehir as RTÉ
radio's principal radio commentator. His distinctive
lyrical descriptions of matches and bilingual asides
are the subject of email exchanges and inspired
the title poem in a collection of poetry by Paul
Durcan. Many followers watch matches with
the television sound turned down, opting for
Ó Muircheartaigh's radio commentary.

Nine-year-old Olambambi Fasanya acts as umpire
during the mini games at half-time in a match between
Monaghan and Mayo in 2002. The GAA brings primary
schoolchildren on to the field at half-time for displays
during major matches, conscious that participation at
local level is as integral to the sports as its high-profile
inter-county competition.

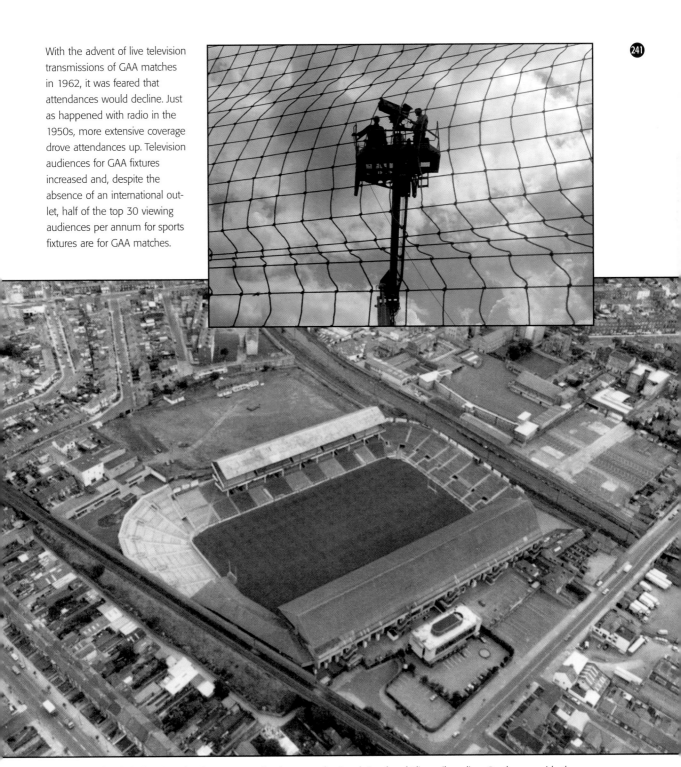

With the advent of live television transmissions of GAA matches in 1962, it was feared that attendances would decline. Just as happened with radio in the 1950s, more extensive coverage drove attendances up. Television audiences for GAA fixtures increased and, despite the absence of an international outlet, half of the top 30 viewing audiences per annum for sports fixtures are for GAA matches.

Croke Park shortly before its redevelopment, nestling between the Royal Canal and Sligo railway line. On the near side the Hogan stand was built in 1959 to replace the old Hogan stand, which was moved to Limerick, and what was known as the Long stand from the 1922–4 period. In the bottom left-hand corner is the Nally stand which was built in 1954. At the top right is Hill 16 which was originally built from rubble accumulated after the 1916 Rising but had been reconstructed in 1992. The Cusack stand (top right) had been built in 1938 and the Canal End terracing (on the right) concreted over in 1948. The four sides of the new Croke Park are named in honour of Bloody Sunday victim Michael Hogan, GAA founder Michael Cusack, the 1870s 'athletics for the people' campaigner Pat Nally and GAA founding president Maurice Davin.

A decision in September 1983 that Ireland's biggest sports stadium should be demolished and rebuilt, while remaining in continuous use, proved far-sighted for the GAA. They completed the project in 2005, having paid 80 per cent of the capital cost from their own resources.

A Garda bandsman plays in front of 82,000 spectators in Croke Park at a Leinster championship match in 2005. Summer championship matches at the national stadium draw an average attendance of 52,000.

All-Ireland Hurling Finals

1887 Tipperary 1-1 (1) Galway 0-0 (0) Birr *c*.5,000
1888 Cork v Clare unresolved, Kilkenny Leinster champions
1889 Dublin 5-1 Clare 1-6 Inchicore *c*.1,500
1890 Wexford 2-2 Cork 1-6 Clonturk Park *c*.1,000
  (unfinished). Cork awarded match
1891 Kerry 2-3 Wexford 1-5 Clonturk Park *c*.2,000
  (after extra time)
1892 Cork 2-4 Dublin 1-1 Clonturk Park *c*.5,000
  (unfinished)
1893 Cork 6-8 Kilkenny 0-2 Phoenix Park *c*.1,000
1894 Cork 5-20 Dublin 2-0 Clonturk Park *c*.2,000
1895 Tipperary 6-8 Kilkenny 1-10 Jones's Road *c*.8,000
1896 Tipperary 8-14 Dublin 0-4 Jones's Road *c*.3,500
1897 Limerick 3-4 Kilkenny 2-4 Tipperary *c*.5,000
1898 Tipperary 7-13 Kilkenny 3-10 Jones's Road *c*.2,500
1899 Tipperary 3-12 Wexford 1-4 Jones's Road *c*.3,500
1900 Tipperary 2-5 London 0-6 Jones's Road *c*.8,000
  Home Final: Tipperary 6-13 Galway 1-5 Terenure *c*.2,000
1901 London 1-5 Cork 0-4 Jones's Road *c*.1,000
  Home Final: Cork 2-8 Wexford 0-6 Carrick-on-Suir *c*.6,000
1902 Cork 3-13 London 0-0 Cork *c*.10,000
  Home Final: Cork 1-7 Dublin 1-7 Tipperary *c*.4,000
  Replay: Cork 2-6 Dublin 0-1 Tipperary *c*.3,000
1903 Cork 3-16 London 1-1 Jones's Road *c*.10,000
  Home Final: Cork 8-9 Kilkenny 0-8 Dungarvan 5,000
1904 Kilkenny 1-9 Cork 1-8 Carrick-on-Suir *c*.10,000
1905 Cork 5-10 Kilkenny 3-13 Tipperary *c*.6,000
  Replay: Kilkenny 7-7 Cork 2-9 Dungarvan *c*.9,000
1906 Tipperary 3-16 Dublin 3-8 Kilkenny *c*.5,000
1907 Kilkenny 3-12 Cork 4-8 Dungarvan 15,000
1908 Tipperary 2-5 Dublin 1-8 Jones's Road *c*.6,000
  Replay: Tipperary 3-15 Dublin 1-5 Athy *c*.3,000
1909 Kilkenny 4-6 Tipperary 0-12 Cork *c*.11,000
1910 Wexford 7-0 Limerick 6-2 Jones's Road 4,780
1911 Kilkenny awarded. Limerick withdrew
  (Alternative to final: Kilkenny 3-3 Tipperary 2-1 Thurles)
1912 Kilkenny 2-1 Cork 1-3 Jones's Road *c*.18,000
1913 Kilkenny 2-4 Tipperary 1-2 Jones's Road *c*.15,000
1914 Clare 5-1 Laois 1-0 Croke Park *c*.12,000
1915 Laois 6-2 Cork 4-1 Croke Park *c*.14,000
1916 Tipperary 5-4 Kilkenny 3-2 Croke Park *c*.5,000
1917 Dublin 5-4 Tipperary 4-2 Croke Park *c*.11,500
1918 Limerick 9-5 Wexford 1-3 Croke Park *c*.12,000
1919 Cork 6-4 Dublin 2-4 Croke Park 14,300
1920 Dublin 4-9 Cork 4-3 Croke Park *c*.22,000
1921 Limerick 8-5 Dublin 3-2 Croke Park *c*.18,000
1922 Kilkenny 4-2 Tipperary 2-6 Croke Park 26,119
1923 Galway 7-3 Limerick 4-5 Croke Park *c*.7,000
1924 Dublin 5-3 Galway 2-6 Croke Park *c*.9,000
1925 Tipperary 5-6 Galway 1-5 Croke Park *c*.20,000
1926 Cork 4-6 Kilkenny 2-0 Croke Park 26,829
1927 Dublin 4-8 Cork 1-3 Croke Park 23,824
1928 Cork 6-12 Galway 1-0 Croke Park 15,259
1929 Cork 4-9 Galway 1-3 Croke Park *c*.14,000
1930 Tipperary 2-7 Dublin 1-3 Croke Park 21,730
1931 Cork 1-6 Kilkenny 1-6 Croke Park 26,460
  Replay: Cork 2-5 Kilkenny 2-5 Croke Park 33,124
  Replay: Cork 5-8 Kilkenny 3-4 Croke Park 31,935
1932 Kilkenny 3-3 Clare 2-3 Croke Park 34,392
1933 Kilkenny 1-7 Limerick 0-6 Croke Park 45,176
1934 Limerick 2-7 Dublin 3-4 Croke Park 34,867
  Replay: Limerick 5-2 Dublin 2-6 Croke Park 30,250
1935 Kilkenny 2-5 Limerick 2-4 Croke Park 46,591
1936 Limerick 5-6 Kilkenny 1-5 Croke Park 51,235
1937 Tipperary 3-11 Kilkenny 0-3 Killarney 43,638
1938 Dublin 2-5 Waterford 1-6 Croke Park 37,129
1939 Kilkenny 2-7 Cork 3-3 Croke Park 39,302

1940 Limerick 3-7 Kilkenny 1-7 Croke Park 49,260
1941 Cork 5-11 Dublin 0-6 Croke Park 26,150
1942 Cork 2-14 Dublin 3-4 Croke Park 27,313
1943 Cork 5-16 Antrim 0-4 Croke Park 48,843
1944 Cork 2-13 Dublin 1-2 Croke Park 26,896
1945 Tipperary 5-6 Kilkenny 3-6 Croke Park 69,459
1946 Cork 7-5 Kilkenny 3-8 Croke Park 64,415
1947 Kilkenny 0-14 Cork 2-7 Croke Park 61,510
1948 Waterford 6-7 Dublin 4-2 Croke Park 61,742
1949 Tipperary 3-11 Laois 0-3 Croke Park 67,168
1950 Tipperary 1-9 Kilkenny 1-8 Croke Park 67,629
1951 Tipperary 7-7 Wexford 3-9 Croke Park 68,515
1952 Cork 2-14 Dublin 0-7 Croke Park 64,332
1953 Cork 3-3 Galway 0-8 Croke Park 71,195
1954 Cork 1-9 Wexford 1-6 Croke Park 84,856
1955 Wexford 3-13 Galway 2-8 Croke Park 72,854
1956 Wexford 2-14 Cork 2-8 Croke Park 83,096
1957 Kilkenny 4-10 Waterford 3-12 Croke Park 70,594
1958 Tipperary 4-9 Galway 2-5 Croke Park 47,276
1959 Waterford 1-17 Kilkenny 5-5 Croke Park 73,707
  Replay: Waterford 3-12 Kilkenny 1-10 Croke Park 77,285
1960 Wexford 2-15 Tipperary 0-11 Croke Park 77,154
1961 Tipperary 0-16 Dublin 1-12 Croke Park 67,866
1962 Tipperary 3-10 Wexford 2-11 Croke Park 75,039
1963 Kilkenny 4-17 Waterford 6-8 Croke Park 73,123
1964 Tipperary 5-13 Kilkenny 2-8 Croke Park 71,282
1965 Tipperary 2-16 Wexford 0-10 Croke Park 67,498
1966 Cork 3-9 Kilkenny 1-10 Croke Park 68,249
1967 Kilkenny 3-8 Tipperary 2-7 Croke Park 64,241
1968 Wexford 5-8 Tipperary 3-12 Croke Park 63,461
1969 Kilkenny 2-15 Cork 2-9 Croke Park 66,844
1970 Cork 6-21 Wexford 5-10 Croke Park 65,062
1971 Tipperary 5-17 Kilkenny 5-14 Croke Park 61,393
1972 Kilkenny 3-24 Cork 5-11 Croke Park 66,137
1973 Limerick 1-21 Kilkenny 1-14 Croke Park 58,009
1974 Kilkenny 3-19 Limerick 1-13 Croke Park 62,071
1975 Kilkenny 2-22 Galway 2-10 Croke Park 63,711
1976 Cork 2-21 Wexford 4-11 Croke Park 62,684
1977 Cork 1-17 Wexford 3-8 Croke Park 63,168
1978 Cork 1-15 Kilkenny 2-8 Croke Park 64,155
1979 Kilkenny 2-12 Galway 1-8 Croke Park 53,535
1980 Galway 2-15 Limerick 3-9 Croke Park 64,895
1981 Offaly 2-12 Galway 0-15 Croke Park 71,348
1982 Kilkenny 3-18 Cork 1-15 Croke Park 59,550
1983 Kilkenny 2-14 Cork 2-12 Croke Park 58,381
1984 Cork 3-16 Offaly 1-12 Thurles 59,814
1985 Offaly 2-11 Galway 1-12 Croke Park 61,451
1986 Cork 4-13 Galway 2-15 Croke Park 63,451
1987 Galway 1-12 Kilkenny 0-9 Croke Park 65,586
1988 Galway 1-15 Tipperary 0-14 Croke Park 63,545
1989 Tipperary 4-24 Antrim 3-9 Croke Park 65,496
1990 Cork 5-15 Galway 2-21 Croke Park 63,954
1991 Tipperary 1-16 Kilkenny 0-15 Croke Park 64,500
1992 Kilkenny 3-10 Cork 1-12 Croke Park 64,534
1993 Kilkenny 2-17 Galway 1-15 Croke Park 63,460
1994 Offaly 3-16 Limerick 2-13 Croke Park 54,458
1995 Clare 1-13 Offaly 2-8 Croke Park 65,092
1996 Wexford 1-13 Limerick 0-14 Croke Park 65,849
1997 Clare 0-20 Tipperary 2-13 Croke Park 65,575
1998 Offaly 2-16 Kilkenny 1-13 Croke Park 65,491
1999 Cork 0-13 Kilkenny 0-12 Croke Park 62,989
2000 Kilkenny 5-15 Offaly 1-14 Croke Park 61,493
2001 Tipperary 2-18 Galway 2-15 Croke Park 68,515
2002 Kilkenny 2-20 Clare 0-19 Croke Park 76,254
2003 Kilkenny 1-14 Cork 1-11 Croke Park 79,383
2004 Cork 0-17 Kilkenny 0-9 Croke Park 78,212
2005 Cork 1-21 Galway 1-16 Croke Park 81,136

All-Ireland Football Finals

1887 Limerick 1-4 Louth 0-3 Clonskeagh *c.*9,000
1888 Unfinished. Tipperary, Kilkenny and Monaghan qualified
1889 Tipperary 3-6 Queens County 0-0 Inchicore *c.*1,500
1890 Cork 2-4 Wexford 0-1 Clonturk Park *c.*1,000
1891 Dublin 2-1 Cork 1-9 Clonturk Park *c.*2,000
          (Goal outweighed any number of points until 1892)
1892 Dublin 1-4 Kerry 0-3 Clonturk Park *c.*5,000
1893 Wexford 1-1 Cork 0-2 Phoenix Park *c.*1,000 (unfinished)
1894 Dublin 0-6 Cork 1-1 Clonturk Park *c.*2,000
          Replay: Cork 1-2 Dublin 0-5 Thurles *c.*10,000 (unfinished)
          Dublin awarded championship
1895 Tipperary 0-4 Meath 0-3 Jones's Road *c.*8,000
1896 Limerick 1-5 Dublin 0-7 Jones's Road *c.*3,500
1897 Dublin 2-6 Cork 0-2 Jones's Road *c.*4,000
1898 Dublin 2-8 Waterford 0-4 Tipperary *c.*1,000
1899 Dublin 1-10 Cork 0-6 Jones's Road *c.*2,000
1900 Tipperary 3-7 London 0-2 Jones's Road *c.*2,000
          Home Final: Tipperary 2-17 Galway 0-1 Terenure *c.*2,000
1901 Dublin 0-14 London 0-2 Jones's Road *c.*2,000
          Home Final: Dublin 1-2 Cork 0-4 Tipperary 4,500
1902 Dublin 2-8 London 0-4 Cork *c.*10,000
          Home Final: Dublin 0-6 Tipperary 0-5 Kilkenny *c.*4,000
1903 Kerry 0-11 London 0-3 Jones's Road *c.*10,000
          Home Final: Kerry 1-4 Kildare 1-3 Tipperary 12,000
          (disputed score)
          Replay: Kerry 0-7 Kildare 1-4 Cork *c.*18,000
          Replay: Kerry 0-8 Kildare 0-2 Croke Park *c.*20,000
1904 Kerry 0-5 Dublin 0-2 Cork *c.*10.000
1905 Kildare 1-7 Kerry 0-5 Thurles *c.*15,000
1906 Dublin 0-5 Cork 0-4 Athy *c.*8,000
1907 Dublin 0-6 Cork 0-2 Tipperary 5,000
1908 Dublin 1-10 London 0-4 Jones's Road *c.*10,000
          Home Final: Dublin 0-10 Kerry 0-3 Thurles *c.*5,000
1909 Kerry 1-9 Louth 0-6 Jones's Road *c.*16,000
1910 Louth walkover from Kerry
1911 Cork 6-6 Antrim 1-2 Jones's Road *c.*11,000
1912 Louth 1-7 Antrim 1-2 Jones's Road *c.*13,000
1913 Kerry 2-2 Wexford 0-3 Croke Park *c.*17,000
1914 Kerry 1-3 Wexford 0-6 Croke Park *c.*13,000
          Replay: Kerry 2-3 Wexford 0-6 Croke Park *c.*20,000
1915 Wexford 2-4 Kerry 2-1 Croke Park *c.*27,000
1916 Wexford 2-4 Mayo 1-2 Croke Park *c.*3,000
1917 Wexford 0-9 Clare 0-5 Croke Park *c.*6,500
1918 Wexford 0-5 Tipperary 0-4 Croke Park *c.*12,000
1919 Kildare 2-5 Galway 0-1 Croke Park *c.*32,000
1920 Tipperary 1-6 Dublin 1-2 Croke Park *c.*17,000
1921 Dublin 1-9 Mayo 0-2 Croke Park *c.*16,000
1922 Dublin 0-6 Galway 0-4 Croke Park 11,792
1923 Dublin 1-5 Kerry 1-3 Croke Park *c.*18,500
1924 Kerry 0-4 Dublin 0-3 Croke Park 28,844
1925 Galway awarded
1926 Kerry 1-3 Kildare 0-6 Croke Park 37,500
          Replay: Kerry 1-4 Kildare 0-4 Croke Park 35,500
1927 Kildare 0-5 Kerry 0-3 Croke Park 36,529
1928 Kildare 2-6 Cavan 2-5 Croke Park 24,700
1929 Kerry 1-8 Kildare 1-5 Croke Park 43,839
1930 Kerry 3-11 Monaghan 0-2 Croke Park 33,280
1931 Kerry 1-11 Kildare 0-8 Croke Park 42,350
1932 Kerry 2-7 Mayo 2-4 Croke Park 25,816
1933 Cavan 2-5 Galway 1-4 Croke Park 45,188
1934 Galway 3-5 Dublin 1-9 Croke Park 36,143
1935 Cavan 3-6 Kildare 2-5 Croke Park 50,380
1936 Mayo 4-11 Laois 0-5 Croke Park 50,168
1937 Kerry 2-5 Cavan 1-8 Croke Park 52,325
          Replay: Kerry 4-4 Cavan 1-7 Croke Park 51,234
1938 Galway 3-3 Kerry 2-6 Croke Park 68,950
          Replay: Galway 2-4 Kerry 0-7 Croke Park 47,851
1939 Kerry 2-5 Meath 2-3 Croke Park 46,828
1940 Kerry 0-7 Galway 1-3 Croke Park 60,821
1941 Kerry 1-8 Galway 0-7 Croke Park 45,512

1942 Dublin 1-10 Galway 1-8 Croke Park 37,105
1943 Roscommon 1-6 Cavan 1-6 Croke Park 68,023
          Replay: Roscommon 2-7 Cavan 2-2 Croke Park 47,193
1944 Roscommon 1-9 Kerry 2-4 Croke Park 79,245
1945 Cork 2-5 Cavan 0-7 Croke Park 67,329
1946 Kerry 2-4 Roscommon 1-7 Croke Park 75,771
          Replay: Kerry 2-8 Roscommon 0-10 Croke Park 65,661
1947 Cavan 2-11 Kerry 2-7 Polo Grounds, New York 34,491
1948 Cavan 4-5 Mayo 4-4 Croke Park 74,645
1949 Meath 1-10 Cavan 1-6 Croke Park 79,460
1950 Mayo 2-5 Louth 1-6 Croke Park 76,174
1951 Mayo 2-8 Meath 0-9 Croke Park 78,201
1952 Cavan 2-4 Meath 1-7 Croke Park 64,200
          Replay: Cavan 0-9 Meath 0-5 Croke Park 62,515
1953 Kerry 0-13 Armagh 1-6 Croke Park 86,155
1954 Meath 1-13 Kerry 1-7 Croke Park 75,276
1955 Kerry 0-12 Dublin 1-6 Croke Park 87,102
1956 Galway 2-13 Cork 3-7 Croke Park 70,772
1957 Louth 1-9 Cork 1-7 Croke Park 72,732
1958 Dublin 2-12 Derry 1-9 Croke Park 73,371
1959 Kerry 3-7 Galway 1-4 Croke Park 85,897
1960 Down 2-10 Kerry 0-8 Croke Park 87,768
1961 Down 3-6 Offaly 2-8 Croke Park 90,556
1962 Kerry 1-12 Roscommon 1-4 Croke Park 75,771
1963 Dublin 1-9 Galway 0-10 Croke Park 87,106
1964 Galway 0-15 Kerry 0-10 Croke Park 76,498
1965 Galway 0-12 Kerry 0-9 Croke Park 77,735
1966 Galway 1-10 Meath 0-7 Croke Park 71,569
1967 Meath 1-9 Cork 0-9 Croke Park 70,343
1968 Down 2-12 Kerry 1-13 Croke Park 71,294
1969 Kerry 0-10 Offaly 0-7 Croke Park 67,828
1970 Kerry 2-19 Meath 0-18 Croke Park 71,775
1971 Offaly 1-14 Galway 2-8 Croke Park 70,789
1972 Offaly 1-13 Kerry 1-13 Croke Park 72,032
          Replay: Offaly 1-19 Kerry 0-13 Croke Park 66,136
1973 Cork 3-17 Galway 2-13 Croke Park 73,308
1974 Dublin 0-14 Galway 1-6 Croke Park 71,898
1975 Kerry 2-12 Dublin 0-11 Croke Park 66,346
1976 Dublin 3-8 Kerry 0-10 Croke Park 73,588
1977 Dublin 5-12 Armagh 3-6 Croke Park 66,542
1978 Kerry 5-11 Dublin 0-9 Croke Park 71,503
1979 Kerry 3-13 Dublin 1-8 Croke Park 72,185
1980 Kerry 1-9 Roscommon 1-6 Croke Park 63,854
1981 Kerry 1-12 Offaly 0-8 Croke Park 61,489
1982 Offaly 1-15 Kerry 0-17 Croke Park 62,309
1983 Dublin 1-10 Galway 1-8 Croke Park 71,988
1984 Kerry 0-14 Dublin 1-6 Croke Park 68,365
1985 Kerry 2-12 Dublin 2-8 Croke Park 69,389
1986 Kerry 2-15 Tyrone 1-10 Croke Park 68,628
1987 Meath 1-14 Cork 0-11 Croke Park 68,431
1988 Meath 0-12 Cork 1-9 Croke Park 65,000
          Replay: Meath 0-13 Cork 0-12 Croke Park 64,069
1989 Cork 0-17 Mayo 1-11 Croke Park 65,519
1990 Cork 0-11 Meath 0-9 Croke Park 65,723
1991 Down 1-16 Meath 1-14 Croke Park 64,500
1992 Donegal 0-18 Dublin 0-14 Croke Park 64,547
1993 Derry 1-14 Cork 2-8 Croke Park 64,500
1994 Down 1-12 Dublin 0-13 Croke Park 58,684
1995 Dublin 1-10 Tyrone 0-12 Croke Park 65,000
1996 Meath 0-12 Mayo 1-9 Croke Park 65,898
          Replay: Meath 2-9 Mayo 1-11 Croke Park 65,802
1997 Kerry 0-13 Mayo 1-7 Croke Park 65,601
1998 Galway 1-14 Kildare 1-10 Croke Park 65,886
1999 Meath 1-11 Cork 1-8 Croke Park 63,276
2000 Galway 0-14 Kerry 0-14 Croke Park 63,349
          Replay: Kerry 0-17 Galway 1-10 Croke Park 64,094
2001 Galway 0-17 Meath 0-8 Croke Park 70,482
2002 Armagh 1-12 Kerry 0-14 Croke Park 79,500
2003 Tyrone 0-12 Armagh 0-9 Croke Park 79,394
2004 Kerry 1-20 Mayo 2-9 Croke Park 79,749
2005 Tyrone 1-16 Kerry 2-10 Croke Park 82,112

All-Ireland Club Finals

Football

1971 East Kerry 5-9 Bryansford 2-7 Croke Park *c*.300
1972 Bellaghy 0-15 UCC 1-11 Croke Park *c*.500
1973 Nemo Rangers 2-11 St Vincent's 2-11 Portlaoise *c*.3,000
1974 UCD 1-6 Lurgan Clan Na Gael 1-6 Croke Park *c*.6,000
      Replay: UCD 0-14 Lurgan Clan Na Gael 1-4 UCD *c*.12,000
1975 UCD 1-11 Nemo Rangers 0-12 Croke Park *c*.5,000
1976 St Vincent's 4-10 Roscommon Gaels 0-5 Portlaoise *c*.4,000
1977 Austin Stacks 1-13 Ballerin 2-7 Croke Park 8,971
1978 Thomond College 2-14 St John's 1-3 Croke Park *c*.3,000
1979 Nemo Rangers 2-9 Scotstown 1-3 Croke Park 4,443
1980 St Finbarr's 3-9 Ballinasloe 0-8 Tipperary *c*.3,000
1981 St Finbarr's 1-8 Walterstown 0-6 Croke Park 4,066
1982 Nemo Rangers 6-11 Garrymore 1-8 Ennis 3,600
1983 Portlaoise 0-12 Clan Na Gael 2-0 Cloughjordan *c*.2,000
1984 Nemo Rangers 2-10 Walterstown 0-5 Athlone *c*.2,000
1985 Castleisland 2-2 St Vincent's 0-7 Tipperary *c*.4,000
1986 Burren 1-10 Castleisland 1-6 Croke Park 10,176
1987 St Finbarr's 0-10 Clan Na Gael 0-7 Croke Park 9,550
1988 Burren 1-9 Clan Na Gael 0-8 Croke Park *c*.7,000
1989 Nemo Rangers 1-13 Clan Na Gael 1-3 Croke Park 9,158
1990 Baltinglass 2-7 Clan na Gael 0-7 Croke Park 15,708
1991 Lavey 2-9 Salthill 0-10 Croke Park 8,316
1992 Killarney Crokes 1-11 Thomas Davis 0-13 Croke Park 13,885
1993 O'Donovan Rossa 1-12 Éire Óg 3-6 Croke Park 21,714
      Replay: O'Donovan Rossa 1-7 Éire Óg 0-8 Limerick 25,000
1994 Nemo Rangers 3-11 Castlebar Mitchels 0-8 Croke Park 13,392
1995 Kilmacud Crokes 0-8 Bellaghy 0-5 Croke Park 18,544
1996 Laune Rangers 4-5 Éire Óg 0-11 Croke Park 21,986
1997 Crossmaglen 2-13 Knockmore 0-11 Croke Park 34,852
1998 Corofin 0-15 Erin's Isle 0-10 Croke Park 36,545
1999 Crossmaglen 0-9 Ballina 0-8 Croke Park 40,106
2000 Crossmaglen 1-14 Na Fianna 0-12 Croke Park 31,965
2001 Crossmolina 0-16 Nemo Rangers 1-12 Croke Park 20,025
2002 Ballinderry 2-10 Nemo Rangers 0-9 Thurles 16,112 (excluding children)
2003 Nemo Rangers 0-14 Crossmolina 1-9 Croke Park 26,235
2004 Caltra 0-13 An Gaeltacht 0-12 Croke Park 38,500
2005 Ballina Stephenites 1-12 Portlaoise 2-8 Croke Park 31,236

Hurling

1971 Roscrea 4-5 St Rynagh's 2-5 Birr *c*.1,000
1972 Blackrock 5-13 Rathnure 6-9 Waterford *c*.1,500
1973 Glen Rovers 2-18 St Rynagh's 2-8 Croke Park *c*.500
1974 Blackrock 2-14 Rathnure 3-11 Croke Park *c*.6,000
      Replay: Blackrock 3-8 Rathnure 1-9 Dungarvan *c*.3,000
1975 St Finbarr's 3-8 Fenians 1-6 Croke Park *c*.3,000
1976 James Stephens 2-10 Blackrock 2-4 Thurles *c*.3,000
1977 Glen Rovers 2-12 Camross 0-8 Thurles *c*.4,000
1978 St Finbarr's 2-7 Rathnure 0-9 Thurles *c*.3,000
1979 Blackrock 5-7 Ballyhale Shamrocks 5-5 Thurles *c*.3,000
1980 Castlegar 1-11 Ballycastle 1-8 Navan *c*.4,000
1981 Ballyhale Shamrocks 1-15 St Finbarr's 1-11 Thurles *c*.3,000
1982 James Stephens 3-13 Mount Sion 3-8 Thurles 6,300
1983 Loughgiel 1-8 St Rynagh's 2-5 Croke Park *c*.3,000
      Replay: Loughgiel 2-12 St Rynagh's 1-12 Casement Park 10,000
1984 Ballyhale Shamrocks 1-10 Gort 1-10 Birr *c*.3,000
      Replay: Ballyhale Shamrocks 1-10 Gort 0-7 Thurles *c*.3,000
1985 St Martin's 2-9 Castlegar 3-6 Croke Park *c*.4,000
      Replay: St Martin's 1-13 Castlegar 1-10 Thurles *c*.3,000
1986 Kilruane McDonaghs 1-15 Buffer's Alley 2-10 Croke Park 10,176
1987 Borrisoleigh 2-9 Rathnure 0-9 Croke Park 9,550
1988 Midleton 3-8 Athenry 0-9 Croke Park *c*.3,000
1989 Buffer's Alley 2-12 Rossa 0-12 Croke Park 9,158
1990 Ballyhale Shamrocks 1-16 Ballybrown 0-16 Croke Park 15,708
1991 Glenmore 1-13 Patrickswell 0-12 Croke Park 8,316
1992 Kiltormer 0-15 Birr 1-8 Thurles 13,855
1993 Sarsfields 1-17 Kilmallock 2-7 Croke Park 21,714
1994 Sarsfields 1-14 Toomevara 3-6 Croke Park 13,392
1995 Birr 0-9 Dunloy 0-9 Croke Park 18,544
      Replay: Birr 3-13 Dunloy 2-3 Croke Park 6,395
1996 Sixmilebridge 5-10 Dunloy 2-8 Croke Park 21,986
1997 Athenry 0-14 Shannon Wolfe Tones 1-8 Croke Park 34,852
1998 Birr 1-13 Sarsfields 0-9 Croke Park 36,545
1999 St Joseph's 2-14 Rathnure 0-8 Croke Park 40,106
2000 Athenry 0-16 St Joseph's 0-12 Croke Park 31,965
2001 Athenry 3-24 Graigue-Ballycallan 2-19 20,025
2002 Birr 2-10 Clarinbridge 1-5 Thurles 16,112 (excluding children)
2003 Birr 1-19 Dunloy 0-11 Croke Park 26,235
2004 Newtownshandrum 0-17 Dunloy 1-6 Croke Park 38,500
2005 James Stephens 0-19 Athenry 0-14 Croke Park 31,236